T0149172

A HILLTOP
on the
MARNE

A HILLTOP
on the
MARNE

MILDRED ALDRICH

Hesperus Press Limited
28 Mortimer Street
London W1W 7RD
www.hesperuspress.com

A Hilltop on the Marne first published 1916, also included in this
collection *On the Edge of the War Zone*, published 1917.
First published by Hesperus Press Limited, 2014

Typeset by Roland Codd
Printed and bound by CPI Group (UK) Ltd, Croydon, CR0 4YY

ISBN: 978-1-84391-501-0

To My Grandmother Judith Trask Baker, that staunch New Englander and pioneer Universalist, to the memory of whose courage and example I owe a debt of eternal gratitude.

Part I

A Hilltop on the Marne

Being Letters Written
June 3–September 8, 1914

The author wishes to apologize for the constant use of the word English in speaking of the British Expedition to France. At the beginning of the war this was a colloquial error into which we all fell over here, even the French press. Everything in khaki was spoken of as 'English', even though we knew perfectly well that Scotch, Irish, and Welsh were equally well represented in the ranks, and the colors they followed were almost universally spoken of as the 'English flag'. These letters were written in the days before the attention of the French press was called to this error of speech, which accounts for the mistake's persisting in the book.

I

Well, the deed is done. I have not wanted to talk with you much about it until I was here. I know all your objections. You remember that you did not spare me when, a year ago, I told you that this was my plan. I realize that you – more active, younger, more interested in life, less burdened with your past – feel that it is cowardly on my part to seek a quiet refuge and settle myself into it, to turn my face peacefully to the exit, feeling that the end is the most interesting event ahead of me – the one truly interesting experience left to me in this incarnation.

I am not proposing to ask you to see it from my point of view. You cannot, no matter how willing you are to try. No two people ever see life from the same angle. There is a law which decrees that two objects may not occupy the same place at the same time – result: two people cannot see things from the same point of view, and the slightest difference in angle changes the thing seen.

I did not decide to come away into a little corner in the country, in this land in which I was not born, without looking at the move from all angles. Be sure that I know what I am doing, and I have found the place where I can do it. Some time you will see the new home, I hope, and then you will understand. I have lived more than sixty years. I have lived a fairly active life, and it has been, with all its hardships – and they have been many – interesting. But I have had enough of the city – even of Paris, the most beautiful city in the world. Nothing can take any of that away from me. It is treasured up in my memory. I am even prepared to own that there was a sort of arrogance in my persistence in choosing for so many years the most seductive city in the world, and saying, 'Let others live where they will – here I propose to stay.' I lived there until I seemed to take it for my own – to know it on the surface and under it, and over it, and around it; until I had a sort of morbid jealousy when I found any one who knew it half as well as I did, or presumed to love it half as much, and dared to say so. You will please note that I have not gone far from it.

But I have come to feel the need of calm and quiet – perfect peace. I know again that there is a sort of arrogance in expecting it, but I am going to make a bold bid for it. I will agree, if you like, that it is cowardly to say that my work is done. I will even agree that we both know plenty of women who have cheerfully gone on struggling to a far greater age, and I do think it downright pretty of you to find me younger than my years. Yet you must forgive me if I say that none of us know one another, and, likewise, that appearances are often deceptive.

What you are pleased to call my 'pride' has helped me a little. No one can decide for another the proper moment for striking one's colors.

I am sure that you – or for that matter any other American – never heard of Huiry. Yet it is a little hamlet less than thirty miles from Paris. It is in that district between Paris and Meaux little known to the ordinary traveler. It only consists of less than a dozen rude farmhouses, less than five miles, as a bird flies, from Meaux, which, with a fair cathedral, and a beautiful chestnut-shaded promenade on the banks of the Marne, spanned just there bylines of old mills whose water-wheels churn the river into foaming eddies, has never been popular with excursionists. There are people who go there to see where Bossuet wrote his funeral orations, in a little summer-house standing among pines and cedars on the wall of the garden of the Archbishop's palace, now, since the 'separation', the property of the State, and soon to be a town museum. It is not a very attractive town. It has not even an out-of-doors restaurant to tempt the passing automobilist.

My house was, when I leased it, little more than a peasant's hut. It is considerably over 150 years old, with stables and outbuildings attached whimsically, and boasts six gables. Is it not a pity, for early association's sake, that it has not one more?

I have, as Traddles used to say, 'Oceans of room, Copperfield', and no joking. I have on the ground floor of the main building a fair-sized salon, into which the front door opens directly. Over that I have a long, narrow bedroom and dressing room, and above that, in the eaves, a sort of attic workshop. In an attached, one-story addition with a gable, at the west of the salon, I have a library lighted from both east and west. Behind the salon on the west side I have a double room which serves as dining and breakfast room, with a guest chamber above. The kitchen, at the north side of the salon, has its own gable, and there is an old stable extending forward at the north side, and an old grange extending west from the dining room. It is a jumble of roofs and chimneys, and looks very much like the houses I used to combine from my Noah's Ark box in the days of my babyhood.

All the rooms on the ground floor are paved in red tiles, and the staircase is built right in the salon. The ceilings are raftered. The cross-beam in the salon fills my soul with joy – it is over a foot wide and a foot and a half thick. The walls and the rafters are painted green, – my color – and so good, by long trial, for my eyes and my nerves, and my disposition.

But much as I like all this, it was not this that attracted me here. That was the situation. The house stands in a small garden, separated from the road by an old gnarled hedge of hazel. It is almost on the crest of the hill on the south bank of the Marne – the hill that is the watershed between the Marne and the Grand Morin. Just here the Marne makes a wonderful loop, and is only fifteen minutes walk away from my gate, down the hill to the north.

From the lawn, on the north side of the house, I command a panorama which I have rarely seen equaled. To me it is more beautiful than that we have so often looked at together from the terrace at Saint-Germain. In the west the new part of Esbly climbs the hill, and from there to a hill at the northeast I have a wide view of the valley of the Marne, backed by a low line of hills which is the watershed between the Marne and the Aisne. Low down in the valley, at the northwest, lies Isles-lès-Villenoy, like a toy town, where the big bridge spans the Marne to carry the railroad into Meaux. On the horizon line to the west the tall chimneys of Claye send lines of smoke into the air. In the foreground to the north, at the foot of the hill, are the roofs of two little hamlets – Joncheroy and Voisins – and beyond them the trees that border the canal.

On the other side of the Marne the undulating hill, with its wide stretch of fields, is dotted with little villages that peep out of the trees or are silhouetted against the skyline – Vignely, Trilbardou, Penchard, Monthyon, Neufmortier, Chauconin, and in the foreground to the north, in the valley, just halfway between me and Meaux, lies Mareuil-on-the-Marne, with its red roofs, gray walls, and church spire. With a glass I can find where Chambry and Barcy are, on the slope behind Meaux, even if the trees conceal them.

But these are all little villages of which you may never have heard. No guidebook celebrates them. No railroad approaches them. On clear days I can see the square tower of the cathedral at Meaux, and I have only to walk a short distance on the *route nationale* – which runs from Paris, across the top of my hill a little to the east, and thence to Meaux and on to the frontier – to get a profile view of it standing up above the town, quite detached, from foundation to clock tower.

This is a rolling country of grain fields, orchards, masses of blackcurrant bushes, vegetable plots – it is a great sugar-beet country – and asparagus beds; for the Department of the Seine et Marne is one of the most productive in France, and every inch under cultivation. It is what the French call *un paysage riant*, and I assure you, it does more than smile these lovely June mornings. I am up every morning almost as soon as the sun, and I slip my feet into sabots, wrap myself in a big cloak, and run right on to the lawn to make sure that the panorama has not disappeared in the night. There always lie – too good almost to be true – miles and miles of laughing country, little white towns just smiling in the early light, a thin strip of river here and there, dimpling and dancing, stretches of fields of all colors – all so peaceful and so gay, and so 'chummy' that it gladdens the opening day, and makes me rejoice to have lived to see it. I never weary of it. It changes every hour, and I never can decide at which hour it is the loveliest. After all, it is a rather nice world.

Now get out your map and locate me.

You will not find Huiry. But you can find Esbly, my nearest station on the mainline of the Eastern Railroad. Then you will find a little narrow-gauge road running from there to Crecy-la-Chapelle. Halfway between you will find Couilly-Saint-Germain. Well, I am right up the hill, about a third of the way between Couilly and Meaux.

It is a nice historic country. But for that matter so is all France. I am only fifteen miles northeast of Bondy, in whose forest the naughty Queen Fredegonde, beside whose tomb, in Saint-Denis, we have often stood together, had her husband killed, and nearer still to Chelles, where the Merovingian kings once had a palace stained with the blood of many crimes, about which you read, in many awful details, in Maurice Strauss's *Tragique Histoire des Reines Brunhaut et Fredegonde*, which I remember to have sent you when it first came out. Of course no trace of those days of the Merovingian dynasty remains here or anywhere else. Chelles is now one of the fortified places in the outer belt of forts surrounding Paris.

So, if you will not accept all this as an explanation of what you are pleased to call my 'desertion', may I humbly and reluctantly put up a plea for my health, and hope for a sympathetic hearing?

If I am to live much longer – and I am on the road down the hill, you know – I demand of Life my physical well-being. I want a robust old age. I feel that I could never hope to have that much longer in town – city-born and city-bred though I am. I used to think, and I continued to think for a long time, that I could not live if my feet did not press a city pavement. The fact that I have changed my mind seems to me, at my age, a sufficient excuse for, as frankly, changing my habits. It surely proves that I have not a sick will – yet. In the simple life I crave – digging in the earth, living out of doors – I expect to earn the strength of which city life and city habits were robbing me. I believe I can. Faith half wins a battle. No one ever dies up on this hill, I am told, except of hard drink. Judging by my experience with workmen here, not always of that. I never saw so many very old, very active, robust people in so small a space in all my life as I have seen here.

Are you answered?

Yet if, after all this expenditure of words, you still think I am shirking – well, I am sorry. It seems to me that, from another point of view, I am doing my duty, and giving the younger generation more room – getting out of the limelight, so to speak, which, between you and me, was getting trying for my mental complexion. If I have blundered, the consequences be on my own head. My hair could hardly be whiter – that's something. Besides, retreat is not cut off. I have sworn no eternal oath not to change my mind again.

In any case you have no occasion to worry about me: I've a head full of memories. I am going to classify them, as I do my books. Some of them I am going to forget, just as I reject books that have ceased to interest me. I know the latter is always a wrench. The former may be impossible. I shall not be lonely. No one who reads is ever that. I may miss talking. Perhaps that is a good thing. I may have talked too much. That does happen.

Remember one thing – I am not inaccessible. I may now and then get an opportunity to talk again, and in a new background. Who knows? I am counting on nothing but the facts about me. So come on, Future. I've my back against the past. Anyway, as you see, it is too late to argue. I've crossed the Rubicon, and can return only when I have built a new bridge.

II

That's right. Accept the situation. You will soon find that Paris will seem the same to you. Besides, I had really given all I had to give there.

Indeed you shall know, to the smallest detail, just how the material side of my life is arranged – all my comforts and discomforts – since you ask.

I am now absolutely settled into my little 'hole' in the country, as you call it. It has been so easy. I have been here now nearly three weeks. Everything is in perfect order. You would be amazed if you could see just how everything fell into place. The furniture has behaved itself beautifully. There are days when I wonder if either I or it ever lived anywhere else. The shabby old furniture with which you were long so familiar just slipped right into place. I had not a stick too little, and could not have placed another piece. I call that 'bull luck'.

I have always told you – you have not always agreed – that France was the easiest place in the world to live in, and the love of a land in which to be a pauper. That is why it suits me.

Don't harp on that word 'alone'. I know I am living alone, in a house that has four outside doors into the bargain. But you know I am not one of the 'afraid' kind. I am not boasting. That is a characteristic, not a quality. One is afraid or one is not. It happens that I am not. Still, I am very prudent. You would laugh if you could see me 'shutting up' for the night. All my windows on the ground floor are heavily barred. Such of the doors as have glass in them have shutters also. The window shutters are primitive affairs of solid wood, with diamond-shaped holes in the upper part. First, I put up the shutters on the door in the dining room which leads into the

16

garden on the south side; then I lock the door. Then I do a similar service for the kitchen door on to the front terrace, and that into the orchard, and lock both doors. Then I go out the salon door and lock the stable and the grange and take out the keys. Then I come into the salon and lock the door after me, and push two of the biggest bolts you ever saw.

After which I hang up the keys, which are as big as the historic key of the Bastille, which you may remember to have seen at the Musée Carnavalet. Then I close and bolt all the shutters downstairs. I do it systematically every night – because I promised not to be foolhardy. I always grin, and feel as if it were a scene in a play. It impresses me so much like a tremendous piece of business – dramatic suspense – which leads up to nothing except my going quietly upstairs to bed.

When it is all done I feel as I used to in my strenuous working days, when, after midnight, all the rest of the world – my little world – being calmly asleep, I cuddled down in the corner of my couch to read; – the world is mine!

Never in my life – anywhere, under any circumstances – have I been so well taken care of. I have a *femme de ménage* – a sort of cross between a housekeeper and a maid-of-all-work. She is a married woman, the wife of a farmer whose house is three minutes away from mine. My dressing-room window and my dining-room door look across a field of currant bushes to her house. I have only to blow on the dog's whistle and she can hear. Her name is Amélie, and she is a character, a nice one, but not half as much of a character as her husband – her second. She is a Parisian. Her first husband was a jockey, half Breton, half English. He died years ago when she was young: broke his neck in a big race at Auteuil.

She has had a checkered career, and lived in several smart families before, to assure her old age, she married this gentle, queer little farmer. She is a great find for me. But the thing balances up beautifully, as I am a blessing to her, a new interest in her monotonous life, and she never lets me forget how much happier she is since I came here to live. She is very bright and gay, intelligent enough to be a companion when I need one, and well-bred enough to fall right into her proper place when I don't.

Her husband's name is Abelard. Oh, yes, of course, I asked him about Héloise the first time I saw him, and I was staggered when the little old toothless chap giggled and said, 'That was before my time.' What do you think of that? Everyone calls him 'Père Abelard', and about the house it is shortened down to 'Père'. He is over twenty years older than Amélie – well along in his seventies. He is a native of the *commune* – was born at Pont-aux-Dames, at the foot of the hill, right next to the old *abbaye* of that name. He is a type familiar enough to those who know French provincial life. His father was a well-to-do farmer. His mother was the typical mother of her class. She kept her sons under her thumb as long as she lived. Père Abelard worked on his father's farm. He had his living, but never a *sou* in his pocket. The only diversion he ever had was playing the violin, which some passer in the *commune* taught him. When his parents died, he and his brothers sold the old place at Pont-aux-Dames to Coquelin, who was preparing to turn the historic old convent into a *maison de retraite* for aged actors, and he came up here on the hill and bought his present farm in this hamlet, where almost everyone is some sort of a cousin of his.

Oddly enough, almost every one of these female cousins has a history. You would not think it, to look at the place and the people, yet I fancy that it is pretty universal for women in such places to have 'histories'. You will see an old woman with a bronzed face – sometimes still handsome, often the reverse – in her short skirt, her big apron tied round where

18

a waist is not, her still beautiful hair concealed in a colored handkerchief. You ask the question of the right person, and you will discover that she is rich; that she is avaricious; that she pays heavy taxes; denies herself all but the bare necessities; and that the foundation of her fortune dates back to an *affaire du coeur*, or perhaps of interest, possibly of cupidity; and that very often the middle-aged daughter who still 'lives at home with mother', had also had a profitable *affaire* arranged by mother herself. Everything has been perfectly *convenable*. Everyone either knows about it or has forgotten it. No one is bothered or thinks the worse of her so long as she has remained of the 'people' and put on no airs. But let her attempt to rise out of her class, or go up to Paris, and the Lord help her if she ever wants to come back, and, French fashion, end her days where she began them. This is typically, provincially French. When you come down here I shall tell you tales that will make Balzac and De Maupassant look tame.

You have no idea how little money these people spend. It must hurt them terribly to cough up their taxes. They all till the land, and eat what they grow. Amélie's husband spends exactly four cents a week – to get shaved on Sunday. He can't shave himself. A razor scares him to death. He looks as if he were going to the guillotine when he starts for the barber's, but she will not stand for a beard of more than a week's growth. He always stops at my door on his way back to let his wife kiss his clean old face, all wreathed with smiles – the ordeal is over for another week. He never needs a *sou* except for that shave. He drinks nothing but his own cider: he eats his own vegetables, his own rabbits; he never goes anywhere except to the fields – does not want to – unless it is to play the violin for a dance or a fête. He just works, eats, sleeps, reads his newspaper, and is content. Yet he pays taxes on nearly a hundred thousand francs' worth of real estate.

But, after all, this is not what I started to tell you – that was about my domestic arrangements. Amélie does everything for me. She comes early in the morning, builds a fire, then goes across the field for the milk while water is heating. Then she arranges my bath, gets my coffee, tidies up the house. She buys everything I need, cooks for me, waits on me, even mends for me – all for the magnificent sum of eight dollars a month. It really isn't as much as that, it is forty francs a month, which comes to about a dollar and eighty cents a week in your currency. She has on her farm everything in the way of vegetables that I need, from potatoes to 'asparagras', from peas to tomatoes. She has chickens and eggs. Bread, butter, cheese, meat come right to the gate; so does the letter carrier, who not only brings my mail but takes it away. The only thing we have to go for is the milk.

To make it seem all the more primitive there is a rickety old diligence which runs from Quincy – Huiry is really a suburb of Quincy – to Esbly twice a day, to connect with trains for Paris with which the branch road does not connect. It has an imperial, and when you come out to see me, at some future time, you will get a lovely view of the country from a top seat. You could walk the four miles quicker than the horse does – it is uphill nearly all the way – but time is no longer any object with *me*. Amélie has a donkey and a little cart to drive me to the station at Couilly when I take that line, or when I want to do an errand or go to the laundress, or merely to amuse myself.

If you can really match this for a cheap, easy, simple way for an elderly person to live in dignity, I wish you would. It is far easier than living in Paris was, and living in Paris was easier for me than the States. I am sorry, but it is the truth.

You ask me what I do with the 'long days'. My dear! they are short, and yet I am out of bed a little after four every morning. To be sure I get into bed again at half past eight, or, at latest, nine, every night. Of course the weather is simply lovely. As soon as I have made sure that my beloved panorama has not disappeared in the night I dress in great haste. My morning toilette consists of a long black studio apron such as the French children wear to school – it takes the place of a dress – felt shoes inside my sabots, a big hat, and long gardening-gloves. In that get-up I weed a little, rake up my paths, examine my fruit trees, and, at intervals, lean on my rake in a Maud Muller posture and gaze at the view. It is never the same two hours of the day, and I never weary of looking at it.

My garden would make you chortle with glee. You will have to take it by degrees, as I do. I have a sort of bowing acquaintance with it myself – en masse, so to speak. I hardly know a thing in it by name. I have wall fruit on the south side and an orchard of plum, pear, and cherry trees on the north side. The east side is half lawn and half disorderly flowerbeds. I am going to let the tangle in the orchard grow at its own sweet will – that is, I am going to as far as Amélie allows me. I never admire some trailing, flowering thing there that, while I am admiring it, Amélie does not come out and pull it out of the ground, declaring it *une salet*é and sure to poison the whole place if allowed to grow. Yet some of these same *saletés* are so pretty and grow so easily that I am tempted not to care. One of these trials of my life is what I am learning to know as *liserone* – we used to call it wild morning-glory. *That* I am forbidden to have – if I want anything else. But it is pretty.

I remember years ago to have heard Ysolet, in a lecture at the Sorbonne, state that the 'struggle for life' among the plants was fiercer and more tragic than that among human beings. It was mere words to me then. In the short three weeks that I have been out here in my hilltop garden I have learned to know how true that was. Sometimes I am tempted to have a garden of weeds. I suppose my neighbors would object if I let them all go to seed and sow these sins of agriculture all over the tidy farms about me.

Often these lovely mornings I take a long walk with the dog before breakfast. He is an Airedale, and I am terribly proud of him and my neighbors terribly afraid of him. I am half inclined to believe that he is as afraid of them as they are of him, but I keep that suspicion, for prudential reasons, to myself. At any rate, all passers keep at a respectful distance from me and him.

Our usual walk is down the hill to the north, toward the shady route that leads by the edge of the canal to Meaux. We go along the fields, down the long hill until we strike into a footpath which leads through the woods to the road called 'Pavés du Roi' and on to the canal, from which a walk of five minutes takes us to the Marne. After we cross the road at the foot of the hill there is not a house, and the country is so pretty – undulating ground, in every tint of green and yellow. From the high bridge that crosses the canal the picture is – well, is French-canally, and you know what that means – green-banked, tree-shaded, with a towpath bordering the straight line of water, and here and there a row of broad long canal-boats moving slowly through the shadows.

By the time I get back I am ready for breakfast. You know I never could eat or drink early in the morning. I have my coffee in the orchard under a big pear tree, and I have the inevitable book propped against the urn. Needless to say I never read a word. I simply look at the panorama. All the same I have to have the book there or I could not eat, just as I can't go to sleep without books on the bed.

After breakfast I write letters. Before I know it Amélie appears at the library door to announce that '*Madame est servie*' – and the morning is gone. As I am alone, as a rule I take my lunch in the breakfast room. It is on the north side of the house, and is the coolest room in the house at noon. Besides, it has a window overlooking the plain. In the afternoon I read and write and mend, and then I take a light supper in the arbor on the east side of the house under a crimson rambler, one of the first ever planted here over thirty years ago.

I must tell you about that crimson rambler. You know when I hired this house it was only a peasant's hut. In front of what is now the kitchen – it was then a dark hole for fuel – stood four dilapidated posts, moss-covered and decrepit, over which hung a tangle of something. It was what I called a 'mess'. I was not as educated as I am now. I saw – it was winter – what looked to me an unsightly tangle of disorder. I ordered those posts down. My workmen, who stood in some awe of me – I was the first American they had ever seen – were slow in obeying. They did not dispute the order, only they did not execute it.

One day I was very stern. I said to my head mason, 'I have ordered that thing removed half a dozen times. Be so good as to have those posts taken down before I come out again.'

He touched his cap, and said, 'Very well, *madame*.'

It happened that the next time I came out the weather had become spring-like.

The posts were down. The tangle that had grown over them was trailing on the ground – but it had begun to put out leaves. I looked at it – and for the first time it occurred to me to say, 'What is that?'

The mason looked at me a moment, and replied, 'That, *madame*! That is a "creamson ramblaire" – the oldest one in the *commune*.'

Poor fellow, it had never occurred to him that I did not know.

Seven feet to the north of the climbing rose bush was a wide hedge of tall lilac bushes. So I threw up an arbor between them, and the crimson rambler now mounts eight feet in the air. It is a glory of color today, and my pride. But didn't I come near to losing it?

The long evenings are wonderful. I sit out until nine, and can read until almost the last minute. I never light a lamp until I go up to bed. That is my day. It seems busy enough to me. I am afraid it will – to you, still so willing to fight, still so absorbed in the struggle, and still so over-fond of your species – seem futile. Who knows which of us is right? – or if our difference of opinion may not be a difference in our years? If all who love one another were of the same opinion, living would be monotonous, and conversation flabby. So cheer up. You are content. Allow me to be.

III

I have just received your letter – the last, you say, that you can send before you sail away again for 'The Land of the Free and the Home of the Brave', where you still seem to feel that it is my duty to return to die. I vow I will not discuss that with you again. Poverty is an unpretty thing, and poverty plus old age simply horrid in the wonderful land which saw my birth, and to which I take off my sun-bonnet in reverent admiration, in much the same spirit that the peasants still uncover before a shrine. But it is the land of the young, the energetic, and the ambitious, the ideal home of the very rich and the laboring classes. I am none of those – hence here I stay. I turn my eyes to the west often with a queer sort of amazed pride. If I were a foreigner – of any race but French – I'd work my passage out there in an emigrant ship. As it is, I did forty-five years of hard labor there, and I consider that I earned the freedom to die where I please.

I can see in 'my mind's eye' the glitter in yours as you wrote – and underscored – I'll wager you spend half your days in writing letters back to the land you have willfully deserted. As well have stayed among us and talked – and you talk so much better than you write. 'Tut! tut! That *is* nasty.' Of course I do not deny that I shall miss the inspiration of your contradictions – or do you call it repartee? I scorn your arguments, and I hereby swear that you shall not worry another remonstrance from me.

You ask me how it happens that I wandered in this direction, into a part of the country about which you do not remember to have ever heard me talk, when there were so many places that would have seemed to you to be more interesting. Well, this is more interesting than you think. You must not fancy that a place is not interesting because you can't find it in Hare, and because Henry James never talked about it. That was James's misfortune and not his fault.

The truth is I *did* look in many more familiar directions before fortunate accident led me here. I had an idea that I wanted to live on the heights of Montmorency, in the Jean Jacques Rousseau country. But it was terribly expensive – too near to Enghien and its Casino and baccarat tables. Then I came near to taking a house near Viroflay, within walking distance of Versailles. But at the very mention of that all my French friends simply howled. 'It was too near to Paris'; 'it was the chosen route of the Apaches'; and so on and so forth. I did not so much care for the situation. It was too familiar, and it was not really country, it was only suburbs. But the house attracted me. It was old and quaint, and the garden was pretty, and it was high. Still it *was* too expensive. After that I found a house well within my means at Poigny, about an hour, by diligence, from Rambouillet. That did attract me. It was real country, but it had no view and the house was very small. Still I had got so tired of hunting that I was actually on the point of taking it when one of my friends accidentally found this place. If it had been made to order it could not have suited me better – situation, age, price, all just to my taste. I put over a year and a half into the search. Did I keep it to myself well?

Besides, the country here had a certain novelty to me. I know the country on the other side of the Petit Morin, but all this is new to me except Meaux. At first the house did not look habitable to me. It was easily made so, however, and it has great possibilities, which will keep me busy for years.

Although you do not know this part of the country, it has, for me, every sort of attraction – historical as well as picturesque. Its historical interest is rather for the student than the tourist, and I love it none the less for that.

If ever you relent and come to see me, I can take you for some lovely walks. I can, on a Sunday afternoon, in good weather, even take you to the theater – what is more, to the theater to see the players of the *Comédie Française*. It is only half an hour's walk from my house to Pont-aux-Dames, where Coquelin set up his *maison de retraite* for aged actors, and where he died and is buried. In the old park, where the du Barry used to walk in the days when Louis XVI clapped her in prison on a warrant wrung from the dying old king, her royal lover, there is an open-air theater, and there, on Sundays, the actors of the *Theatre Français* play, within sight of the tomb of the founder of the retreat, under the very trees – and they are stately and noble – where the du Barry walked.

Of course I shall only take you there if you insist. I have outgrown the playhouse. I fancy that I am much more likely to sit out on the lawn and preach to you on how the theater has missed its mission than I am – unless you insist – to take you down to the hill to listen to Molière or Racine.

If, however, that bores you – it would me –you can sit under the trees and close your eyes while I give you a Stoddard lecture without the slides. I shall tell you about the little walled town of Crécy, still surrounded by its moat, where the tiny little houses stand in gardens with their backs on the moat, each with its tiny footbridge, that pulls up, just to remind you that it was once a royal city, with drawbridge and portcullis, a city in which kings used to stay, and in which Jeanne d'Arc slept one night on her way back from crowning *her* king at Rheims: a city that once boasted ninety-nine towers. Half a dozen of these towers still stand. Their thick walls are now pierced with windows, in which muslin curtains blow in the wind, to say that today they are the humble homes of simple people, and to remind you of what warfare was in the days when such towers were a defense. Why, the very garden in which you will be sitting when I tell you this was once a part of the royal estate, and the last Lord of the Land was the Duke de Penthièvre. I thought that fact rather amusing when I found it out, considering that the house I came so near to taking at Poigny was on the Rambouillet estate where his father, the Duke de Toulouse, one of Louis XIV's illegitimate sons, died, where the Duke de Penthièvre was born, and where he buried his naughty son, the Duke de Lamballe.

Of course, while I am telling you things like this you will have to bring your imagination into play, as very few vestiges of the old days remain. I still get just as much fun out of *Il y avait une fois*, even when the 'once on a time' can only be conjured up with closed eyes. Still, I can show you some dear little old chapels, and while I am telling you about it you will probably hear the far-off, sad tolling of a bell, and I shall say to you 'Ça sonne à Bouleurs.' It will be the church bells at Bouleurs, a tiny, tree-shaded hamlet, on another hilltop, from which, owing to its situation, the bells, which rarely ring save for a funeral, can be heard at a great distance, as they have rung over the valley for years. They sound so sad in the still air that the expression, Ça sonne à Bouleurs, has come to mean bad luck. In all the towns where the bell can be heard, a man who is having bad luck at cards, or has made a bad bargain, or has been tricked in any way, invariably remarks, 'Ça sonne à Bouleurs.'

I could show you something more modern in the way of historical association. For example, from the road at the south side of my hill I can show you the Château de la Haute Maison, with its mansard and Louis XVI pavilions, where Bismarck and Favre had their first unsuccessful meeting, when this hill was occupied by the Germans in 1870 during the siege of Paris. And fifteen minutes' walk from here is the pretty Château de Condé, which was then the home of Casimir-Perier, and if you do not remember him as the President of the Republic who resigned rather than face the Dreyfus case, you may remember him as the father-in-law of Madame Simone, who unsuccessfully stormed the American theater, two years ago.

You ask me how isolated I am. Well, I am, and I am not. My house stands in the middle of my garden. That is a certain sort of isolation. There is a house on the opposite side of the road, much nearer than I wish it were. Luckily it is rarely occupied. Still, when it is, it is over-occupied. At the foot of the hill – perhaps five hundred yards away – are the tiny hamlet of Joncheroy and the little village of Voisins. Just above me is the hamlet of Huiry – half a dozen houses. You see that is not sad. So cheer up. So far as I know the *commune* has no criminal record, and I am not on the route of tramps. Remember, please, that, in those last winters in Paris, I did not prove immune to contagions. There is nothing for me to catch up here – unless it be the gayety with which the air is saturated.

You ask me also how it happens that I am living again 'near by Quincy'? As true as you live, I never thought of the coincidence. If you please, we pronounce it 'Kansee'. When I read your question I laughed. I remembered that Abelard, when he was first condemned, retired to the Hermitage of Quincy, but when I took down Larousse to look it up, what do you think I found? Simply this and nothing more: 'Quincy: Ville des Etats-Unis (Massachusetts), 28,000 habitants.'

Isn't that droll? However, I know that there was a Sire de Quincy centuries ago, so I will look him up and let you know what I find.

The morning paper – always late here – brings the startling news of the assassination of the Crown Prince of Austria. What an unlucky family that has been! Franz Josef must be a tough old gentleman to have stood up against so many shocks.

I used to feel so sorry for him when Fate dealt him another blow that would have been a 'knock-out' for most people. But he has stood so many, and outlived happier people, that I begin to believe that if the wind is tempered to the shorn lamb, the hides, or the hearts, of some people are toughened to stand the gales of Fate.

Well, I imagine that Austria will not grieve much – though she may be mad – over the loss of a none too popular crown prince, whose morganatic wife could never be crowned, whose children cannot inherit, and who could only have kept the throne warm for a while for the man who now steps into line a little sooner than he would have had this not happened. If a man will be a crown prince in these times he must take the consequences. We do get hard-hearted, and no mistake, when it is not in our family that the lightning strikes. The 'Paths of Glory lead but to the grave', so what matters it, really, out by what door one goes?

This will reach you soon after you arrive in the great city of tall buildings. More will follow, and I expect they will be so gay that you will rejoice to have even a postal tie with *La Belle France*, to which, if you are a real good American, you will come back when you die – if you do not before.

IV

Your Fourth of July letter came this morning. It was lively reading, especially coming so soon after my first *quatorze de juillet* in the country. The day was a great contrast to the many remembrances I have of Bastille Day in Paris. How I remember my first experience of that fête, when my bedroom window overlooked one of the squares where the band played for the three nights of dancing. That was a fierce experience after the novelty of the first night had worn off, when hour after hour the dance music droned on, and hour after hour the dancing feet on the pavement nearly drove me frantic. To offset it I have memories of the Champs-Elysées and the Place de l'Hôtel de Ville turned into a fairyland. I am glad I saw all that. The memory hangs in my mind like a lovely picture. Out here it was all as still as – I was going to say Sunday, but I should have to say a New England Sunday, as out here Sunday is just like any other day. There was not even a ringing of bells. The only difference there was to me was that Amélie drove Père over to Coutevroult, on the other side of the valley of the Grand Morin, where he played for the dance, and did not get back until long after daylight. I did put out my flags in honor of the day. That was the extent of my celebrating.

In the evening there was a procession at Voisins, and from Meaux and the other towns on the hill there was an occasional rocket. It was not really an exciting day.

The procession at Voisins was a primitive affair, but, to me, all the prettier for that. It looked so quaint with its queer lanterns, its few flags, its children and men in blouses, strolling through the crooked, hilly streets of the old town, to the tap of the drum. No French procession, except it be soldiers, ever

31

marches. If you ever saw a funeral procession going through the street, or one going about a church, you do not need to be told that.

I was glad that this little procession here kept so much of its old-time character, but I was sorry it was not gayer. Still, it was so picturesque that it made me regret anew, what I have so many times regretted of late years, that so many of the old habits of country life in France are passing away, as they are, for that matter, all over Europe, along with ignorance and national costumes.

I must tell you that up to three years ago it was the custom in this *commune*, which, simply because it is not on a railroad, has preserved its old-days air and habits, for wedding and baptismal parties to walk in procession through the streets from the house to the church and back again. Père Abelard used to head the procession, playing on his violin. There has been but one event of that kind since I came, and I am afraid it will be the last. That was for the baptism of the first grandchild of a French officer who had married a woman born in this *commune*, and the older members of the family had a desire to keep up the old traditions. The church is at Quincy, just a step off the *route nationale* to Meaux. Père walked ahead – he could not be accused of marching – fiddling away for dear life. The pretty young godmother carried the baby, in its wonderful christening finery, walking between the grandmother and the father, and the guests, all in their gayest clothes, followed on as they liked behind, all stepping out a little on account of the fiddle ahead. They came back from the church in the same way, only father carried the baby, and the godmother scattered her largesse among the village children.

It is a pity that such pretty customs die out. Wedding parties must have looked so attractive going along these country roads. The fashion that has replaced it is unattractive. Today

32

they think it much more *chic* to hire a big barge and drive down to Esbly and have a rousing breakfast and dance in the big hall which every country hotel has for such festivities. Such changes are in the spirit of the times, so I suppose one must not complain. I should not if people were any happier, but I cannot see that they are. However, I suppose that will come when the Republic is older. The responsibility which that has put on the people has made them more serious than they used to be.

I don't blame you for laughing at the idea of me in a donkey cart. You would laugh harder if you could *see* the cart and me. I do look droll. But this is the land where nothing astonishes any one, thank Heaven. But you wait until I get my *complet de velours* – which is to say my velveteens. I shall match up with the rig then, never fear. Rome was not built in a day, nor can a lady from the city turn into a country-looking lady in the wink of an eye. By the time you have sufficiently overcome your prejudices as to come out and see me with your own eyes, I'll fit into the landscape and the cart in great style.

Absolutely no news to write you, unless you will consider it news that my hedge of dahlias, which I planted myself a month ago, is coming up like nothing else in the world but Jack's Beanstalk. Nothing but weeds ever grew so rank before. Père says I was too generous with my biogene – the latest French thing in fertilizers. But I did want them to be nourished in a rich soil – and come up quick. They did. I can actually see them grow. I am almost afraid to tell you that they are over two feet high now. Of course you won't believe me. But it is not a fairy tale. I would not have believed it myself if I had not seen it.

Alas! I find that I cannot break myself of reading the news-papers, and reading them eagerly. It is all the fault of that nasty affair in Servia. I have a dim recollection that I was very flippant about it in my last letter to you. After all, woman proposes and politics upset her proposition. There seems to be no quick remedy for habit, more's the pity. It is a nasty outlook. We are simply holding our breaths here.

V

This will be only a short letter – more to keep my promise to you than because I feel in the mood to write. Events have broken that. It looks, after all, as if the Servian affair was to become a European affair, and that, what looked as if it might happen during the Balkan War is really coming to pass – a general European uprising.

It is an odd thing. It seems it is an easy thing to change one's environment, but not so easy to change one's character. I am just as excited over the ugly business as I should have been had I remained near the boulevards, where I could have got a newspaper half a dozen times a day. I only get one a day, and this morning I got that one with difficulty. My *Figaro*, which comes out by mail, has not come at all.

Well, it seems that the so-called 'alarmists' were right. Germany has NOT been turning her nation into an army just to divert her population, nor spending her last mark on ships just to amuse herself, and keep Prince Henry busy.

I am sitting here this morning, as I suppose all France is doing, simply holding my breath to see what England is going to do. I imagine there is small doubt about it. I don't see how she can do anything but fight. It is hard to realize that a big war is inevitable, but it looks like it. It was staved off, in spite of Germany's perfidy, during the Balkan troubles. If it has to come now, just imagine what it is going to mean! It will be the bloodiest affair the world has ever seen – a war in the air, a war under the sea as well as on it, and carried out with the most effective man-slaughtering machines ever used in battle.

I need not tell you – you know, we have so often talked about it – how I feel about war. Yet many times since I came to

France to live, I have felt as if I could bear another one, if only it gave Alsace and Lorraine back to us – us meaning me and France. France really deserves her revenge for the humiliation of 1870 and that beastly Treaty of Frankfort. I don't deny that 1870 was the making of modern France, or that, since the Treaty of Frankfort, as a nation she has learned a lesson of patience that she sorely needed. But now that Germany is preparing – is really prepared to attack her again – well, the very hair on my head rises up at the idea. There have been times in the last ten years when I have firmly believed that she could not be conquered again. But Germany! Well, I don't know. If she is, it will not be for lack of nerve or character. Still, it is no secret that she is not ready, or that the anti-military party is strong – and with that awful Caillaux affair; I swore to myself that nothing should tempt me to speak of it. It has been so disgraceful. Still, it is so in the air just now that it has to be recognized as pitifully significant and very menacing to political unity.

The tension here is terrible. Still, the faces of the men are stern, and everyone is so calm – the silence is deadly. There is an absolute suspension of work in the fields. It is as if all France was holding its breath.

One word before I forget it again. You say that you have asked me twice if I have any friend near me. I am sure I have already answered that – yes! I have a family of friends at Voulangis, about two miles the other side of Crécy-en-Brie. Of course neighbors do not see one another in the country as often as in the city, but there they are; so I hasten to relieve your mind just now, when there is a menace of war, and I am sitting tight on my hilltop on the road to the frontier.

VI

Well, dear, what looked impossible is evidently coming to pass.

Early yesterday morning the *garde champêtre* – who is the only thing in the way of a policeman that we have – marched up the road beating his drum. At every crossroad he stopped and read an order. I heard him at the foot of the hill, but I waited for him to pass. At the top of the hill he stopped to paste a bill on the door of the carriage-house on Père Abelard's farm. You can imagine me – in my long studio apron, with my head tied up in a muslin cap – running up the hill to join the group of poor women of the hamlet, to read the proclamation to the armies of land and sea – the order for the mobiliza-tion of the French military and naval forces – headed by its crossed French flags. It was the first experience in my life of a thing like that. I had a cold chill down my spine as I realized that it was not so easy as I had thought to separate myself from Life. We stood there together – a little group of women – and silently read it through – this command for the rising up of a Nation. No need for the men to read it. Each with his military papers in his pocket knew the moment he heard the drum what it meant, and knew equally well his place. I was a foreigner among them, but I forgot that, and if any of them remembered they made no sign. We did not say a word to one another. I silently returned to my garden and sat down. War again! This time war close by – not war about which one can read, as one reads it in the newspapers, as you will read it in the States, far away from it, but war right here – if the Germans can cross the frontier.

It came as a sort of shock, though I might have realized it yesterday when several of the men of the *commune* came to say *au revoir*, with the information that they were joining their regiments, but I felt as if some way other than cannon might be found out of the situation. War had not been declared – has not today. Still, things rarely go to this length and stop there. Judging by this morning's papers Germany really wants it. She could have, had she wished, held stupid Austria back from the throat of poor Servia, not yet recovered from her two Balkan wars.

I imagine this letter will turn into a sort of diary, as it is difficult to say when I shall be able to get any mail matter off. All our communications with the outside world – except by road – were cut this morning by order of the War Bureau. Our railroad is the road to all the eastern frontiers – the trains to Belgium as well as to Metz and Strasbourg pass within sight of my garden. If you don't know what that means – just look on a map and you will realize that the army that advances, whether by road or by train, will pass by me.

During the mobilization, which will take weeks – not only is France not ready, all the world knows that her fortified towns are mostly only fortified on the map – civilians, the mails, and such things must make way for soldiers and war materials. I shall continue to write. It will make me feel in touch still; it will be something to do: besides, any time someone may go up to town by road and I thus have a chance to send it.

VII

August 3, 1914

Well – war is declared.

I passed a rather restless night. I fancy everyone in France did. All night I heard a murmur of voices, such an unusual thing here. It simply meant that the town was awake and, the night being warm, everyone was out of doors.

All day today aeroplanes have been flying between Paris and the frontier. Everything that flies seems to go right over my roof. Early this morning I saw two machines meet, right over my garden, circle about each other as if signaling, and fly off together. I could not help feeling as if one chapter of Wells's *War in the Air* had come to pass. It did make me realize how rapidly the aeroplane had developed into a real weapon of war. I remember so well, no longer ago than Exposition year – that was 1900 – that I was standing, one day, in the old *Galerie des Machines*, with a young engineer from Boston. Over our heads was a huge model of a flying machine. It had never flown, but it was the nearest thing to success that had been accomplished – and it expected to fly some time. So did Darius Green, and people were still skeptical. As he looked up at it, the engineer said: 'Hang it all, that dashed old thing will fly one day, but I shall probably not live to see it.'

He was only thirty at that time, and it was such a few years after that it did fly, and no time at all, once it rose in the air to stay there, before it crossed the Channel. It is wonderful to think that after centuries of effort the thing flew in my time – and that I am sitting in my garden today, watching it sail overhead, like a bird, looking so steady and so sure. I can see them for miles as they approach and for miles after they pass. Often they disappear from view, not because they have passed a horizon line, but simply because they have passed out of the range of my vision – becoming smaller and smaller, until they seem no bigger than a tiny bird, so small that if I take my eyes off the speck in the sky I cannot find it again. It is awe-compelling to remember how these cars in the air change all military tactics. It will be almost impossible to make any big movement that may not be discovered by the opponent.

Just after breakfast my friend from Voulangis drove over in a great state of excitement, with the proposition that I should pack up and return with her. She seemed alarmed at the idea of my being alone, and seemed to think a group of us was safer. It was a point of view that had not occurred to me, and I was not able to catch it. Still, I was touched at her thoughtfulness, even though I had to say that I proposed to stay right here. When she asked me what I proposed to do if the army came retreating across my garden, I instinctively laughed. It seems so impossible this time that the Germans can pass the frontier, and get by Verdun and Toul. All the same, that other people were thinking it possible rather brought me up standing. I just looked at the little house I had arranged such a little time ago – I have only been here two months.

She had come over feeling pretty glum – my dear neighbor from Voulangis. She went away laughing. At the gate she said, 'It looks less gloomy to me than it did when I came. I felt such a brave thing driving over here through a country preparing for war. I expected you to put a statue up in your garden "To a Brave Lady".'

I stood in the road watching her drive away, and as I turned back to the house it suddenly took on a very human sort of look. There passed through my mind a sudden realization, that, according to my habit, I had once again stuck my feet in the ground of a new home – and taken root. It is a fact. I have often looked at people who seem to keep foot-free.

40

I never can. If I get pulled up violently by the roots, if I have my earthly possessions pruned away, I always hurry as fast as I can, take root in a new place, and proceed to sprout a new crop of possessions which fix me there. I used, when I was younger, to envy people who could just pack a bag and move on. I am afraid that I never envied them enough to do as they did. If I had I should have done it. I find that life is pretty logical. It is like chemical action – given certain elements to begin with, contact with the fluids of Life give a certain result. After all I fancy everyone does about the best he can with the gifts he has to do with. So I imagine we do what is natural to us; if we have the gift of knowing what we want and wanting it hard enough we get it. If we don't, we compromise.

I am closing this up rather hurriedly as one of the boys who joins his regiment at Fontainebleau will mail it in Paris as he passes through. I suppose you are glad that you got away before this came to pass.

VIII

August 10, 1914

I have your cable asking me to come 'home' as you call it. Alas, my home is where my books are – they are here. Thanks all the same.

It is a week since I wrote you – and what a week. We have had a sort of intermittent communication with the outside world since the 6th, when, after a week of deprivation, we began to get letters and an occasional newspaper, brought over from Meaux by a boy on a bicycle.

After we were certain, on the 4th of August, that war was being declared all around Germany and Austria, and that England was to back France and Russia, a sort of stupor settled on us all. Day after day Amélie would run to the *mairie* at Quincy to read the telegraphic bulletin – half a dozen lines of facts – that was all we knew from day to day. It is all we know now.

Day after day I sat in my garden watching the aeroplanes flying over my head, and wishing so hard that I knew what they knew. Often I would see five in the day, and one day ten. Day after day I watched the men of the *commune* on their way to join their *classe*. There was hardly an hour of the day that I did not nod over the hedge to groups of stern, silent men, accompanied by their women, and leading the children by the hand, taking the short cut to the station which leads over the hill, right by my gate, to Couilly. It has been so thrilling that I find myself forgetting that it is tragic. It is so different from anything I ever saw before. Here is a nation – which two weeks ago was torn by political dissension – suddenly united, and with a spirit that I have never seen before.

I am old enough to remember well the days of our Civil War, when regiments of volunteers, with flying flags and bands of music, marched through our streets in Boston, on the way to the front. Crowds of stay-at-homes, throngs of women and children lined the sidewalks, shouting deliriously, and waving handkerchiefs, inspired by the marching soldiers, with guns on their shoulders, and the strains of martial music, varied with the then popular 'The girl I left behind me', or, 'When this cruel war is over'. But this is quite different. There are no marching soldiers, no flying flags, no bands of music. It is the rising up of a Nation as one man – all classes shoulder to shoulder, with but one idea – 'Lift up your hearts, and long live France.' I rather pity those who have not seen it.

Since the day when war was declared, and when the Chamber of Deputies – all party feeling forgotten – stood on its feet and listened to Paul Deschanel's terse, remarkable speech, even here in this little *commune*, whose silence is broken only by the rumbling of the trains passing, in view of my garden, on the way to the frontier, and the footsteps of the groups on the way to the train, I have seen sights that have moved me as nothing I have ever met in life before has done. Day after day I have watched the men and their families pass silently, and an hour later have seen the women come back leading the children. One day I went to Couilly to see if it was yet possible for me to get to Paris. I happened to be in the station when a train was going out. Nothing goes over the line yet but men joining their regiments. They were packed in like sardines. There were no uniforms – just a crowd of men – men in blouses, men in patched jackets, well-dressed men – no distinction of class; and on the platform the women and children they were leaving. There was no laughter, none of the gayety with which one has so often reproached this race – but neither were there any tears. As the crowded train began to move, bare heads were thrust out of windows, hats were waved, and a great shout of 'Vive la France' was answered by piping children's voices, and the choked voices of women – 'Vive l'Armée'; and when the train was out of sight the women took the children by the hand, and quietly climbed the hill.

Ever since the 4th of August all our crossroads have been guarded, all our railway gates closed, and also guarded – guarded by men whose only sign of being soldiers is a cap and a gun, men in blouses with a mobilization badge on their left arms, often in patched trousers and sabots, with stern faces and determined eyes, and one thought – 'The country is in danger.'

There is a crossroad just above my house, which commands the valley on either side, and leads to a little hamlet on the *route nationale* from Couilly to Meaux, and is called 'La Demi-Lune' – why 'Half-Moon' I don't know. It was there, on the 6th, that I saw, for the first time, an armed barricade. The gate at the railway crossing had been opened to let a cart pass, when an automobile dashed through Saint-Germain, which is on the other side of the track. The guard raised his bayonet in the air, to command the car to stop and show its papers, but it flew by him and dashed up the hill. The poor guard – it was his first experience of that sort – stood staring after the car; but the idea that he ought to fire at it did not occur to him until it was too late. By the time it occurred to him, and he could telephone to the Demi-Lune, it had passed that guard in the same way – and disappeared. It did not pass Meaux. It simply disappeared. It is still known as the 'Phantom Car'. Within half an hour there was a barricade at the Demi-Lune mounted by armed men – too late, of course. However, it was not really fruitless – that barricade – as the very next day they caught three Germans there, disguised as Sisters of Charity – papers all in order – and who would have got by,

44

after they were detected by a little boy's calling attention to their ungloved hands, if it had not been for the number of armed old men on the barricade.

What makes things especially serious here, so near the frontier, and where the military movements must be made, is the presence of so many Germans, and the bitter feeling there is against them. On the night of August 2, just when the troops were beginning to move east, an attempt was made to blow up the railroad bridge at Isles-lès-Villenoy, between here and Meaux. The three Germans were caught with the dynamite on them – so the story goes – and are now in the barracks at Meaux. But the most absolute secrecy is preserved about all such things. Not only is all France under martial law: the censorship of the press is absolute. Everyone has to carry his papers, and be provided with a passport for which he is liable to be asked in simply crossing a road.

Meaux is full of Germans. The biggest department shop there is a German enterprise. Even Couilly has a German or two, and we had one in our little hamlet. But they've got to get out. Our case is rather pathetic. He was a nice chap, employed in a big fur house in Paris. He came to France when he was fifteen, has never been back, consequently has never done his military service there. Oddly enough, for some reason, he never took out his naturalization papers, so never did his service here. He has no relatives in Germany – that is to say, none with whom he has kept up any correspondence, he says. He earns a good salary, and has always been one of the most generous men in the *commune*, but circumstances are against him. Even though he is an intimate friend of our mayor, the *commune* preferred to be rid of him. He begged not to be sent back to Germany, so he went sadly enough to a concentration camp, pretty well convinced that his career here was over. Still, the French do forget easily.

Couilly had two Germans. One of them – the barber – got out quick. The other did not. But he was quietly informed by some of his neighbors – with pistols in their hands – that his room was better than his company.

The barber occupied a shop in the one principal street in the village, which is, by the way, a comparatively rich place. He had a front shop, which was a café, with a well-fitted-up bar. The back, with a well-dressed window on the street, full of toilette articles, was the barber and hairdressing-room, very neatly arranged, with modern set bowls and mirrors, cabinets full of towels, well-filled shelves of all the things that make such a place profitable. You should see it now. Its broken windows and doors stand open to the weather. The entire interior has been 'efficiently' wrecked. It is as systematic a work of destruction as I have ever seen. Not a thing was stolen, but not an article was spared. All the bottles full of things to drink and all the glasses to drink out of are smashed, so are counters, tables, chairs, and shelving. In the barber shop there is a litter of broken porcelain, broken combs, and smashed-up chairs and boxes among a wreck of hair dyes, perfumes, *brillantine*, and torn towels, and an odor of *apéritifs* and cologne over it all.

Everyone pretends not to know when it happened. They say, 'It was found like that one morning.' Everyone goes to look at it – no one enters, no one touches anything. They simply say with a smile of scorn, 'Good – and so well done.'

There are so many things that I wish you could see. They would give you such a new point of view regarding this race – traditionally so gay, so indifferent to many things that you consider moral, so fond of their individual comfort and personal pleasure, and often so rebellious to discipline. You would be surprised – surprised at their unity, surprised at their seriousness, and often touched by their philosophical acceptance of it all.

Amélie has a stepson and daughter. The boy – named Marius – like his father plays the violin. Like many humble musicians his music is his life and he adds handsomely to his salary as a clerk by playing at dances and little concerts, and by giving lessons in the evening. Like his father he is very timid. But he accepted the war without a word, though nothing is more foreign to his nature. It brought it home to me – this rising up of a Nation in self-defense. It is not the marching into battle of an army that has chosen soldiering. It is the marching out of all the people – of every temperament – the rich, the poor, the timid and the bold, the sensitive and the hardened, the ignorant and the scholar – all men, because they happen to be males, called on not only to cry, 'Vive la France', but to see to it that she does live if dying for her can keep her alive. It is a compelling idea, isn't it?

Amélie's stepdaughter is married to a big burly chap by the name of Georges Godot. He is a thick-necked, red-faced man – in the dynamite corps on the railroad, the construction department. He is used to hardships. War is as good as anything else to him. When he came to say 'goodbye' he said, 'Well, if I have the luck to come back – so much the better. If I don't, that will be all right. You can put a plaque down below in the cemetery with "Godot, Georges: Died for the country"; and when my boys grow up they can say to their comrades, "Papa, you know, he died on the battlefield." It will be a sort of distinction I am not likely to earn for them any other way'; and off he went. Rather fine for a man of that class.

Even the women make no cry. As for the children – even when you would think that they were old enough to understand the meaning of these partings they make no sign, though they seem to understand all the rest of it well enough. There isn't a boy of eight in our *commune* who cannot tell you how it all came about, and who is not just now full of stories of 1870, which he has heard from grandma and grandpa, for, as is natural, everyone talks of 1870 now. I have lived among these people, loved them and believed in them, even when their politics annoyed me, but I confess that they have given me a surprise.

IX

I have Belgium on my soul. Brave little country that has given new proof of its courage and nobility, and surprised the world with a ruler who is a man, as well as king. It occurs to me more than ever today in what a wonderful epoch we have lived. I simply can't talk about it. The suspense is so great. I heard this morning from an officer that the English troops are landing, though he tells me that in London they don't yet know that the Expedition has started. If that is true, it is wonderful. Not a word in the papers yet, but your press is not censored as ours is. I fancy you know these things in New York before we do, although we are now getting a newspaper from Meaux regularly. But there is never anything illuminating in it. The attitude of the world to the Belgian question is a shock to me. I confess to have expected more active indignation at such an outrage.

Everything is very quiet here. Our little *commune* sent 200 men only, but to take 200 able-bodied men away makes a big hole, and upsets life in many ways. For some days we were without bread: bakers gone. But the women took hold and, though the bread is not yet very good, it serves and will as long as flour holds out. No one complains, though we already lack many things. No merchandise can come out yet on the railroads, all the automobiles and most of the horses are gone, and shops are shy of staple things.

Really I don't know which are the more remarkable, the men or the women. You may have read the proclamation of the Minister of Agriculture to the women of France, calling on them to go into the fields and get in the crops and prepare the ground for the sowing of the winter wheat that the men on returning might not find their fields neglected nor their crops lost. You should have seen the old men and the women and the youngsters respond. It is harvest-time, you know, just as it was in the invasion of 1870.

In a few weeks it will be time to gather the fruit. Even now it is time to pick the blackcurrants, all of which go to England to make the jams and jellies without which no English breakfast table is complete.

For days now the women and children have been climbing the hill at six in the morning, with big hats on their heads, deep baskets on their backs, low stools in their hands. There is a big field of blackcurrant bushes beside my garden to the south. All day, in the heat, they sit under the bushes picking away. At sundown they carry their heavy baskets to the weighing-machine on the roadside at the foot of the hill, and stand in line to be weighed in and paid by the English buyers for Crosse and Blackwell, Beach, and such houses, who have, I suppose, some special means of transportation.

That work is, however, the regular work for the women and children. Getting in the grain is not. Yet if you could see them take hold of it you would love them. The old men do double work. Amélie's husband is over seventy. His own work in his fields and orchard would seem too much for him. Yet he and Amélie and the donkey are in the field by three o'clock every morning, and by nine o'clock he is marching down the hill, with his rake and hoe on his shoulder, to help his neighbors.

There is many a woman working in the fields today who was not trained to it. I have a neighbor, a rich peasant, whose two sons are at the front. Her only daughter married an officer in the Engineer Corps. When her husband joined his regiment she came home to her mother with her little boy. I see her every day, in a short skirt and a big hat, leading her boy by the hand, going to the fields to help her mother. If you don't think that is fine, I do. It is only one of many cases right under my eyes.

There are old men here who thought that their days of hard work were over, who are in the fields working like boys. There is our blacksmith – old Père Marie – lame with rheumatism, with his white-haired wife working in the fields from sunrise to sunset. He cheerfully limps up the hill in his big felt slippers, his wife carrying the lunch basket, and a tiny black-and-tan English dog called 'Missy', who is the family baby, and knows lots of tricks, trotting behind, 'because', as he says, 'she is so much company'. The old blacksmith is a veteran of 1870, and was for a long time a prisoner at Königsburg. He likes nothing better than to rest a bit on a big stone at my gate and talk of 1870. Like all Frenchmen of his type he is wonderfully intelligent, full of humor, and an omnivorous reader. Almost every day he has a bit of old newspaper in his pocket out of which he reads to *la dame Américaine* as he calls me, not being able to pronounce my name. It is usually something illuminating about the Germans, when it is not something prophetic. It is wonderful how these old chaps take it all to heart.

All the time my heart is out there in the northeast. It is not my country nor my war – yet I feel as if it were both. All my French friends are there, all my neighbors, and any number of English friends will soon be, among them the brother of the sculptor you met at my house last winter and liked so much. He is with the Royal Field Artillery. His case is rather odd. He came back to England in the spring, after six years in the civil service, to join the army. His leave expired just in time for him to re-enter the army and see his first active service in this war. Fortunately men seem to take it all as a matter of course. That consoles some, I find.

I have just heard that there are two trains a day on which civilians can go up to Paris *if there are places left* after the army is accommodated. There is no guaranty that I can get back the same day. Still, I am going to risk it. I am afraid to be any longer without money, though goodness knows what I can do with it. Besides, I find that all my friends are flying, and I feel as if I should like to say 'goodbye' – I don't know why, but I feel like indulging the impulse. Anyway, I am going to try it. I am going armed with every sort of paper – provisional passport from our consul, *permis de séjour* from my mayor here, and a local permit to enter and leave Paris, which does not allow me to stay inside the fortifications after six o'clock at night, unless I get myself identified at the préfecture of the arrondissement in which I propose to stay and have my passport viséd.

X

I seem to be able to get my letters off to you much more regularly than I dared to hope.

I went up to Paris on the 19th, and had to stay over one night. The trip up was long and tedious, but interesting. There were soldiers everywhere. It amused me almost to tears to see the guards all along the line. We hear so much of the wonderful equipment of the German army. Germany has been spending fortunes for years on its equipment. French taxpayers have kicked for years against spending public moneys on war preparations. The guards all along the railroad were not a jot better got up than those in our little *commune*. There they stand all along the track in their patched trousers and blouses and sabots, with a band round the left arm, a broken soldier cap, and a gun on the shoulder. Luckily the uniform and shaved head do not make the soldier.

Just before we reached Chelles we saw the first signs of actual war preparations, as there we ran inside the wire entanglements that protect the approach to the outer fortifications at Paris, and at Pantin we saw the first concentration of trains – miles and miles of made-up trains all carrying the Red Cross on their doors, and line after line of trucks with gray ammunition wagons, and cannons. We were being constantly held up to let trainloads of soldiers and horses pass. In the station we saw a long train being made up of men going to some point on the line to join their regiments. It was a crowd of men who looked the lower laboring class. They were in their working clothes, many of them almost in rags, each carrying in a bundle, or a twine bag, his few belongings, and some of them with a loaf of bread under the arm. It looked as little martial as possible but for the stern look in the eyes of even the commonest of them. I waited on the platform to see the train pull out. There was no one to see these men off. They all seemed to realize. I hope they did. I remembered the remark of the woman regarding her husband when she saw him go: 'After all, I am only his wife. France is his mother'; and I hoped these poor men, to whom Fate seemed not to have been very kind, had at least that thought in the back of their minds.

I found Paris quiet, and everyone calm – that is to say, everyone but the foreigners, struggling like people in a panic to escape. In spite of the sad news – Brussels occupied Thursday, Namur fallen Monday – there is no sign of discouragement, and no sign of defeat. If it were not for the excitement around the steamship offices the city would be almost as still as death. But all the foreigners, caught here by the unexpectedness of the war, seemed to be fighting to get off by the same train and the same day to catch the first ship, and they seemed to have little realization that, first of all, France must move her troops and war material. I heard it said – it may not be true – that some of the consular officers were to blame for this, and that there was a rumor abroad among foreigners that Paris was sure to be invested, and that foreigners had been advised to get out, so that there should be as few people inside the fortifications as possible. This rumor, however, was prevalent only among foreigners. No French people that I saw seemed to have any such feeling. Apart from the excitement which prevailed in the vicinity of the steamship offices and banks the city had a deserted look. The Paris that you knew exists no longer. Compared with it this Paris is a dead city. Almost every shop is closed, and must be until the great number of men gone to the front can be replaced in some way. There are streets in which every closed front bears, under a paper flag pasted on shutter or door, a sign saying, 'Closed on account of the mobilization'; or, 'All the men with the colors.'

There are almost no men in the streets. There are no busses or tramways, and cabs and automobiles are rare. Some branches of the underground are running at certain hours, and the irregular service must continue until women, and men unfit for military service, replace the men so suddenly called to the flag, and that will take time, especially as so many of the organizers as well as conductors and engineers have gone. It is the same with the big shops. However, that is not important. No one is in the humor to buy anything except food.

It took me a long time to get about. I had to walk everywhere and my friends live a long way apart, and I am a miserable walker. I found it impossible to get back that night, so I took refuge with one of my friends who is sailing on Saturday. Everyone seems to be sailing on that day, and most of them don't seem to care much how they get away – 'ameliorated steerage', as they call it, seems to be the fate of many of them. I can assure you that I was glad enough to get back the next day. Silent as it is here, it is no more so than Paris, and not nearly so sad, for the change is not so great. Paris is no longer our Paris, lovely as it still is.

I do not feel in the mood to do much. I work in my garden intermittently, and the harvest bug (bête rouge we call him here) gets in his work unintermittently on me. If things were normal this introduction to the bête rouge would have seemed to me a tragedy. As it is, it is unpleasantly unimportant. I clean house intermittently; read intermittently; write letters intermittently. That reminds me, do read Leon Daudet's *Fantomes et Vivantes* – the first volumes of his memoirs. He is a terrible example of 'Le fils à papa'. I don't know why it is that a vicious writer, absolutely lacking in reverence, can hold one's attention so much better than a kindly one can. In this book Daudet simply smashes idols, tears down illusions, dances gleefully on sacred traditions, and I lay awake half the night reading him – and forgot the advancing Germans. The book comes down only to 1880, so most of the men he writes about are dead, and most of them, like Victor Hugo, for example, come off very sadly.

Well, I am reconciled to living a long time now – much longer than I wanted to before this awful thing came to pass – just to see all the mighty good that will result from the struggle. I am convinced, no matter what happens, of the final result. I am sure even now, when the Germans have actually crossed the frontier, that France will not be crushed this time, even if she be beaten down to Bordeaux, with her back against the Bay of Biscay. Besides, did you ever know the English bulldog to let go? But it is the horror of such a war in our times that bears so heavily on my soul. After all, 'civilization' is a word we have invented, and its meaning is hardly more than relative, just as is the word 'religion'.

There are problems in the events that the logical spirit finds it hard to face. In every Protestant church the laws of Moses are printed on tablets on either side of the pulpit. On those laws our civil code is founded. 'Thou shalt not kill', says the law. For thousands of years the law has punished the individual who settled his private quarrels with his fists or any more effective weapon, and reserved to itself the right to exact 'an eye for an eye and a tooth for a tooth'. And here we are today, in the twentieth century, when intelligent people have long been striving after a spiritual explanation of the meaning of life, trying to prove its upward trend, trying to beat out of it materialism, endeavoring to find in altruism a road to happiness, and governments can still find no better way to settle their disputes than wholesale slaughter, and that with weapons no so-called civilized man should ever have invented nor any so-called civilized government ever permitted to be made. The theory that the death penalty was a preventive of murder has long ago been exploded. The theory that by making war horrible, war could be prevented, is being exploded today.

And yet – I *know* that if the thought be taken out of life that it is worthwhile to die for an idea a great factor in the making of national spirit will be gone. I *know* that a long peace makes for weakness in a race. I *know* that without war there is still death. To me this last fact is the consolation. It is finer to die voluntarily for an idea deliberately faced, than to die of old age in one's bed; and the grief of parting no one ever born can escape. Still it is puzzling to us simple folk – the feeling that fundamental things do not change: that the balance of good and evil has not changed. We change our fashions, we change our habits, we discover now and then another of the secrets Nature has hidden, that delving man may be kept busy and interested. We pride ourselves that science at least has progressed, that we are cleaner than our progenitors. Yet we are no cleaner than the Greeks and Romans in the days when Athens and Rome ruled the world, nor do we know in what cycle all we know today was known and lost. Oh, I can hear you claiming more happiness for the masses! I wonder. There is no actual buying and selling in open slave markets, it is true, but the men who built the Pyramids and dragged the stone for Hadrian's Villa, were they any worse off really than the workers in the mines today? Upon my soul, I don't know. Life is only a span between the Unknown and the Unknowable. Living is made up in all centuries of just so many emotions. We have never, so far as I know, invented any new one. It *is* too bad to throw these things at you on paper which can't answer back as you would, and right sharply I know.

Nothing going on here except the passing now and then of a long line of Paris street busses on the way to the front. They are all mobilized and going as heroically to the front as if they were human, and going to get smashed up just the same. It does give me a queer sensation to see them climbing this hill. The little Montmartre-Saint-Pierre bus, that climbs up the hill to the funicular in front of Sacré-Coeur, came up the hill bravely. It was built to climb a hill. But the Bastille-Madeleine and the Ternes-Fille de Calvaine, and Saint-Sulpice-Villette just groaned and panted and had to have their traction changed every few steps. I thought they would never get up, but they did.

Another day it was the automobile delivery wagons of the Louvre, the Bon Marché, the Printemps, Petit-Saint-Thomas, La Belle Jardinière, Potin – all the automobiles with which you are so familiar in the streets of Paris. Of course those are much lighter, and came up bravely. As a rule they are all loaded. It is as easy to take men to the front, and material, that way as by railroad, since the cars go. Only once have I seen any attempt at pleasantry on these occasions. One procession went out the other day with all sorts of funny inscriptions, some not at all pretty, many blackguarding the Kaiser, and of course one with the inevitable '*A Berlin*' the first battle-cry of 1870. This time there has been very little of that. I confess it gave me a kind of shiver to see '*A Berlin – pour notre plaisir*' all over the bus. 'On to Berlin!' I don't see that that can be hoped for unless the Germans are beaten to a finish on the Rhine and the allied armies cross Germany as conquerors, unopposed. If they only could! It would only be what is due to Belgium that King Albert should lead the procession 'Under the Lindens'. But I doubt if the maddest war optimist hopes for anything so well deserved as that. I don't dare to, sure as I am of seeing Germany beaten to her knees before the war is closed.

XI

September 8, 1914

Oh, the things I have seen and felt since I last wrote to you over two weeks ago. Here I am again cut off from the world, and have been since the first of the month. For a week now I have known nothing of what was going on in the world outside the limits of my own vision. For that matter, since the Germans crossed the frontier our news of the war has been meager. We got the calm, constant reiteration – 'Left wing – held by the English – forced to retreat a little.' All the same, the general impression was, that in spite of that, 'all was well'. I suppose it was wise.

On Sunday week – that was August 30 – Amélie walked to Esbly, and came back with the news that they were rushing trains full of wounded soldiers and Belgian *réfugiés* through toward Paris, and that the ambulance there was quite insufficient for the work it had to do. So Monday and Tuesday we drove down in the donkey cart to carry bread and fruit, water and cigarettes, and to 'lend a hand'.

It was a pretty terrible sight. There were long trains of wounded soldiers. There was train after train crowded with Belgians – well-dressed women and children (evidently all in their Sunday best) – packed on to open trucks, sitting on straw, in the burning sun, without shelter, covered with dust, hungry and thirsty. The sight set me to doing some hard thinking after I got home that first night. But it was not until Tuesday afternoon that I got my first hint of the truth. That afternoon, while I was standing on the platform, I heard a drum beat in the street, and sent Amélie out to see what was going on. She came back at once to say that it was the *garde champêtre* calling on the inhabitants to carry all their guns, revolvers,

59

etc., to the *mairie* before sundown. That meant the disarming of our *département*, and it flashed through my mind that the Germans must be nearer than the official announcements had told us.

While I stood reflecting a moment – it looked serious – I saw approaching from the west side of the track a procession of wagons. Amélie ran down the track to the crossing to see what it meant, and came back at once to tell me that they were evacuating the towns to the north of us.

I handed the basket of fruit I was holding into a coach of the train just pulling into the station, and threw my last package of cigarettes after it; and, without a word, Amélie and I went out into the street, untied the donkey, climbed into the wagon, and started for home.

By the time we got to the road which leads east to Montry, whence there is a road over the hill to the south, it was full of the flying crowd. It was a sad sight. The procession led in both directions as far as we could see. There were huge wagons of grain; there were herds of cattle, flocks of sheep; there were wagons full of household effects, with often as many as twenty people sitting aloft; there were carriages; there were automobiles with the occupants crowded in among bundles done up in sheets; there were women pushing overloaded handcarts; there were women pushing baby-carriages; there were dogs and cats, and goats; there was every sort of a vehicle you ever saw, drawn by every sort of beast that can draw, from dogs to oxen, from boys to donkeys. Here and there was a man on horseback, riding along the line, trying to keep it moving in order and to encourage the weary. Everyone was calm and silent. There was no talking, no complaining.

The whole road was, however, blocked, and, even had our donkey wished to pass – which she did not – we could not. We simply fell into the procession, as soon as we found a place.

Amélie and I did not say a word to each other until we reached the road that turns off to the Château de Condé; but I did speak to a man on horseback, who proved to be the *intendant* of one of the châteaux at Daumartin, and with another who was the mayor. I simply asked from where these people had come, and was told that they were evacuating Daumartin and all the towns on the plain between there and Meaux, which meant that Monthyon, Neufmortier, Penchard, Chauconin, Barcy, Chambry – in fact, all the villages visible from my garden were being evacuated by order of the military powers.

One of the most disquieting things about this was to see the effect of the procession as it passed along the road. All the way from Esbly to Montry people began to pack at once, and the speed with which they fell into the procession was disconcerting.

When we finally escaped from the crowd into the poplar-shaded avenue which leads to the Château de Condé, I turned to look at Amélie for the first time. I had had time to get a good hold of myself.

'Well, Amélie?' I said.

'Oh, *madame*,' she replied, 'I shall stay.'

'And so shall I,' I answered; but I added, 'I think I must make an effort to get to Paris tomorrow, and I think you had better come with me. I shall not go, of course, unless I am sure of being able to get back. We may as well face the truth: if this means that Paris is in danger, or if it means that we may in our turn be forced to move on, I must get some money so as to be ready.'

'Very well, *madame*,' she replied as cheerfully as if the rumble of the procession behind us were not still in our ears.

The next morning – that was September 2 – I woke just before daylight. There was a continual rumble in the air. At first I thought it was the passing of more *refugiés* on the road.

I threw open my blinds, and then realized that the noise was in the other direction – from the *route nationale*. I listened. I said to myself, 'If that is not artillery, then I never heard any.'

Sure enough, when Amélie came to get breakfast, she announced that the English soldiers were at the Demi-Lune. The infantry was camped there, and the artillery had descended to Couilly and was mounting the hill on the other side of the Morin – between us and Paris.

I said a sort of 'Hm', and told her to ask Père to harness at once. As we had no idea of the hours of the trains, or even if there were any, it was best to get to Esbly as early as possible. It was nine o'clock when we arrived, to find that there should be a train at half past. The station was full. I hunted up the *chef de gare*, and asked him if I could be sure of being able to return if I went up to Paris.

He looked at me in perfect amazement.

'You want to come back?' he asked.

'Sure,' I replied.

'You can,' he answered, 'if you take a train about four o'clock. That may be the last.'

I very nearly said, 'Jiminy-cricket!'

The train ran into the station on time, but you never saw such a sight. It was packed as the Brookline street-cars used to be on the days of a baseball game. Men were absolutely hanging on the roof; women were packed on the steps that led up to the imperials to the third-class coaches. It was a perilous-looking sight. I opened a dozen coaches – all packed, standing room as well as seats, which is ordinarily against the law. I was about to give it up when a man said to me, '*Madame*, there are some coaches at the rear that look as if they were empty.'

I made a dash down the long platform, yanked open a door, and was about to ask if I might get in, when I saw that the coach was full of wounded soldiers in khaki, lying about on the floor as well as the seats. I was so shocked that if the station master, who had run after me, had not caught me I should have fallen backward.

'Sh! *madame*,' he whispered, 'I'll find you a place'; and in another moment I found myself, with Amélie, in a compartment where there were already eight women, a young man, two children, and heaps of hand-luggage – bundles in sheets, twine bags just bulging, paper parcels, and valises. Almost as soon as we were in, the train pulled slowly out of the station.

I learned from the women that Meaux was being evacuated. No one was remaining but the soldiers in the barracks and the Archbishop. They had been ordered out by the army the night before, and the railroad was taking them free. They were escaping with what they could carry in bundles, as they could take no baggage. Their calm was remarkable – not a complaint from any one. They were of all classes, but the barriers were down.

The young man had come from farther up the line – a newspaper chap, who had given me his seat, and was sitting on a bundle. I asked him if he knew where the Germans were, and he replied that on this wing they were at Compiègne, that the center was advancing on Coulommier, but he did not know where the Crown Prince's division was.

I was glad I had made the effort to get to town, for this began to look as if they might succeed in arriving before the circle of steel that surrounds Paris, and God knows what good that seventy-five miles of fortifications will be against the long-range cannon that battered down Liege. I had only one wish – to get back to my hut on the hill; I did not seem to want anything else.

Just before the train ran into Lagny – our first stop – I was surprised to see British soldiers washing their horses in the river, so I was not surprised to find the station full of men in khaki. They were sleeping on the benches along the wall, and standing about, in groups. As to many of the French on the train this was their first sight of the men in khaki, and as there were Scotch there in their kilts, there was a good deal of excitement.

The train made a long stop in the effort to put more people into the already overcrowded coaches. I leaned forward, wishing to get some news, and the funny thing was that I could not think how to speak to those boys in English. You may think that an affectation. It wasn't. Finally I desperately sang out:

'Hulloa, boys.'

You should have seen them dash for the window. I suppose that their native tongue sounded good to them so far from home.

'Where did you come from?' I asked.

'From up yonder – a place called La Fère,' one of them replied.

'What regiment?' I asked.

'Anyone else here speak English?' he questioned, running his eyes along the faces thrust out of the windows.

I told him no one did.

'Well,' he said, 'we are all that is left of the North Irish Horse and a regiment of Scotch Borderers.'

'What are you doing here?'

'Retreating – and waiting for orders. How far are we from Paris?'

I told him about seventeen miles. He sighed, and remarked that he thought they were nearer, and as the train started I had the idea in the back of my head that these boys actually expected to retreat inside the fortifications. La! la!

Instead of the half-hour the train usually takes to get up from here to Paris, we were two hours.

I found Paris much more normal than when I was there two weeks ago, though still quite unlike itself; everyone perfectly calm and no one with the slightest suspicion that the battle line was so near – hardly more than ten miles beyond the outer forts. I transacted my business quickly – saw only one person, which was wiser than I knew then, and caught the four o'clock train back – we were almost the only passengers.

I had told Père not to come after us – it was so uncertain when we could get back, and I had always been able to get a carriage at the hotel in Esbly.

We reached Esbly at about six o'clock to find the stream of emigrants still passing, although the roads were not so crowded as they had been the previous day. I ran over to the hotel to order the carriage – to be told that Esbly was evacuated, the ambulance had gone, all the horses had been sold that afternoon to people who were flying. There I was faced with a walk of five miles – lame and tired. Just as I had made up my mind that what had to be done could be done – die or no die – Amélie came running across the street to say:

'Did you ever see such luck? Here is the old cart horse of Cousine Georges and the wagon!'

Cousine Georges had fled, it seems, since we left, and her horse had been left at Esbly to fetch the schoolmistress and her husband. So we all climbed in. The schoolmistress and her husband did not go far, however. We discovered before we had got out of Esbly that Couilly had been evacuated during the day, and that a great many people had left Voisins; that the civil government had gone to Coutevroult; that the Croix Rouge had gone. So the schoolmistress and her husband, to whom all this was amazing news, climbed out of the wagon, and made a dash back to the station to attempt to get back to Paris. I do hope they succeeded.

Amélie and I dismissed the man who had driven the wagon down, and jogged on by ourselves. I sat on a board in the back of the covered cart, only too glad for any sort of locomotion which was not 'shank's mare'.

Just after we left Esbly I saw first an English officer, standing in his stirrups and signaling across a field, where I discovered a detachment of English artillery going toward the hill. A little farther along the road we met a couple of English officers – pipes in their mouths and sticks in their hands – strolling along as quietly and smilingly as if there were no such thing as war. Naturally I wished to speak to them. I was so shut in that I could see only directly in front of me, and if you ever rode behind a big cart horse I need not tell you that although he walks slowly and heavily he walks steadily, and will not stop for any pulling on the reins unless he jolly well chooses. As we approached the officers, I leaned forward and said, 'Beg your pardon,' but by the time they realized that they had been addressed in English we had passed. I yanked at the flap at the back of the cart, got it open a bit, looked out to find them standing in the middle of the road, staring after us in amazement.

The only thing I had the sense to call out was:

'Where'd you come from?'

One of them made an emphatic gesture with his stick, over his shoulder in the direction from which they had come.

'Where are you going?' I called.

He made the same gesture toward Esbly, and then we all laughed heartily, and by that time we were too far apart to continue the interesting conversation, and that was all the enlightenment I got out of that meeting. The sight of them and their cannon made me feel a bit serious. I thought to myself: 'If the Germans are not expected here – well, it looks like it.' We finished the journey in silence, and I was so tired when I got back to the house that I fell into bed, and only drank a glass of milk that Amélie insisted on pouring down my throat.

XII

September 8, 1914

You can get some idea of how exhausted I was on that night of Wednesday, September 2, when I tell you that I waked the next morning to find that I had a picket at my gate. I did not know until Amélie came to get my coffee ready the next morning – that was Thursday, September 3 – can it be that it is only five days ago! She also brought me news that they were preparing to blow up the bridges on the Marne; that the post office had gone; that the English were cutting the telegraph wires.

While I was taking my coffee, quietly, as if it were an everyday occurrence, she said: 'Well, *madame*, I imagine that we are going to see the Germans. Père is breaking an opening into the underground passage under the stable, and we are going to put all we can out of sight. Will you please gather up what you wish to save, and it can be hidden there?'

I don't know that I ever told you that all the hill is honeycombed with those old subterranean passages, like the one we saw at Provins. They say that they go as far as Crécy-en-Brie, and used to connect the royal palace there with one on this hill.

Naturally I gave a decided refusal to any move of that sort, so far as I was concerned. My books and portraits are the only things I should be eternally hurt to survive. To her argument that the books could be put there – there was room enough – I refused to listen. I had no idea of putting my books underground to be mildewed. Besides, if it had been possible I would not have attempted it – and it distinctly was impossible. I felt a good deal like the Belgian *réfugiés* I had seen – all so well dressed; if my house was going up, it was going up in its best clothes. I had just been uprooted once – a horrid operation – and I did not propose to do it again so soon. To that my mind was made up.

Luckily for me – for Amélie was as set as I was – the argument was cut short by a knock at the front door. I opened it to find standing there a pretty French girl whom I had been seeing every day, as, morning and evening, she passed my gate to and from the railway station. Sooner or later I should have told you about her if all this excitement had not put it out of my mind and my letters. I did not know her name. I had never got to asking Amélie who she was, though I was a bit surprised to find anyone of her type here where I had supposed there were only farmers and peasants.

She apologized for presenting herself so informally: said she had come, '*de la part de maman*', to ask me what I proposed to do. I replied at once, 'I am staying.'

She looked a little surprised: said her mother wished to do the same, but that her only brother was with the colors; that he had confided his young wife and two babies to her, and that the Germans were so brutal to children that she did not dare risk it.

'Of course, you know,' she added, 'that everyone has left Couilly; all the shops are closed, and nearly everyone has gone from Voisins and Quincy. The mayor's wife left last night. Before going she came to us and advised us to escape at once, and even found us a horse and cart – the trains are not running. So mother thought that, as you were a foreigner, and all alone, we ought not to go without at least offering you a place in the wagon – the chance to go with us.'

I was really touched, and told her so, but explained that I should stay. She was rather insistent – said her mother would be so distressed at leaving me alone with only a little group of women and children about me, who might, at the last moment, be panic-stricken.

I explained to her as well as I could that I was alone in the world, poor myself, and that I could not see myself leaving all that I valued – my home; to have which I had made a supreme effort, and for which I had already a deep affection – to join the band of *réfugiés*, shelterless, on the road, or to look for safety in a city, which, if the Germans passed here, was likely to be besieged and bombarded. I finally convinced her that my mind was made up. I had decided to keep my face turned toward Fate rather than run away from it. To me it seemed the only way to escape a panic – a thing of which I have always had a horror.

Seeing that nothing could make me change my mind, we shook hands, wished each other luck, and, as she turned away, she said, in her pretty French: 'I am sorry it is disaster that brought us together, but I hope to know you better when days are happier'; and she went down the hill.

When I returned to the dining room I found that, in spite of my orders, Amélie was busy putting my few pieces of silver, and such bits of china from the buffet as seemed to her valuable – her ideas and mine on that point do not jibe – into the waste-paper baskets to be hidden underground.

I was too tired to argue. While I stood watching her there was a tremendous explosion. I rushed into the garden. The picket, his gun on his shoulder, was at the gate.

'What was that?' I called out to him.

'Bridge,' he replied. 'The English divisions are destroying the bridges on the Marne behind them as they cross. That means that another division is over.'

I asked him which bridge it was, but of course he did not know. While I was standing there, trying to locate it by the smoke, an English officer, who looked of middle age, tall, clean-cut, rode down the road on a chestnut horse, as slight, as clean-cut, and well groomed as himself. He rose in his stirrups to look off at the plain before he saw me. Then he looked at me, then up at the flags flying over the gate – saw the Stars and Stripes – smiled, and dismounted.

'American, I see,' he said.

I told him I was.

'Live here?' said he.

I told him that I did.

'Staying on?' he asked.

I answered that it looked like it.

He looked me over a moment before he said, 'Please invite me into your garden and show me that view.'

I was delighted. I opened the gate, and he strolled in and sauntered with a long, slow stride – a long-legged stride – out on to the lawn and right down to the hedge, and looked off.

'Beautiful,' he said, as he took out his field-glass, and turned up the map case which hung at his side. 'What town is that?' he asked, pointing to the foreground.

I told him that it was Mareuil-on-the-Marne.

'How far off is it?' he questioned.

I told him that it was about two miles, and Meaux was about the same distance beyond it.

'What town is that?' he asked, pointing to the hill.

I explained that the town on the horizon was Penchard – not really a town, only a village; and lower down, between Penchard and Meaux, were Neufmortier and Chauconin.

All this time he was studying his map.

'Thank you. I have it,' he said. 'It is a lovely country, and this is a wonderful view of it, the best I have had.'

For a few minutes he stood studying it in silence – alternatively looking at his map and then through his glass. Then he dropped his map, put his glasses into the case, and turned to me – and smiled. He had a winning smile, sad and yet consoling, which lighted up a bronzed face, stern and weary. It was the sort of smile to which everything was permitted.

'Married?' he said.

You can imagine what he was like when I tell you that I answered right up, and only thought it was funny hours after – or at least I shook my head cheerfully.

'You don't live here alone?' he asked.

'But I do,' I replied.

He looked at me bravely a moment, then off at the plain.

'Lived here long?' he questioned.

I told him that I had lived in this house only three months, but that I had lived in France for sixteen years.

Without a word he turned back toward the house, and for half a minute, for the first time in my life, I had a sensation that it looked strange for me to be an exile in a country that was not mine, and with no ties. For a penny I would have told him the history of my life. Luckily he did not give me time. He just strode down to the gate, and by the time he had his foot in the stirrup I had recovered.

'Is there anything I can do for you, captain?' I asked.

He mounted his horse, looked down at me. Then he gave me another of his rare smiles.

'No,' he said, 'at this moment there is nothing that you can do for me, thank you; but if you could give my boys a cup of tea, I imagine that you would just about save their lives.' And nodding to me, he said to the picket, 'This lady is kind enough to offer you a cup of tea,' and he rode off, taking the road down the hill to Voisins.

I ran into the house, put on the kettle, ran up the road to call Amélie, and back to the arbor to set the table as well as I could. The whole atmosphere was changed. I was going to be useful.

I had no idea how many men I was going to feed. I had only seen three. To this day I don't know how many I did feed. They came and came and came. It reminded me of hens running toward a place where another hen has found something good. It did not take me many minutes to discover that these men needed something more substantial than tea. Luckily I had brought back from Paris an emergency stock of things like biscuit, dry cakes, jam, etc., for even before our shops were closed there was mighty little in them. For an hour and a half I brewed pot after pot of tea, opened jar after jar of jam and jelly, and tin after tin of biscuit and cakes, and although it was hardly hearty fodder for men, they put it down with a relish. I have seen hungry men, but never anything as hungry as these boys.

I knew little about military discipline – less about the rules of active service; so I had no idea that I was letting these hungry men – and evidently hunger laughs at laws – break all the regulations of the army. Their guns were lying about in any old place; their kits were on the ground; their belts were unbuckled. Suddenly the captain rode up the road and looked over the hedge at the scene. The men were sitting on the benches, on the ground, anywhere, and were all smoking my best Egyptian cigarettes, and I was running round as happy as a queen, seeing them so contented and comfortable.

It was a rude awakening when the captain rode up the street.

There was a sudden jumping up, a hurried buckling up of belts, a grab for kits and guns, and an unceremonious cut for the gate. I heard a volley from the officer. I marked a serious effort on the part of the men to keep the smiles off their faces as they hurriedly got their kits on their backs and their guns on their shoulders, and, rigidly saluting, dispersed up the hill, leaving two very straight men marching before the gate as if they never in their lives had thought of anything but picket duty.

The captain never even looked at me, but rode up the hill after his men. A few minutes later he returned, dismounted at the gate, tied his horse, and came in. I was a bit confused. But he smiled one of those smiles of his, and I got right over it.

'Dear little lady,' he said, 'I wonder if there is any tea left for me?'

Was there! I should think so; and I thought to myself, as I led the way into the dining room, that he was probably just as hungry as his men.

While I was making a fresh brew he said to me:

'You must forgive my giving my men Hades right before you, but they deserved it, and know it, and under the circumstances I imagine they did not mind taking it. I did not mean you to give them a party, you know. Why, if the major had ridden up that hill – and he might have – and seen that party inside your garden, I should have lost my commission and those boys got the guardhouse. These men are on active service.'

Then, while he drank his tea, he told me why he felt a certain indulgence for them – these boys who were hurried away from England without having a chance to take leave of their families, or even to warn them that they were going.

'This is the first time that they have had a chance to talk to a woman who speaks their tongue since they left England; I can't begrudge it to them and they know it. But discipline is discipline, and if I had let such a breach of it pass they would have no respect for me. They understand. They had no business to put their guns out of their hands. What would they have done if the detachment of Uhlans we are watching for had dashed up that hill – as they might have?'

Before I could answer or remark on this startling speech there was a tremendous explosion, which brought me to my feet, with the inevitable, 'What's that?'

He took a long pull at his tea before he replied quietly, 'Another division across the Marne.'

Then he went on as if there had been no interruption:

'This Yorkshire regiment has had hard luck. Only one other regiment in the Expedition has had worse. They have marched from the Belgian frontier, and they have been in four big actions in the retreat – Mons, Cambrai, Saint-Quentin, and La Fère. Saint-Quentin was pretty rough luck. We went into the trenches a full regiment. We came out to retreat again with four hundred men – and I left my younger brother there.'

I gasped; I could not find a word to say. He did not seem to feel it necessary that I should. He simply winked his eyelids, stiffened his stern mouth, and went right on; and I forgot all about the Uhlans:

'At La Fère we lost our commissary on the field. It was burned, and these lads have not had a decent feed since – that was three days ago. We have passed through few towns since, and those were evacuated – drummed out; and fruit from the orchards on the roadsides is about all they have had – hardly good feed for a marching army in such hot weather. Besides, we were moving pretty fast – but in order – to get across the Marne, toward which we have been drawing the Germans, and in every one of these battles we have been fighting with one man to their ten.'

I asked him where the Germans were.

'Can't say,' he replied.

'And the French?'

'No idea. We've not seen them – yet. We understood that we were to be reinforced at Saint-Quentin by a French detachment at four o'clock. They got there at eleven – the battle was over – and lost. But these boys gave a wonderful account of themselves, and in spite of the disaster retreated in perfect order.'

Then he told me that at the last moment he ordered his company to lie close in the trench and let the Germans come right up to them, and not to budge until he ordered them to give them what they hate – the bayonet. The Germans were within a few yards when a German automobile carrying a machine gun bore down on them and discovered their position, but the English sharpshooters picked off the five men the car carried before they could fire a shot, and after that it was every man for himself – what the French call '*sauve qui peut*'.

The Uhlans came back to my mind, and it seemed to me a good time to ask him what he was doing here. Oddly enough, in spite of the several shocks I had had, and perhaps because of his manner, I was able to do it as if it was the sort of tea-table conversation to which I had always been accustomed.

'What are you doing here?' I said.

'Waiting for orders,' he answered.

'And for Uhlans?'

'Oh,' replied he, 'if incidentally while we are sitting down here to rest, we could rout out a detachment of German cavalry, which our aeroplane tells us crossed the Marne ahead of us, we would like to. Whether this is one of those flying squads they are so fond of sending ahead, just to do a little terrorizing, or whether they escaped from the battle of La Fère, we don't know. I fancy the latter, as they do not seem to have done any harm or to have been too anxious to be seen.'

I need not tell you that my mind was acting like lightning. I remembered, in the pause, as I poured him another cup of tea, and pushed the jam pot toward him, that Amélie had heard at Voisins last night that there were horses in the woods near the canal; that they had been heard neighing in the night; and that we had jumped to the conclusion that there were English cavalry there. I mentioned this to the captain, but for some reason it did not seem to make much impression on him; so I did not insist, as there was something that seemed more important which I had been getting up the courage to ask him. It had been on my lips all day. I put it.

'Captain,' I asked, 'do you think there is any danger in my staying here?'

He took a long drink before he answered:

'Little lady, there is danger everywhere between Paris and the Channel. Personally – since you have stayed until getting away will be difficult – I do not really believe that there is any reason why you should not stick it out. You may have a disagreeable time. But I honestly believe you are running no real risk of having more than that. At all events, I am going to do what I can to assure your personal safety. As we understand it – no one really knows anything except the orders given out – it is not intended that the Germans shall cross the Marne here. But who knows? Anyway, if I move on, each division of the Expeditionary Force that retreats to this hill will know that you are here. If it is necessary, later, for you to leave, you will be notified and precautions taken for your safety. You are not afraid?'

I could only tell him, 'Not yet,' but I could not help adding, 'Of course I am not so stupid as to suppose for a moment that you English have retreated here to amuse yourselves, or that you have dragged your artillery up the hill behind me just to exercise your horses or to give your gunners a pretty promenade.'

He threw back his head and laughed aloud for the first time, and I felt better.

'Precautions do not always mean a battle, you know'; and as he rose to his feet he called my attention to a hole in his coat, saying, 'It was a miracle that I came through Saint-Quentin with a whole skin. The bullets simply rained about me. It was pouring – I had on a mackintosh – which made me conspicuous as an officer, if my height had not exposed me. Every German regiment carries a number of sharpshooters whose business is to pick off the officers. However, it was evidently not my hour.'

As we walked out to the gate I asked him if there was anything else I could do for him.

'Do you think,' he replied, 'that you could get me a couple of fresh eggs at half-past seven and let me have a cold wash-up?'

'Well, rather,' I answered, and he rode away.

As soon as he was gone one of the picket called from the road to know if they could have 'water and wash'.

I told them of course they could – to come right in.

He said that they could not do that, but that if they could have water at the gate – and I did not mind – they could wash up in relays in the road. So Père came and drew buckets and buckets of water, and you never saw such a stripping and such a slopping, as they washed and shaved – and with such dispatch. They had just got through, luckily, when, at about half-past six, the captain rode hurriedly down the hill again. He carried a slip of white paper in his hand, which he seemed intent on deciphering.

As I met him at the gate he said:

'Sorry I shall miss those eggs – I've orders to move east,' and he began to round up his men.

I foolishly asked him why. I felt as if I were losing a friend.

'Orders,' he answered. Then he put the slip of paper into his pocket, and leaning down he said:

'Before I go I am going to ask you to let my corporal pull down your flags. You may think it cowardly. I think it prudent. They can be seen a long way. It is silly to wave a red flag at a bull. Any needless display of bravado on your part would be equally foolish.'

So the corporal climbed up and pulled down the big flags, and together we marched them off to the stable. When I returned to the gate, where the captain was waiting for the rest of the picket to arrive, I was surprised to find my French caller of the morning standing there, with a pretty blonde

77

girl, whom she introduced as her sister-in-law. She explained that they had started in the morning, but that their wagon had been overloaded and broken down and they had had to return, and that her mother was 'glad of it'. It was perfectly natural that she should ask me to ask the 'English officer if it was safe to stay'. I repeated the question. He looked down at them, asked if they were friends of mine. I explained that they were neighbors and acquaintances only.

'Well,' he said, 'I can only repeat what I said to you this morning – I think you are safe here. But for God's sake, don't give it to them as coming from me. I can assure your personal safety, but I cannot take the whole village on my conscience.' I told him that I would not quote him.

All this time he had been searching in a letter-case, and finally selected an envelope from which he removed the letter, passing me the empty cover.

'I want you,' he said, 'to write me a letter – that address will always reach me. I shall be anxious to know how you came through, and every one of these boys will be interested. You have given them the only happy day they have had since they left home. As for me – if I live – I shall some time come back to see you. Goodbye and good luck.' And he wheeled his horse and rode up the hill, his boys marching behind him; and at the turn of the road they all looked back and I waved my hand, and I don't mind telling you that I nodded to the French girls at the gate and got into the house as quickly as I could – and wiped my eyes. Then I cleared up the tea-mess. It was not until the house was in order again that I put on my glasses and read the envelope that the captain had given me:

Capt. T. E. Simpson,
King's Own Yorkshire L. I. VIth Infantry Brigade,
15th Division, British Expeditionary Force.

And I put it carefully away in my address book until the time should come for me to write and tell 'how I came through'; the phrase did disturb me a little.

I did not eat any supper. Food seemed to be the last thing I wanted. I sat down in the study to read. It was about eight when I heard the gate open. Looking out I saw a man in khaki, his gun on his shoulder, marching up the path. I went to the door.

'Good evening, ma'am,' he said. 'All right?'

I assured him that I was.

'I am the corporal of the guard,' he added. 'The commander's compliments, and I was to report to you that your road was picketed for the night and that all is well.'

I thanked him, and he marched away, and took up his post at the gate, and I knew that this was the commander's way of letting me know that Captain Simpson had kept his word. I had just time while the corporal stood at the door to see 'Bedford' on his cap, so I knew that the new regiment was from Bedfordshire.

I sat up a while longer, trying to fix my mind on my book, trying not to look round constantly at my pretty green interior, at all my books, looking so ornamental against the walls of my study, at all the portraits of the friends of my life of active service above the shelves, and the old sixteenth-century Buddha, which Oda Neilson sent me on my last birthday, looking so stoically down from his perch to remind me how little all these things counted. I could not help remembering at the end that my friends at Voulangis had gone – that they were at that very moment on their way to Marseilles, that almost everyone else I knew on this side of the water was either at Havre waiting to sail, or in London, or shut up in Holland or Denmark; that except for the friends I had at the front I was alone with my beloved France and her Allies. Through it all there ran a thought that made me laugh at last – how all through August I had felt so outside of things, only suddenly to find it right at my door. In the back of my mind – pushed back as hard as I could – stood the question – what was to become of all this?

Yet, do you know, I went to bed, and what is more I slept well. I was physically tired. The last thing I saw as I closed up the house was the gleam of the moonlight on the muskets of the picket pacing the road, and the first thing I heard, as I waked suddenly at about four, was the crunching of the gravel as they still marched there.

I got up at once. It was the morning of Friday, the 4th of September. I dressed hurriedly, ran down to put the kettle on, and start the coffee, and by five o'clock I had a table spread in the road, outside the gate, with hot coffee and milk and bread and jam. I had my lesson, so I called the corporal and explained that his men were to come in relays, and when the coffee-pot was empty there was more in the house; and I left them to serve themselves, while I finished dressing. I knew that the officers were likely to come over, and one idea was fixed in my mind: I must not look demoralized. So I put on a clean white frock, white shoes and stockings, a big black bow in my hair, and I felt equal to anything – in spite of the fact that before I dressed I heard far off a booming – could it be cannon? – and more than once a nearer explosion – more bridges down, more English across.

It was not much after nine when two English officers strolled down the road – Captain Edwards and Major Ellison, of the Bedfordshire Light Infantry. They came into the garden, and the scene with Captain Simpson of the day before was practically repeated. They examined the plain, located the towns, looked long at it with their glasses; and that being over I put the usual question, 'Can I do anything for you?' and got the usual answer, 'Eggs'.love o

I asked how many officers there were in the mess, and he replied 'Five'; so I promised to forage, and away they went.

As soon as they were out of sight the picket set up a howl for baths. These Bedfordshire boys were not hungry, but they had retreated from their last battle leaving their kits in the trenches, and were without soap or towels, or combs or razors. But that was easily remedied. They washed up in relays in the court at Amélie's – it was a little more retired. As Amélie had put all her towels, etc., down underground, I ran back and forward between my house and hers for all sorts of things, and, as they slopped until the road ran tiny rivulets, I had to change shoes and stockings twice. I was not conscious till afterward how funny it all was. I must have been a good deal like an excited duck, and Amélie like a hen with a duckling. When she was not twitching my sash straight, she was running about after me with dry shoes and stockings, and a chair, for fear '*madame* was getting too tired'; and when she was not doing that she was clapping my big garden hat on my head, for fear '*madame* would get a sunstroke'. The joke was that I did not know it was hot. I did not even know it was funny until afterward, when the whole scene seemed to have been by a sort of dual process photographed unconsciously on my memory.

When the boys were all washed and shaved and combed – and they were so larky over it – we were like old friends. I did not know one of them by name, but I did know who was married, and who had children; and how one man's first child had been born since he left England, and no news from home because they had seen their mail wagon burn on the battle-field; and how one of them was only twenty, and had been six years in the army – lied when he enlisted; how none of them had ever seen war before; how they had always wanted to, and 'Now,' said the twenty-year old, 'I've seen it – good Lord –

and all I want is to get home,' and he drew out of his breast pocket a photograph of a young girl in all her best clothes, sitting up very straight.

When I said, 'Best girl?' he said proudly, 'Only one, and we were to have been married in January if this hadn't happened. Perhaps we may yet, if we get home at Christmas, as they tell us we may.'

I wondered who he meant by 'they'. The officers did not give any such impression.

While I was gathering up towels and things before returning to the house, this youngster advanced toward me, and said with a half-shy smile, 'I take it you're a lady.'

I said I was glad he had noticed it – I did make such an effort.

'No, no,' he said, 'I'm not joking. I may not say it very well, but I am quite serious. We all want to say to you that if it is war that makes you and the women you live amongst so different from English women, then all we can say is that the sooner England is invaded and knows what it means to have a fighting army on her soil, and see her fields devastated and her homes destroyed, the better it will be for the race. You take my word for it, they have no notion of what war is like; and there ain't no English woman of your class could have, or would have, done for us what you have done this morning. Why, in England the common soldier is the dirt under the feet of women like you.'

I had to laugh, as I told him to wait and see how they treated them when war was there; that they probably had not done the thing simply because they never had had the chance.

'Well,' he answered, 'they'll have to change mightily. Why, our own women would have been uncomfortable and ashamed to see a lot of dirty men stripping and washing down like we have done. You haven't looked as if you minded it a bit, or thought of anything but getting us cleaned up as quick and comfortable as possible.'

I started to say that I felt terribly flattered that I had played the role so well, but I knew he would not understand. Besides, I was wondering if it were true. I never knew the English except as individuals, never as a race. So I only laughed, picked up my towels, and went home to rest.

Not long before noon a bicycle scout came over with a message from Captain Edwards, and I sent by him a basket of eggs, a cold chicken, and a bottle of wine as a contribution to the breakfast at the officers' mess; and by the time I had eaten my breakfast, the picket had been changed, and I saw no more of those boys.

During the afternoon the booming off at the east became more distinct. It surely was cannon. I went out to the gate where the corporal of the guard was standing, and asked him, 'Do I hear cannon?'

'Sure,' he replied.

'Do you know where it is?' I asked.

He said he hadn't an idea – about twenty-five or thirty miles away. And on he marched, up and down the road, perfectly indifferent to it.

When Amélie came to help get tea at the gate, she said that a man from Voisins, who had started with the crowd that left here Wednesday, had returned. He had brought back the news that the sight on the road was simply horrible. The *réfugiés* had got so blocked in their hurry that they could move in neither direction; cattle and horses were so tired that they fell by the way; it would take a general to disentangle them. My! wasn't I glad that I had not been tempted to get into that mess!

Just after the boys had finished their tea, Captain Edwards came down the road, swinging my empty basket on his arm, to say 'Thanks' for his breakfast. He looked at the table at the gate.

'So the men have been having tea – lucky men – and bottled water! What extravagance!'

'Come in and have some, too,' I said.

'Love to,' he answered, and in he came.

While I was making the tea he walked about the house, looked at the pictures, examined the books. Just as the table was ready there was a tremendous explosion. He went to the door, looked off, and remarked, as if it were the most natural thing in the world, 'Another division across. That should be the last.'

'Are all the bridges down?' I asked.

'All, I think, except the big railroad bridge behind you – Chalifert. That will not go until the last minute.'

I wanted to ask, 'When will it be the "last minute" – and what does the "last minute" mean?' – but where was the good? So we went into the dining room. As he threw his hat on to a chair and sat down with a sigh, he said, 'You see before you a very humiliated man. About half an hour ago eight of the Uhlans we are looking for rode right into the street below you, in Voisins. We saw them, but they got away. It is absolutely our own stupidity.'

'Well,' I explained to him, 'I fancy I can tell you where they are hiding. I told Captain Simpson so last night.' And I explained to him that horses had been heard in the woods at the foot of the hill since Tuesday; that there was a cart road, rough and winding, running in toward Condé for over two miles; that it was absolutely screened by trees, had plenty of water, and not a house in it – a shelter for a regiment of cavalry. And I had the impertinence to suggest that if the picket had been extended to the road below it would have been impossible for the Germans to have got into Voisins.

'Not enough of us,' he replied. 'We are guarding a wide territory, and cannot put our pickets out of sight of one another.' Then he explained that, as far as he knew from his aeroplane men, the detachment had broken up since it was first discovered on this side of the Marne. It was reported that there were only about twenty-four in this vicinity; that they were believed to be without ammunition; and then he dropped the subject, and I did not bother him with questions that were bristling in my mind.

He told me how sad it was to see the ruin of the beautiful country through which they had passed, and what a mistake it had been from his point of view not to have foreseen the methods of Germans and drummed out all the towns through which the armies had passed. He told me one or two touching and interesting stories. One was of the day before a battle, I think it was Saint-Quentin. The officers had been invited to dine at a pretty chateau near which they had bivouacked. The French family could not do too much for them, and the daughters of the house waited on the table. Almost before the meal was finished the *alerte* sounded, and the battle was on them. When they retreated by the house where they had been so prettily entertained such a few hours before, there was not one stone standing on another, and what became of the family he had no idea.

The other that I remember was of the way the Germans passed the river at Saint-Quentin and forced the battle at La Fère on them. The bridge was mined, and the captain was standing beside the engineer waiting to give the order to touch off the mine. It was a nasty night – a Sunday (only last Sunday, think of that!) – and the rain was coming down in torrents. Just before the Germans reached the bridge he ordered it blown up. The engineer touched the button. The fuse did not act. He was in despair, but the captain said to him, 'Brace up, my lad – give her another chance.' The second effort failed like the first. Then, before anyone could stop him, the engineer made a dash for the end of the bridge, drawing his revolver as he ran, and fired six shots into the mine, knowing that, if he succeeded, he would go up with the bridge. No good, and he was literally dragged off the spot weeping with rage at his failure – and the Germans came across.

All the time we had been talking I had heard the cannonade in the distance – now at the north and now in the east. This seemed a proper moment, inspired by the fact that he was talking war, of his own initiative, to put a question or two, so I risked it.

'That cannonading seems much nearer than it did this morning,' I ventured.

'Possibly,' he replied.

'What does that mean?' I persisted.

'Sorry I can't tell you. We men know absolutely nothing. Only three men in this war know anything of its plans – Kitchener, Joffre, and French. The rest of us obey orders, and know only what we see. Not even a brigade commander is any wiser. Once in a while the colonel makes a remark, but he is never illuminating.'

'How much risk am I running by remaining here?'

He looked at me a moment before he asked, 'You want to know the truth?'

'Yes,' I replied.

'Well, this is the situation as near as I can work it out. We infer from the work we were given to do – destroying bridges, railroads, telegraphic communications – that an effort is to be made here to stop the march on Paris; in fact, that the Germans are not to be allowed to cross the Marne at Meaux, and march on the city by the main road from Rheims to the capital. The communications are all cut. That does not mean that it will be impossible for them to pass; they've got clever engineers. It means that we have impeded them and may stop them. I don't know. Just now your risk is nothing. It will be nothing unless we are ordered to hold this hill, which is the line of march from Meaux to Paris. We have had no such order yet. But if the Germans succeed in taking Meaux and attempt to put their bridges across the Marne, our artillery, behind you there on the top of the hill, must open fire on them over your head. In that case the Germans will surely reply by bombarding this hill.' And he drank his tea without looking to see how I took it.

I remember that I was standing opposite him, and I involuntarily leaned against the wall behind me, but suddenly thought, 'Be careful. You'll break the glass in the picture of Whistler's Mother, and you'll be sorry.' It brought me up standing, and he didn't notice. Isn't the mind a queer thing?

He finished his tea, and rose to go. As he picked up his cap he showed me a hole right through his sleeve – in one side, out the other – and a similar one in his puttee, where the ball had been turned aside by the leather lacing of his boot. He laughed as he said, 'Odd how near a chap comes to going out, and yet lives to drink tea with you. Well, goodbye and good luck if I don't see you again.'

And off he marched, and I went into the library and sat down and sat very still.

It was not more than half an hour after Captain Edwards left that the corporal came in to ask me if I had a window in the roof. I told him that there was, and he asked if he might go up. I led the way, picking up my glasses as I went. He explained, as we climbed the two flights of stairs, that the aeroplane had reported a part of the Germans they were hunting 'not a thousand feet from this house'. I opened the skylight. He scanned in every direction. I knew he would not see anything, and he did not. But he seemed to like the view, could command the roads that his posse was guarding, so he sat on the window ledge and talked. The common soldier is far fonder of talking than his officer and apparently he knows more. If he doesn't, he thinks he does. So he explained to me the situation as the 'men saw it'. I remembered what Captain Edwards had told me, but I listened all the same. He told me that the Germans were advancing in two columns about ten miles apart, flanked in the west by a French division pushing them east, and led by the English drawing them toward the Marne. 'You know,' he said, 'that we are the sacrificed corps, and we have known it from the first – went into the campaign knowing it. We have been fighting a force ten times superior in numbers, and retreating, doing rear-guard action, whether we were really outfought or not – to draw the Germans where Joffre wants them. I reckon we've got them there. It is great strategy – Kitchener's, you know.'

Whether any of the corporal's ideas had any relation to facts I shall never know until history tells me, but I can assure you that, as I followed the corporal downstairs, I looked about my house – and, well, I don't deny it, it seemed to me a doomed thing, and I was sorry for it. However, as I let him out into the road again, I pounded into myself lots of things like 'It hasn't happened yet'; 'Sufficient unto the day'; and, 'What isn't to be, won't be'; and found I was quite calm. Luckily I did not have much time to myself, for I had hardly sat down quietly when there was another tap at the door and I opened to find an officer of the bicycle corps standing there.

'Captain Edwards's compliments,' he said, 'and will you be so kind as to explain to me exactly where you think the Uhlans are hidden?'

I told him that if he would come down the road a little way with me I would show him.

'Wait a moment,' he said, holding the door. 'You are not afraid?'

I told him that I was not.

'My orders are not to expose you uselessly. Wait there a minute.'

He stepped back into the garden, gave a quick look overhead – I don't know what for, unless for a Taube. Then he said, 'Now, you will please come out into the road and keep close to the bank at the left, in the shadow. I shall walk at the extreme right. As soon as I get where I can see the roads ahead, at the foot of the hill, I shall ask you to stop, and please stop at once. I don't want you to be seen from the road below, in case anyone is there. Do you understand?'

I said I did. So we went into the road and walked silently down the hill. Just before we got to the turn, he motioned me to stop and stood with his map in hand while I explained that he was to cross the road that led into Voisins, take the cart track down the hill past the washhouse on his left, and turn into the wood road on that side. At each indication he said, 'I have it.' When I had explained, he simply said, 'Rough road?'

I said it was, very, and wet in the driest weather.

'Wooded all the way?' he asked.

I told him that it was, and, what was more, so winding that you could not see ten feet ahead anywhere between here and Condé.

'Humph,' he said. 'Perfectly clear, thank you very much. Please wait right there a moment.'

He looked up the hill behind him, and made a gesture in the air with his hand above his head. I turned to look up the hill also. I saw the corporal at the gate repeat the gesture; then a big bicycle corps, four abreast, guns on their backs, slid round the corner and came gliding down the hill. There was not a sound, not the rattle of a chain or a pedal.

'Thank you very much,' said the captain. 'Be so kind as to keep close to the bank.'

When I reached my gate I found some of the men of the guard dragging a big, long log down the road, and I watched them while they attached it to a tree at my gate, and swung it across to the opposite side of the road, making in that way a barrier about five feet high. I asked what that was for? 'Captain's orders,' was the laconic reply. But when it was done the corporal took the trouble to explain that it was a barricade to prevent the Germans from making a dash up the hill.

'However,' he added, 'don't you get nervous. If we chase them out it will only be a little rifle practice, and I doubt if they even have any ammunition.'

As I turned to go into the house, he called after me,

'See here, I notice that you've got doors on all sides of your house. Better lock all those but this front one.'

As all the windows were barred and so could be left open, I didn't mind; so I went in and locked up. The thing was getting to be funny to me – always doing something, and nothing happening. I suppose courage is a cumulative thing, if only one has time to accumulate, and these boys in khaki treated even the cannonading as if it were all 'in the day's work'.

It was just dusk when the bicycle corps returned up the hill. They had to dismount and wheel their machines under the barricade, and they did it so prettily, dismounting and remounting with a precision that was neat.

'Nothing,' reported the captain. 'We could not go in far – road too rough and too dangerous. It is a cavalry job.'

All the same, I am sure the Uhlans are there.

XIII

September 8, 1914

I had gone to bed early on Friday night, and had passed an uneasy night. It was before four when I got up and opened my shutters. It was a lovely day. Perhaps I have told you that the weather all last week was simply perfect.

I went downstairs to get coffee for the picket, but when I got out to the gate there was no picket there. There was the barricade, but the road was empty. I ran up the road to Amélie's. She told me that they had marched away about an hour before. A bicyclist had evidently brought an order. As no one spoke English, no one understood what had really happened. Père had been to Couilly – they had all left there. So far as anyone could discover there was not an English soldier, or any kind of a soldier, left anywhere in the.

This was Saturday morning, September 5, and one of the loveliest days I ever saw. The air was clear. The sun was shining.

The birds were singing. But otherwise it was very still. I walked out on the lawn. Little lines of white smoke were rising from a few chimneys at Joncheroy and Voisins. The towns on the plain, from Monthyon and Penchard on the horizon to Mareuil in the valley, stood out clear and distinct. But after three days of activity, three days with the soldiers about, it seemed, for the first time since I came here, lonely; and for the first time I realized that I was actually cut off from the outside world. All the bridges in front of me were gone, and the big bridge behind me. No communication possibly with the north, and none with the south except by road over the hill to Lagny. Esbly evacuated, Couilly evacuated, Quincy evacuated. All the shops closed. No government, no post office, and absolutely no knowledge of what had happened since Wednesday. I had a horrible sense of isolation.

Luckily for me, part of the morning was killed by what might be called an incident or a disaster or a farce – just as you look at it. First of all, right after breakfast I had the proof that I was right about the Germans. Evidently well informed of the movements of the English, they rode boldly into the open. Luckily they seemed disinclined to do any mischief. Perhaps the place looked too humble to be bothered with. They simply asked – one of them spoke French, and perhaps they all did – where they were, and were told, 'Huiry, commune of Quincy'. They looked it up on their maps, nodded, and asked if the bridges on the Marne had been destroyed, to which I replied that I did not know – I had not been down to the river. Half a truth and half a lie, but goodness knows that it was hard enough to have to be polite. They thanked me civilly enough and rode down the hill, as they could not pass the barricade unless they had wished to give an exhibition of 'high school'. Wherever they had been they had not suffered. Their horses were fine animals, and both horses and men were well groomed and in prime condition.

The other event was distressing, but about that I held my tongue.

Just after the Germans were here, I went down the road to call on my new French friends at the foot of the hill, to hear how they had passed the night, and incidentally to discover if there were any soldiers about. Just in the front of their house I found an English bicycle scout, leaning on his wheel and trying to make himself understood in a one-sided monosyllabic dialogue, with the two girls standing in their window.

I asked him who he was. He showed his papers. They were all right – an Irishman – Ulster – Royal Innisfall Fusiliers – thirteen years in the service.

I asked him if there were any English soldiers left here. He said there was still a bicycle corps of scouts at the foot of the hill, at Couilly. I thought that funny, as Père had said the town was absolutely deserted. Still, I saw no reason to doubt his word, so when he asked me if I could give him his breakfast, I brought him back to the house, set the table in the arbor, and gave him his coffee and eggs. When he had finished, he showed no inclination to go – said he would rest a bit. As Amélie was in the house, I left him and went back to make the call my encounter with him had interrupted. When I returned an hour later, I found him fast asleep on the bench in the arbor, with the sun shining right on his head. His wheel, with his kit and gun on it was leaning up against the house. It was nearly noon by this time, and hot, and I was afraid he would get a sunstroke; so I waked him and told him that if it was a rest he needed – and he was free to take it – he could go into the room at the head of the stairs, where he would find a couch and lie down comfortably. He had sleepily obeyed, and must have just about got to sleep again, when it occurred to me that it was hardly prudent to leave an English bicycle with a khaki-covered kit and a gun on it right on the terrace in plain sight of the road up which the Germans had ridden so short a time before. So I went to the foot of the stairs, called him, and explained that I did not care to touch the wheel on account of the gun, so he had better come down and put it away, which he did. I don't know whether it was my saying 'Germans' to him that explained it, but his sleepiness seemed suddenly to have disappeared, so he asked for the chance to wash and shave; and half an hour later he came down all slicked up and spruce, with a very visible intention of paying court to the lady of the house. Irish, you see – white hairs no obstacle. I could not help laughing. 'Hoity-toity,' I said to myself, 'I am getting all kinds of impressions of the military.'

While I was, with amusement, putting up fences, the gardener next door came down the hill in great excitement to tell me that the Germans were on the road above, and were riding down across Père's farm into a piece of land called '*la terre blanche*', where Père had recently been digging out great rocks, making it an ideal place to hide. He knew that there was an English scout in my house and thought I ought to know. I suppose he expected the boy in khaki to grab his gun and capture them all. I thanked him and sent him away. I must say my Irishman did not seem a bit interested in the Germans. His belt and pistol lay on the salon table, where he put them when he came downstairs. He made himself comfortable in an easy chair, and continued to give me another dose of his blarney. I suppose I was getting needlessly nervous. It was really none of my business what he was doing here. Still he was a bit too *sans gêne*.

Finally he began to ask questions. 'Was I afraid?' I was not. 'Did I live alone?' I did. As soon as I had said it, I thought it was stupid of me, especially as he at once said – 'If you are, yer know, I'll come back here to sleep tonight. I'm perfectly free to come and go as I like – don't have to report until I'm ready.'

I thought it wise to remind him right here that if his corps was at the foot of the hill, it was wise for him to let his commanding officer know that the Germans, for whom two regiments had been hunting for three days, had come out of hiding. I fancy if I had not taken that tack he'd have settled for the day.

'Put that thing on,' I said, pointing to his pistol; 'get your wheel out of the barn, and I'll take a look up the road and see that it's clear. I don't care to see you attacked under my eyes.'

I knew that there was not the slightest danger of that, but it sounded businesslike. I am afraid he found it so, because he said at once, 'Could you give me a drink before I go?'

'Water?' I said.

'No, not that.'

I was going to say 'no' when it occurred to me that Amélie had told me that she had put a bottle of cider in the buffet, and – well, he was Irish, and I wanted to get rid of him. So I said he could have a glass of cider, and I got the bottle, and a small, deep champagne glass. He uncorked the bottle, filled a brimming glass, recorked the bottle, drank it off, and thanked me more earnestly than cider would have seemed to warrant. While he got his wheel out I went through the form of making sure the road was free. There was no one in sight. So I sent him away with directions for reaching Couilly without going over the part of the hill where the Uhlans had hidden, and drew a sigh of relief when he was off. Hardly fifteen minutes later someone came running up from Voisins to tell me that just round the corner he had slipped off his wheel, almost unconscious – evidently drunk. I was amazed. He had been absolutely all right when he left me. As no one understood a word he tried to say, there was nothing to do but go and rescue him. But by the time I got to where he had fallen off his wheel, he was gone – someone had taken him away – and it was not until later that I knew the truth of the matter, but that must keep until I get to the way of the discovery.

All this excitement kept me from listening too much to the cannon, which had been booming ever since nine o'clock. Amélie had been busy running between her house and mine, but she has, among other big qualities, the blessed habit of taking no notice. I wish it were contagious. She went about her work as if nothing were hanging over us. I walked about the house doing little things aimlessly. I don't believe Amélie shirked a thing. It seemed to me absurd to care whether the dusting were done or not, whether or not the writing table was in order, or the pictures straight on the wall.

As near as I can remember, it was a little after one o'clock when the cannonading suddenly became much heavier, and I stepped out into the orchard, from which there is a wide view of the plain. I gave one look; then I heard myself say, 'Amélie', – as if she could help – and I retreated. Amélie rushed by me. I heard her say, '*Mon Dieu*'. I waited, but she did not come back. After a bit I pulled myself together, went out again, and followed down to the hedge where she was standing, looking off to the plain.

The battle had advanced right over the crest of the hill. The sun was shining brilliantly on silent Mareuil and Chauconin, but Monthyon and Penchard were enveloped in smoke. From the eastern and western extremities of the plain we could see the artillery fire, but owing to the smoke hanging over the crest of the hill on the horizon, it was impossible to get an idea of the positions of the armies. In the west it seemed to be somewhere near Claye, and in the east it was in the direction of Barcy. I tried to remember what the English soldiers had said – that the Germans were, if possible, to be pushed east, in which case the artillery at the west must be either the French or English. The hard thing to bear was that it was all conjecture.

So often, when I first took this place on the hill, I had looked off at the plain and thought, 'What a battlefield!' forgetting how often the Seine et Marne had been that from the days when the kings lived at Chelles down to the days when it saw the worst of the invasion of 1870. But when I thought that, I had visions very different from what I was seeing. I had imagined long lines of marching soldiers, detachments of flying cavalry, like the war pictures at Versailles and Fontainebleau. Now I was actually seeing a battle, and it was nothing like that. There was only noise, belching smoke, and long drifts of white clouds concealing the hill.

By the middle of the afternoon Monthyon came slowly out of the smoke. That seemed to mean that the heaviest firing was over the hill and not on it – or did it mean that the battle was receding? If it did, then the Allies were retreating. There was no way to discover the truth. And all this time the cannon thundered in the southeast, in the direction of Coulommiers, on the route into Paris by Ivry.

Naturally I could not but remember that we were only seeing the action on the extreme west of a battle line which probably extended hundreds of miles. I had been told that Joffre had made a frontier of the Marne. But alas, the Meuse had been made a frontier – but the Germans had crossed it, and advanced to here in little less than a fortnight. If that – why not here? It was not encouraging.

A dozen times during the afternoon I went into the study and tried to read. Little groups of old men, women, and children were in the road, mounted on the barricade which the English had left. I could hear the murmur of their voices. In vain I tried to stay indoors. The thing was stronger than I, and in spite of myself, I would go out on the lawn and, field-glass in hand, watch the smoke. To my imagination every shot meant awful slaughter, and between me and the terrible thing stretched a beautiful country, as calm in the sunshine as if horrors were not. In the field below me the wheat was being cut. I remembered vividly afterward that a white horse was drawing the reaper, and women and children were stacking and gleaning. Now and then the horse would stop, and a woman, with her red hand-kerchief on her head, would stand, shading her eyes a moment, and look off. Then the white horse would turn and go plodding on. The grain had to be got in if the Germans were coming, and these fields were to be trampled as they were in 1870. Talk about the duality of the mind – it is sextuple. I would not dare tell you all that went through mine that long afternoon.

It was just about six o'clock when the first bomb that we could really see came over the hill. The sun was setting. For two hours we saw them rise, descend, explode. Then a little smoke would rise from one hamlet, then from another; then a tiny flame – hardly more than a spark – would be visible; and by dark the whole plain was on fire, lighting up Mareuil in the foreground, silent and untouched. There were long lines of grain-stacks and mills stretching along the plain. One by one they took fire, until, by ten o'clock, they stood like a procession of huge torches across my beloved panorama.

It was midnight when I looked off for the last time. The wind had changed. The fires were still burning. The smoke was drifting toward us – and oh! the odor of it! I hope you will never know what it is like.

I was just going to close up when Amélie came to the door to see if I was all right. My mind was in a sort of riot. It was the suspense – the not knowing the result, or what the next day might bring. You know, I am sure, that physical fear is not one of my characteristics. Fear of Life, dread of Fate, I often have, but not the other. Yet somehow, when I saw Amélie standing there, I felt that I needed the sense of something living near me. So I said, 'Amélie, do you want to do me a great service?'

She said she'd like to try.

'Well, then,' I replied, 'don't you want to sleep here tonight?'

With her pretty smile, she pulled her nightdress from under her arm: that was what she had come for. So I made her go to bed in the big bed in the guest-chamber, and leave the door wide open; and do you know, she was fast asleep in five minutes, and she snored, and I smiled to hear her, and thought it the most comforting sound I had ever heard.

As for me, I did not sleep a moment. I could not forget the poor fellows lying dead out there in the starlight – and it was such a beautiful night.

XIV

It was about my usual time, four o'clock, the next morning
– Sunday, September 6 – that I opened my blinds. Another
lovely day. I was dressed and downstairs when, a little before
five, the battle recommenced.

I rushed out on the lawn and looked off. It had moved
east – behind the hill between me and Meaux. All I could see
was the smoke which hung over it. Still it seemed nearer than
it had the day before. I had just about room enough in my
mind for one idea – 'The Germans wish to cross the Marne at
Meaux, on the direct route into Paris. They are getting there.
In that case today will settle our fate. If they reach the Marne,
that battery at Coutevroult will come into action,' – that was
what Captain Edwards had said – 'and I shall be in a direct
line between the two armies.'

Amélie got breakfast as if there were no cannon, so I took
my coffee, and said nothing. As soon as it was cleared away,
I went up into the attic, and quietly packed a tiny square hat-
trunk. I was thankful that this year's clothes take up so little
room. I put in changes of underwear, stockings, slippers, an
extra pair of low-heeled shoes, plenty of handkerchiefs – just
the essentials in the way of toilette stuff – a few bandages and
such emergency things, and had room for two dresses. When
it was packed and locked, it was so light that I could easily
carry it by its handle on top. I put my long black military cape,
which I could carry over my shoulder, on it, with hat and veil
and gloves. Then I went downstairs and shortened the skirt
of my best walking-suit, and hung it and its jacket handy. I
was ready to fly – if I had to – and in case of that emergency
nothing to do for myself.

I had got all this done systematically when my little French friend – I call her Mlle. Henriette now – came to the door to say that she simply 'could *not* stand another day of it'. She had put, she said, all the ready money they had inside her corset, and a little box which contained all her dead father's decorations also, and she was ready to go. She took out the box and showed the pretty jeweled things – his cross of the *Légion d'Honneur*, his Papal decoration, and several foreign orders – her father, it seems, was an officer in the army, a great friend of the Orleans family, and grandson of an officer of Louis XVI's Imperial Guard. She begged me to join them in an effort to escape to the south. I told her frankly that it seemed to me impossible, and I felt it safer to wait until the English officers at Coutevroult notified us that it was necessary. It would be as easy then as now – and I was sure that it was safer to wait for their advice than to adventure it for ourselves. Besides, I had no intention of leaving my home and all the souvenirs of my life without making every effort I could to save them up to the last moment. In addition to that, I could not see myself joining that throng of homeless *réfugiés* on the road, if I could help it.

'But,' she insisted, 'you cannot save your house by staying. We are in the same position. Our house is full of all the souvenirs of my father's family. It is hard to leave all that – but I am afraid – terribly afraid for the children.'

I could not help asking her how she proposed to get away. So far as I knew there was not a carriage to be had.

She replied that we could start on foot in the direction of Melun, and perhaps find an automobile: we could share the expense. Together we could find a way, and what was more, that I could share my optimism and courage with them and that would help.

That made me laugh, but I didn't think it necessary to explain to her that, once away from the shelter of my own walls, I should be just as liable to a panic as anyone else, or that I knew we should not find a conveyance, or, worse still, that her money and her jewels would hardly be safe inside her corset if she were to meet with some of the Uhlans who were still about us.

Amélie had not allowed me to carry a *sou* on me, nor even my handbag since we knew they were here. Such things as that have been hidden – all ready to be snatched up – ever since I came home from Paris last Wednesday – only four days ago, after all!

Poor Mlle. Henriette went away sadly when she was convinced that my mind was made up.

'Goodbye,' she called over the hedge. 'I seem to be always taking leave of you.'

I did not tell Amélie anything about this conversation. What was the good? I fancy it would have made no difference to her. I knew pretty well to what her mind was made up. Nothing in the world would have made Père budge. He had tried it in 1870, and had been led to the German post with a revolver at his head. He did not have any idea of repeating the experience. It was less than half an hour later that Mlle. Henriette came up the hill again. She was between tears and laughter.

'Mother will *not* go,' she said. 'She says if you can stay we must. She thinks staying is the least of two evils. We can hide the babies in the *cave* if necessary, and they may be as safe there as on the road.'

I could not help saying that I should be sorry if my decision influenced theirs. I could be responsible for myself. I could not bear to have to feel any responsibility for others in case I was wrong. But she assured me that her mother had been of my opinion from the first. 'Only,' she added, 'if I could have coaxed you to go, she would have gone too.'

This decision did not add much to my peace of mind all that long Sunday. It seems impossible that it was only the day before yesterday. I think the suspense was harder to bear than that of the day before, though all we could see of the battle were the dense clouds of smoke rising straight into the air behind the green hill under such a blue sky all aglow with sunshine, with the incessant booming of the cannon, which made the contrasts simply monstrous.

I remember that it was about four in the afternoon when I was sitting in the arbor under the crimson rambler, which was a glory of bloom, that Père came and stood near by on the lawn, looking off. With his hands in the pockets of his blue apron, he stood silent for a long time. Then he said, 'Listen to that. They are determined to pass. This is different from 1870. In 1870 the Germans marched through here with their guns on their shoulders. There was no one to oppose them. This time it is different. It was harvest-time that year, and they took everything, and destroyed what they did not take. They bedded their horses in the wheat.'

You see Père's father was in the Franco-Prussian War, and his grandfather was with Napoleon at Moscow, where he had his feet frozen. Père is over seventy, and his father died at ninety-six. Poor old Père just hates the war. He is as timid as a bird – can't kill a rabbit for his dinner. But with the queer spirit of the French farmer he has kept right on working as if nothing were going on. All day Saturday and all day Sunday he was busy digging stone to mend the road.

The cannonading ceased a little after six – thirteen hours without intermission. I don't mind confessing to you that I hope the war is not going to give me many more days like that one. I'd rather the battle would come right along and be done with it. The suspense of waiting all day for that battery at Coutevroult to open fire was simply nasty.

I went to bed as ignorant of how the battle had turned as I was the night before. Oddly enough, to my surprise, I slept, and slept well.

XV

September 8, 1914

I did not wake on the morning of Monday, September 7 –
yesterday – until I was waked by the cannon at five. I jumped
out of bed and rushed to the window. This time there could
be no doubt of it: the battle was receding. The cannonading
was as violent, as incessant, as it had been the day before, but
it was surely farther off – to the northeast of Meaux. It was
another beautiful day. I never saw such weather.

Amélie was on the lawn when I came down. 'They are
surely retreating,' she called as soon as I appeared.

'They surely are,' I replied. 'It looks as if they were somewhere near Lizy-sur-l'Ourcq,' and that was a guess of which I
was proud a little later. I carry a map around these days as if
I were an army officer.

As Amélie had not been for the milk the night before, she
started off quite gayly for it. She has to go to the other side
of Voisins. It takes her about half an hour to go and return;
so – just for the sake of doing something – I thought I would
run down the hill and see how Mlle. Henriette and the little
family had got through the night.

Amélie had taken the road across the fields. It is rough
walking, but she doesn't mind. I had stopped to tie a fresh
ribbon about my cap – a tricolore – and was about five
minutes behind her. I was about halfway down the hill
when I saw Amélie coming back, running, stumbling,
waving her milk-can and shouting, '*Madame – un anglais,
un anglais.*' And sure enough, coming on behind her, his
face wreathed in smiles, was an English bicycle scout,
wheeling his machine. As soon as he saw me, he waved his
cap, and Amélie breathlessly explained that she had said,

'*Dame américaine*' and he had dismounted and followed her at once.

We went together to meet him. As soon as he was near enough, he called out, 'Good morning. Everything is all right. Germans been as near you as they will ever get. Close shave.'

'Where are they?' I asked as we met.

'Retreating to the northeast – on the Ourcq.'

I could have kissed him. Amélie did. She simply threw both arms round his neck and smacked him on both cheeks, and he said, 'Thank you, ma'am,' quite prettily; and, like the nice clean English boy he was, he blushed.

'You can be perfectly calm,' he said. 'Look behind you.'

I looked, and there along the top of my hill I saw a long line of bicyclists in khaki.

'What are you doing here?' I asked, a little alarmed. For a moment I thought that if the English had returned, something was going to happen right here.

'English scouts,' he replied. 'Colonel Snow's division, clearing the way for the advance. You've a whole corps of fresh French troops coming out from Paris on one side of you, and the English troops are on their way to Meaux.'

'But the bridges are down,' I said.

'The pontoons are across. Everything is ready for the advance. I think we've got 'em.' And he laughed as if it were all a game of cricket.

By this time we were in the road. I sent Amélie on for the milk. He wheeled his machine up the hill beside me. He asked me if there was anything they could do for me before they moved on. I told him there was nothing unless he could drive out the Uhlans who were hidden near us.

He looked a little surprised, asked a few questions – how long they had been there? where they were? how many? and if I had seen them? and I explained.

'Well,' he said, 'I'll speak to the colonel about it. Don't you worry. If he has time he may get over to see you, but we are moving pretty fast.'

By this time we were at the gate. He stood leaning on his wheel a moment, looking over the hedge.

'Live here with your daughter?' he asked.

I told him that I lived here alone with myself.

'Wasn't that your daughter I met?'

I didn't quite fall through the gate backwards. I am accustomed to saying that I am old. I am not yet accustomed to have people notice it when I do not call their attention to it. Amélie is only ten years younger than I am, but she has got the figure and bearing of a girl. The lad recovered himself at once, and said, 'Why, of course not – she doesn't speak any English.' I was glad that he didn't even apologize, for I expect that I look fully a hundred and something. So with a reiterated 'Don't worry – you are all safe here now,' he mounted his wheel and rode up the hills.

I watched him making good time across to the route to Meaux. Then I came into the house and lay down. I suddenly felt horribly weak. My house had taken on a queer look to me. I suppose I had been, in a sort of subconscious way, sure that it was doomed. As I lay on the couch in the salon and looked round the room, it suddenly appeared to me like a thing I had loved and lost and recovered – resurrected, in fact; a living thing to which a miracle had happened. I even found myself asking, in my innermost soul, what I had done to deserve this fortune. How had it happened, and why, that I had come to perch on this hillside, just to see a battle, and have it come almost to my door, to turn back and leave me and my belongings standing here untouched, as safe as if there were no war – and so few miles away destruction extending to the frontier.

The sensation was uncanny. Out there in the northeast still boomed the cannon. The smoke of the battle still rose straight in the still air. I had seen the war. I had watched its destructive bombs. For three days its cannon had pounded on every nerve in my body; but none of the horror it had sowed from the eastern frontier of Belgium to within four miles of me, had reached me except in the form of a threat. Yet out there on the plain, almost within my sight, lay the men who had paid with their lives – each dear to someone – to hold back the battle from Paris – and incidentally from me. The relief had its bitterness, I can tell you. I had been prepared to play the whole game. I had not even had the chance to discover whether or not I could. You, who know me fairly well, will see the irony of it. I am eternally hanging round *dans les coulisses*, I am never in the play. I instinctively thought of Captain Simpson, who had left his brother in the trenches at Saint-Quentin, and still had in him the kindly sympathy that had helped me so much.

When Amélie returned, she said that everyone was out at the Demi-Lune to watch the troops going to Meaux, and that the boys in the neighborhood were already swimming the Marne to climb the hill to the battlefield of Saturday. I had no curiosity to see one scene or the other. I knew what the French boys were like, with their stern faces, as well as I knew the English manner of going forward to the day's work, and the hilarious, *macabre* spirit of the French untried lads crossing the river to look on horrors as if it were a lark.

I passed a strangely quiet morning. But the excitement was not all over. It was just after lunch that Amélie came running down the road to say that we were to have a *cantonnement de régiment* on our hill for the night and perhaps longer – French reinforcements marching out from the south of Paris; that they were already coming over the crest of the hill to the south and could be seen from the road above; that the advance scouts were already here. Before she had done explaining, an officer and a bicyclist were at the gate. I suppose they came here because it was the only house on the road that was open. I had to encounter the expressions of astonishment to which I am now quite accustomed – a foreigner in a little hole on the road to the frontier, in a partially evacuated country. I answered all the usual questions politely; but when he began to ask how many men I could lodge, and how much room there was for horses in the outbuildings, Amélie sharply interfered, assuring him that she knew the resources of the hamlet better than I did, that she was used to 'this sort of thing' and '*madame* was not'; and simply whisked him off.

I can assure you that, as I watched the work of billeting a regiment in evacuated houses, I was mighty glad that I was here, standing, a willing hostess, at my door, but giving to my little house a personality no unoccupied house can ever have to a passing army. They made quick work, and no ceremony, in opening locked doors and taking possession. It did not take the officer who had charge of the billeting half an hour, note-book in hand, to find quarters for his horses as well as his men. Before the head of the regiment appeared over the hill names were chalked up on all the doors, and the number of horses on every door to barn and courtyard, and the fields selected and the number of men to be camped all over the hill. Finally the officer returned to me. I knew by his manner that Amélie, who accompanied him, had been giving him a 'talking to'.

'If you please, *madame*,' he said, 'I will see now what you can do for us'; and I invited him in.

I don't suppose I need to tell you that you would get very little idea of the inside of my house from the outside. I am quite used now to the little change of front in most people when they cross the threshold. The officer nearly went on tiptoes when he got inside. He mounted the polished stairs gingerly, gave one look at the bedroom part-way up, touched his cap, and said: 'That will do for the *chef-major*. We will not trouble you with anyone else. He has his own orderly, and will eat outside, and will be no bother. Thank you very much, *madame*'; and he sort of slid down the stairs, tiptoed out, and wrote in chalk on the gatepost, 'Weitzel'.

By this time the advance guard was in the road and I could not resist going out to talk to them. They had marched out from the south of Paris since the day before – thirty-six miles – without an idea that the battle was going on the Marne until they crossed the hill at Montry and came in sight of its smoke. I tell you their faces were wreathed with smiles when they discovered that we knew the Germans were retreating.

Such talks as I listened to that afternoon – only yesterday – at my gate, from such a fluent, amusing, clever French chap – a bicyclist in the ambulance corps – of the crossing the Meuse and the taking, losing, re-taking, and re-losing of Charleroi. Oddly enough these were the first real battle tales I had heard.

It suddenly occurred to me, as we chatted and laughed, that all the time the English were here they had never once talked battles. Not one of the Tommies had mentioned the fighting. We had talked of 'home', of the girls they had left behind them, of the French children whom the English loved, of the country, its customs, its people, their courage and kindness, but not one had told me a battle story of any kind, and I had not once thought of opening the subject. But this French lad of the ambulance corps, with his Latin eloquence and his national gift of humor and graphic description, with a smile in his eyes, and a laugh on his lips, told me stories that made me see how war affects men, and how often the horrible passes across the line into the grotesque. I shall never forget him as he stood at the gate, leaning on his wheel, describing how the Germans crossed the Meuse – a feat which cost them so dearly that only their superior number made a victory out of a disaster.

'I suppose,' he said, 'that in the history of the war it will stand as a success – at any rate, they came across, which was what they wanted. We could only have stopped them, if at all, by an awful sacrifice of life. Joffre is not doing that. If the Germans want to fling away their men by the tens of thousands – let them. In the end we gain by it. We can rebuild a country; we cannot so easily re-create a race. We mowed them down like a field of wheat, by the tens of thousands, and tens of thousands sprang into the gaps. They advanced shoulder to shoulder. Our guns could not miss them, but they were too many for us. If you had seen that crossing I imagine it would have looked to you like a disaster for Germany. It was so awful that it became comic. I remember one point where a bridge was mined. We let the first divisions of artillery and cavalry come right across on to our guns – they were literally destroyed. As the next division came on to the bridge – up it went – men, horses, guns dammed the flood, and the cavalry literally crossed on their own dead. We are bold enough, but we are not so foolhardy as to throw away men like that. They will be more useful to Joffre later.'

It was the word 'comic' that did for me. There was no sign in the fresh young face before me that the horror had left a mark. If the thought came to him that every one of those tens of thousands whose bodies dammed and reddened the flood was dear to someone weeping in Germany, his eyes gave no sign of it. Perhaps it was as well for the time being. Who knows?

I felt the same revolt against the effect of war when he told me of the taking and losing of Charleroi and set it down as the most 'grotesque' sight he had ever seen. 'Grotesque' simply made me shudder, when he went on to say that even there, in the narrow streets, the Germans pushed on in 'close order', and that the French *mitrailleuses*, which swept the street that he saw, made such havoc in their ranks that the air was so full of flying heads and arms and legs, of boots, and helmets, swords, and guns that it did not seem as if it could be real – 'it looked like some burlesque'; and that even one of the gunners turned ill and said to his commander, who stood beside him: 'For the love of God, colonel, shall I go on?' and the colonel, with folded arms, replied: 'Fire away.'

Perhaps it is lucky, since war is, that men can be like that. When they cannot, what then? But it was too terrible for me, and I changed the subject by asking him if it were true that the Germans deliberately fired on the Red Cross. He instantly became grave and prudent.

'Oh, well,' he said, 'I would not like to go on oath. We have had our field ambulance destroyed. But you know the Germans are often bad marksmen. They've got an awful lot of ammunition. They fire it all over the place. They are bound to hit something. If we screen our hospital behind a building and a shell comes over and blows us up, how can we swear the shell was aimed at us?'

Just here the regiment came over the hill, and I retreated inside the gate where I had pails of water ready for them to drink. They were a sorry-looking lot. It was a hot day. They were covered with dirt, and you know the ill-fitting uniform of the French common soldier would disfigure into trampdom the best-looking man in the world.

The barricade was still across the road. With their packs on their backs, their tin dippers in their hands for the drink they so needed, perspiring in their heavy coats, they crawled, line after line, under the barrier until an officer rode down and called sharply:

'Halt!'

The line came to a standstill.

'What's that thing?' asked the officer sternly.

I replied that obviously it was a barricade.

'Who put it there?' he asked peremptorily, as if I were to blame.

I told him that the English did.

'When?'

I felt as if I were being rather severely cross-examined, but I answered as civilly as I could, 'The night before the battle.'

He looked at me for the first time – and softened his tone a bit – my white hair and beastly accent, I suppose – as he asked:

'What is it for?'

I told him it *was* to prevent a detachment of Uhlans from coming up the hill. He hesitated a moment; then asked if it served any purpose now. I might have told him that the Uhlans were still here, but I didn't, I simply said that I did not know that it did. 'Cut it down!' he ordered, and in a moment it was cut on one end and swung round against the bank and the regiment marched on.

It was just after that that I discovered the explanation of what had happened to my Irish scout on Saturday. An exhausted soldier was in need of a stimulant, and one of his comrades, who was supporting him, asked me if I had anything. I had nothing but the bottle out of which the Irish scout had drunk. I rushed for it, poured some into the tin cup held out to me, and just as the poor fellow was about to drink, his comrade pulled the cup away, smelt it, and exclaimed, 'Don't drink that – here, put some water in it. That's not cider. It's *eau de vie des prunes*.'

I can tell you I was startled. I had never tasted *eau de vie des prunes* – a native brew, stronger than brandy, and far more dangerous – and my Irishman had pulled off a full champagne glass at a gulp, and never winked. No wonder he fell off his wheel. The wonder is that he did not die on the spot. I *was* humiliated. Still, he was Irish and perhaps he didn't care. I hope he didn't. But only think, he will never know that I did not do it on purpose. He was probably gloriously drunk. Anyway, it prevented his coming back to make that visit he threatened me with.

The detachment of the regiment which staggered past my gate camped in the fields below me and in the courtyards at Voisins, and the rest of them made themselves comfortable in the fields at the other side of the hill and the outbuildings on Amélie's place, and the officers and the ambulance corps began to seek their quarters.

I was sitting in the library when my guest, Chef-Major Weitzel, rode up to the gate. I had a good chance to look him over, as he marched up the path. He was a dapper, upright, little chap. He was covered with dust from his head to his heels. I could have written his name on him anywhere. Then I went to the door to meet him. I suppose he had been told that he was to be lodged in the house of an American. He stopped abruptly, halfway up the path, as I appeared, clicked his heels together, and made me his best bow, as he said:

'I am told, *madame*, that you are so gracious as to offer me a bed.'

I might have replied literally, 'Offer? I had no choice,' but I did not. I said politely that if Monsieur le Chef-Major would take the trouble to enter, I should do myself the distinguished honor of conducting him to his chamber, having no servant for the moment to perform for him that service, and he bowed at me again, and marched in – no other word for it – and came up the stairs behind me.

As I opened the door of my guest-room, and stood aside to let him pass, I found that he had paused halfway up and was giving my raftered green salon and the library beyond a curious glance. Being caught, he looked up at once and said: 'So you are not afraid?' I supposed he was inspired by the fact that there were no signs of any preparations to evacuate.

I replied that I could not exactly say that, but that I had not been sufficiently afraid to run away and leave my house to be looted unless I had to.

'Well,' he said, with a pleasant laugh, 'that is about as good an account of himself as many a brave soldier can give the night before his first battle'; and he passed me with a bow and I closed the door.

Half an hour later he came downstairs, all shaved and slicked up – in a white sweater, white tennis shoes, with a silk handkerchief about his neck, and a fatigue cap set rakishly on the side of his head, as if there were no such thing as hot weather or war, while his orderly went up and brought his equipment down to the terrace, and began such a beating, brushing, and cleaning of boots as you never saw.

At the library door he stopped, looked in, and said, 'This is nice'; and before I could get together decent French enough to say that I was honoured – or my house was – at his approval, he asked if he might be so indiscreet as to take the liberty of inviting some of his fellow officers to come into the garden and see the view. Naturally I replied that Monsieur le Chef-Major was at home and his comrades would be welcome to treat the garden as if it were theirs, and he made me another of his bows and marched away, to return in five minutes, accompanied by half a dozen officers and a priest. As they passed the window, where I still sat, they all bowed at me solemnly, and Chef-Major Weitzel stopped to ask if *madame* would be so good as to join them, and explain the country, which was new to them all.

Naturally *madame* did not wish to. I had not been out there since Saturday night – was it less than forty-eight hours before? But equally naturally I was ashamed to refuse. It would, I know, seem super-sentimental to them. So I reluctantly followed them out. They stood in a group about me – these men who had been in battles, come out safely, and were again advancing to the firing line as smilingly as one would go into a ballroom – while I pointed out the towns and answered their questions, and no one was calmer or more keenly interested than the Breton priest, in his long *soutane* with the red cross on his arm. All the time the cannon was booming in the northeast, but they paid no more attention to it than if it were a threshing-machine.

There was a young lieutenant in the group who finally noticed a sort of reluctance on my part – which I evidently had not been able to conceal – to looking off at the plain, which I own I had been surprised to find as lovely as ever. He taxed me with it, and I confessed, upon which he said:

'That will pass. The day will come – Nature is so made, luckily – when you will look off there with pride, not pain, and be glad that you saw what may prove the turning of the tide in the noblest war ever fought for civilization.'

I wonder.

The chef-major turned to me – caught me looking in the other direction – to the west where deserted Esbly climbed the hill.

'May I be very indiscreet?' he asked.

I told him that he knew best.

'Well,' he said, 'I want to know how it happens that you – a foreigner, and a woman – happen to be living in what looks like exile – all alone on the top of a hill – in wartime?'

I looked at him a moment – and – well, conditions like these make people friendly with one another at once. I was, you know, never very reticent, and in days like these even the ordinary reticences of ordinary times are swept away. So I answered frankly, as if these men were old friends, and not the acquaintances of an hour, that, as I was, as they could see, no longer young, very tired, and yet not weary with life, but more interested than my strength allowed. I had sought a pleasant retreat for my old age – not too far from the City of my Love – and that I had chosen this hilltop for the sake of the panorama spread out before me; that I had loved it every day more than the day before; and that exactly three months after I had sat down on this hilltop this awful war had marched to within sight of my gate, and banged its cannon and flung its deadly bombs right under my eyes.

Do you know, every mother's son of them threw back his head – and laughed aloud. I was startled. I knew that I had shown unnecessary feeling – but I knew it too late. I made a dash for the house, but the lieutenant blocked the way. I could not make a scene. I never felt so like it in my life.

'Come back, come back,' he said. 'We all apologize. It was a shame to laugh. But you are so vicious and so personal about it. After all, you know, the gods were kind to you – it *did* turn back – those waves of battle. You had better luck than Canute.'

'Besides,' said the chef-major, 'you can always say that you had front row stage box.'

There was nothing to do to save my face but to laugh with them. And they were still laughing when they tramped across the road to dinner. I returned to the house rather mortified at having been led into such an unnecessary display of feeling, but I suppose I had been in need of some sort of an outlet.

After dinner they came back to the lawn to lie about smoking their cigarettes. I was sitting in the arbor. The battle had become a duel of heavy artillery, which they all found 'magnificent', these men who had been in such things.

Suddenly the chef-major leaped to his feet.

'Listen – listen – an aeroplane.'

We all looked up. There it was, quite low, right over our heads. 'A Taube!' he exclaimed, and before he had got the words out of his mouth, *Crick-crack-crack* snapped the musketry from the field behind us – the soldiers had seen it. The machine began to rise. I stood like a rock – my feet glued to the ground – while the regiment fired over my head. But it was sheer willpower that kept me steady among these men who were treating it as if it were a Fourteenth of July show. I heard a *ping*.

'Touched,' said the officer as the Taube continued to rise. Another *ping*.

Still it rose, and we watched it sail off toward the hills at the southeast.

'Hit, but not hurt,' sighed the officer, dropping down on the grass again, with a sigh. 'It is hard to bring them down at that height with rifles, but it can be done.'

'Perhaps the English battery will get it,' said I; 'it is going right toward it.'

'If there is an English battery up there,' replied he, 'that is probably what he is looking for. It is hardly likely to unmask for a Taube. I am sorry we missed it. You have seen something of the war. It is a pity you should not have seen it come down. It is a beautiful sight.'

I thought to myself that I preferred it should not come down in my garden. But I had no relish for being laughed at again, so I did not say it.

Soon after they all went to bed – very early – and silence fell on the hilltop. I took a look round before I went to bed. I had not seen Amélie since the regiment arrived. But she, who had done everything to spare me inconvenience, had fourteen officers quartered in her place, and goodness knows how many horses, so she had little time to do for me.

The hillside was a picture I shall never forget. Everywhere men were sleeping in the open – their guns beside them. Fires, over which they had cooked, were smouldering; pickets everywhere. The moon shed a pale light and made long shadows. It was really very beautiful if one could have forgotten that tomorrow many of these men would be sleeping for good – 'Life's fitful dream' over.

XVI

September 8, 1914

This morning everything and everybody was astir early. It was another gloriously beautiful day. The birds were singing as if to split their throats. There was a smell of coffee all over the place. Men were hurrying up and down the hill, to and fro from the wash house, bathing, washing out their shirts and stockings and hanging them on the bushes, rubbing down horses and douching them, cleaning saddles and accouterments. There is a lot of work to be done by an army besides fighting. It was all like a play, and everyone was so cheerful.

The chef-major did not come down until his orderly called him, and when he did he looked as rosy and cheerful as a child, and announced that he had slept like one. Soon after he crossed the road for his coffee I heard the officers laughing and chatting as if it were a weekend house party.

When Amélie came to get my breakfast she looked a wreck – I saw one of her famous bilious attacks coming.

It was a little after eleven, while the chef-major was upstairs writing, that his orderly came with a paper and carried it up to him. He came down at once, made me one of his pretty bows at the door of the library, and holding out a scrap of paper said:

'Well, *madame*, we are going to leave you. We advance at two.'

I asked him where he was going.

He glanced at the paper in his hand, and replied:

'Our orders are to advance to Saint-Fiacre – a little east of Meaux – but before I go I am happy to relieve your mind on two points. The French cavalry has driven the Uhlans out – some of them were captured as far east as Bouleurs. And the

English artillery has come down from the hill behind you and is crossing the Marne. We follow them. So you see you can sit here in your pretty library and read all these nice books in security, until the day comes – perhaps sooner than you dare hope – when you can look back to all these days, and perhaps be a little proud to have had a small part in it.' And off he went upstairs.

I sat perfectly still for a long time. Was it possible that it was only a week ago that I had heard the drum beat for the disarming of the Seine et Marne? Was there really going to come a day when all the beauty around me would not be a mockery? All at once it occurred to me that I had promised Captain Simpson to write and tell him how I had 'come through'. Perhaps this was the time. I went to the foot of the stairs and called up to the chef-major. He came to the door and I explained, asking him if, we being without a post office, he could get a letter through, and what kind of a letter I could write, as I knew the censorship was severe.

'My dear lady,' he replied, 'go and write your letter – write anything you like – and when I come down I will take charge of it and guarantee that it shall go through, uncensored, no matter what it contains.'

So I wrote to tell Captain Simpson that all was well at Huiry – that we had escaped, and were still grateful for all the trouble he had taken. When the officer came down I gave it to him, unsealed.

'Seal it, seal it,' he said, and when I had done so, he wrote, 'Read and approved' on the envelope, and gave it to his orderly, and was ready to say 'Goodbye.'

'Don't look so serious about it,' he laughed, as we shook hands. 'Some of us will get killed, but what of that? I wanted this war. I prayed for it. I should have been sad enough if I had died before it came. I have left a wife and children whom

120

I adore, but I am ready to lay down my life cheerfully for the victory of which I am so sure. Cheer up. I think my hour has not yet come. I had three horses killed under me in Belgium. At Charleroi a bomb exploded in a staircase as I was coming down. I jumped – not a scratch to show. Things like that make a man feel immune – but who knows?'

I did my best to smile, as I said, 'I don't wish you courage – you have that, but – good luck.'

'Thank you,' he replied, 'you've had that'; and away he marched, and that was the last I saw of him.

I had a strange sensation about these men who had in so few days passed so rapidly in and out of my life, and in a moment seemed like old friends.

There was a bustle of preparation all about us. Such a harnessing of horses, such a rolling-up of half-dried shirts, but it was all orderly and systematic. Over it all hung a smell of soup-kettles – the preparations for the midday meal, and a buzz of many voices as the men sat about eating out of their tin dishes. I did wish I could see only the picturesque side of it.

It was two o'clock sharp when the regiment began to move. No bands played. No drum beat. They just marched, marched, marched along the road to Meaux, and silence fell again on the hillside.

Off to the northeast the cannon still boomed – it is still booming now as I write, and it is after nine o'clock. There has been no sign of Amélie all day as I have sat here writing all this to you. I have tried to make it as clear a statement of facts as I could. I am afraid that I have been more disturbed in putting it down than I was in living it. Except on Saturday and Sunday I was always busy, a little useful, and that helped. I don't know when I shall be able to get this off to you. But at least it is ready, and I shall take the first opportunity I get to cable to you, as I am afraid before this you have worried, unless your geography is faulty, and the American papers are as reticent as ours.

Part II
On the Edge of the War Zone

I

La Creste, Huiry, Couilly. S et M.

September 16, 1914

Dear Old Girl,

More and more I find that we humans are queer animals.

All through those early, busy, exciting days of September
– can it be only a fortnight ago? – I was possessed, like the
'busy bee', to 'employ each shining hour' by writing out my
adventures. Yet, no sooner was the menace of those days gone,
than, for days at a time, I had no desire to see a pen.

Perhaps it was because we were so absolutely alone, and
because, for days, I had no chance to send you the letters I
had written, nor to get any cable to you to tell you that all
was well.

There was a strange sort of *soulagement* in the conviction
that we had, as my neighbors say, 'échappé bien'. I suppose
it is human. It was like the first days of a real convalescence
– life is so good, the world is so beautiful. The war was still
going on. We still heard the cannon – they are booming this
minute – but we had not seen the spiked helmets dashing up
my hill, nor watched the walls of our little hamlet fall. I imagine that if human nature were not just like that, Life could
never be beautiful to any thinking person. We all know that,
though it be not today, it is to be, but we seem to be fitted for
that, and the idea does not spoil life one bit.

It is very silent here most of the time. We are so few.
Everybody works. No one talks much. With the cannon
booming out there no one feels in the humor, though now
and then we do get shaken up a bit. Everything seems a long

time ago. Yet it is really only nine days since the French troops advanced – nine days since Paris was saved.

The most amazing thing of all is that our communications, which were cut on September 2, were reopened, in a sort of a way, on the 10th. That was only one week of absolute isolation. On that day we were told that postal communication with Paris was to be reopened with an automobile service from Couilly to Lagny, from which place, on the other side of the Marne, trains were running to Paris.

So Amélie gathered up my letters, and carried them down the hill, and dropped them hopefully in the box under the shuttered window of the post office in the deserted town.

That was six days ago, and it is only this morning that I began to feel like writing to you again. I wanted to cable, but there is no way yet, so I can only hope that you know your geography well enough not to have worried since the 7th.

Although we are so shut in, we got news from the other side of the Marne on Wednesday, the 9th, the day after I wrote to you – the fifth day of the battle. Of course we had no newspapers; our *mairie* and post office being closed, there was no telegraphic news. Besides, our telegraph wires are dangling from the poles just as the English engineers left them on September 2. It seems a century ago.

We knew the Germans were still retreating because each morning the booming of the cannon and the columns of smoke were further off, and because the slopes and the hills before us, which had been burning the first three days of the battle, were lying silent in the wonderful sunshine, as if there were no living people in the world except us few on this side of the river.

At no time can we see much movement across the river except with a glass. The plains are undulating. The roads are tree-lined. We trace them by the trees. But the silence over there seems different today. Here and there still thin ribbons of smoke – now rising straight in the air, and now curling in the breeze – say that something is burning, not only in the bombarded towns, but in the woods and plains. But what? No one knows.

One or two of our older men crossed the Marne on a raft on the 10th, the sixth day of the battle. They brought back word that thousands from the battles of the 5th, 6th, and 7th had lain for days unburied under the hot September sun, but that the fire department was already out there from Paris, and that it would only be a few days when the worst marks of the terrible fight would be removed. But they brought back no news. The few people who had remained hidden in cellars or on isolated farms knew no more than we did, and it was impossible, naturally, to get near to the field ambulance at Neufmortier, which we can see from my lawn.

However, on the 9th – the very day after the French advanced from here – we got news in a very amusing way. We had to take it for what it was worth, or seemed to be. It was just after noon. I was working in the garden on the south side of the house. I had instinctively put the house between me and the smoke of battle when Amélie came running down the hill in a high state of excitement, crying out that the French were 'coming back', that there had been a 'great victory', and that I was to 'come and see'.

She was in too much of a hurry to explain or wait for any questions. She simply started across the fields in the direction of the Demi-Lune, where the *route nationale* from Meaux makes a curve to run down the long hill to Couilly.

I grabbed a sunbonnet, picked up my glasses, and followed her to a point in the field from which I could see the road.

Sure enough – there they were – *cuirassiers* – the sun glinting on their helmets, riding slowly towards Paris, as gaily as if returning from a fête, with all sorts of trophies hanging to their saddles.

I was content to go no nearer. It was no army returning. It was only a small detachment. Still, I could not help feeling that if any of them were returning in that spirit, while the cannon were still booming, all must be well.

Amélie ran all the way to the Demi-Lune – a little more than a quarter of a mile. I could see her simply flying over the ground. I waited where I was until she came back, crying breathlessly, long before she reached me:

'Oh, *madame*, what do you think? The regiment which was here yesterday captured a big, big cannon.'

That was good news. They really had not looked it.

'And oh, *madame*,' she went on, as she reached me, 'the war is over. The Germans have asked for peace,' and she sat right down on the ground.

'Peace?' I exclaimed. 'Where? Who told you that?'

'A man out there. He heard it from a soldier. They have asked for peace, those Boches, and General Gallieni, he told them to go back to their own frontier, and ask for it there.'

'And have they gone, Amélie?' I asked.

She replied quite seriously that they were going, and she was terribly hurt because I laughed, and remarked that I hoped they would not be too long about it.

I had the greatest possible difficulty in making her realize that we were only hearing a very small part of a battle, which, judging by the movements which had preceded it, was possibly extending from here to the vicinity of Verdun, where the Crown Prince was said to be vainly endeavoring to break through, his army acting as a sort of a pivot on which the great advance had swung. I could not help wondering if, as often happens in the game of 'snap the whip', von Kluck's right wing had got swung off the line by the very rapidity with which it must have covered that long arc in the great two weeks' offensive.

Amélie, who has an undue confidence in my opinion, was terribly disappointed, quite downcast. Ever since the British landed – she has such faith in the British – she has believed in a short war. Of course I don't know any more than she does. I have to guess, and I'm not a lucky guesser as a rule. I confess to you that even I am absolutely obsessed by the miracle which has turned the invaders back from the walls of Paris. I cannot get over the wonder of it. In the light of the sudden, unexpected pause in that great push I have moments of believing that almost anything can happen. I'll wager you know more about it on your side of the great pond than we do here within hearing of the battle.

I don't even know whether it is true or not that Gallieni is out there. If it is, that must mean that the army covering Paris has advanced, and that Joffre has called out his reserves which have been entrenched all about the seventy-two miles of steel that guards the capital. I wondered then, and today – seven days later – I am wondering still.

It was useless to give these conjectures to Amélie. She was too deep in her disappointment. She walked sadly beside me back to the garden, an altogether different person from the one who had come racing across the field in the sunshine. Once there, however, she braced up enough to say:

'And only think, *madame*, a woman out there told me that the Germans who were here last week were all chauffeurs at the Galeries Lafayette and other big shops in Paris, and that they not only knew all the country better than we do, they knew us all by name. One of them, who stopped at her door to demand a drink, told her so himself, and called her by name. He told her he had lived in Paris for years.'

That was probably true. The delivery automobiles from all the big shops in Paris came out here twice, and some of them three times a week. It is no secret that Paris was full of Germans, and has been ever since that beastly treaty of Frankfort, which would have expired next year.

After Amélie had gone back to her work, I came into the library and sat down at my desk to possess my soul with what patience I could, until official news came. But writing was impossible.

Of course to a person who has known comparatively few restraints of this sort, there is something queer in this kind of isolation. I am afraid I cannot exactly explain it to you. As I could not work, I walked out on to the *chemin Madame*. On one side I looked across the valley of the Marne to the heights crowned by the bombarded towns. On the other I looked across the valley of the Grande Morin, where, on the heights behind the trees, I knew little towns like Coutevoult and Montbarbin were evacuated. In the valley at the foot of the hill, Couilly and Saint-Germain, Montry and Esbly were equally deserted. No smoke rose above the red roofs. Not a soul was on the roads. Even the railway station was closed, and the empty cars stood, locked, on the side tracks. It was strangely silent.

I don't know how many people there are at Voisins. I hear that there is no one at Quincy. As for Huiry? Well, our population – everyone accounted for before the mobilization – was twenty-nine. The hamlet consists of only nine houses. Today we are six grown people and seven children.

There is no doctor if one should be so silly as to fall ill. There are no civil authorities to make out a death certificate if one had the bad taste to die – and one can't die informally in France. If anyone should, so far as I can see, he would have to walk to his grave, dig it, and lie down in it himself, and that would be a scandal, and I am positive it would lead to a *procès*. The French love lawsuits, you know. No respectable family is ever without one.

However, there has not been a case of illness in our little community since we were cut off from the rest of the world.

Somehow, at times, in the silence, I get a strange sensation of unreality – the sort of intense feeling of its all being a dream. I wish I didn't. I wonder if that is not Nature's narcotic for all experiences outside those we are to expect from Life, which, in its normal course, has tragedies enough.

Then again, sometimes, in the night, I have a sensation as if I were getting a special view of a really magnificent spectacle to which the rest of 'my set' had not been invited – as if I were seeing it at a risk, but determined to see it through.

I can imagine you, wrinkling your brows at me and telling me that that frame of mind comes of my theater-going habit. Well, it is not worth while arguing it out. I can't. There is a kind of veil over it.

Nor were the day's mental adventures over.

I was just back from my promenade when my little French friend from the foot of the hill came to the door. I call her 'my little friend', though she is taller than I am, because she is only half my age. She came with the proposition that I should harness Ninette and go with her out to the battlefield, where, she said, they were sadly in need of help.

I asked her how she knew, and she replied that one of our old men had been across the river and brought back the news that the field ambulance at Neufmortier was short of nurses, and that it was thought that there were still many wounded men in the woods who had not yet been picked up.

I asked her if any official call for help had come. She said 'No', but she presented so strong a case in favor of volunteering that, at first, it seemed to me that there was nothing to do but go, and go quickly.

But before she got outside the gate I rushed after her to tell her that it seemed impossible – that I knew they didn't

131

want an old lady like me, however willing, an old lady very unsteady on her feet, absolutely ignorant of the simplest rules of 'first aid to the wounded', that they needed skilled and tried people, that we not only could not lend efficient aid, but should be a nuisance, even if, which I doubted, we were allowed to cross the Marne.

All the time I was explaining myself, with that diabolical dual consciousness which makes us spectator and listener to ourselves, in the back of my brain – or my soul – was running this query: 'I wonder what a raw battlefield looks like? I have a chance to see if I want to – perhaps.' I suppose that was an attack of involuntary, unpremeditated curiosity. I did not want to go.

I wonder if that was not the sort of thing which, if told in the confessional in ancient times, got one convicted of being 'possessed of the devil'?

Of course Mlle. Henriette was terribly disappointed. Her mother would not let her go without me. I imagine the wise lady knew that I would not go. She tried to insist, but my mind was made up.

She argued that we could 'hunt for the dead', and 'carry consolation to the dying'. I shook my head. I even had to cut the argument short by going into the house. I felt an imperative need to get the door closed between us. The habit I have – you know it well, it is often enough disconcerting to me – of getting an ill-timed comic picture in my mind, made me afraid that I was going to laugh at the wrong moment. If I had, I should never have been able to explain to her, and hope to be understood.

The truth was that I had a sudden, cinematographical vision of my chubby self – me, who cannot walk half a mile, nor bend over without getting palpitation – stumbling in my high-heeled shoes over the fields ploughed by cavalry and shell – breathlessly bent on carrying consolation to the dying. I knew that I should surely have to be picked up with the dead and dying, or, worse still, usurp a place in an ambulance, unless eternal justice – in spite of my age, my sex, and my white hairs – left me lying where I fell – and serve me good and right!

I know now that if the need and opportunity had come to my gate – as it might – I should, instinctively, have known what to do, and have done it. But for me to drive deliberately nine miles – we should have had to make a wide detour to cross the Marne on the pontoons – behind a donkey who travels two miles an hour, to seek such an experience, and with several hours to think it over en route, and the conviction that I would be an unwelcome intruder – that was another matter.

I am afraid Mlle. Henriette will never forgive me. She will soon be walking around in a hospital, looking so pretty in her nurse's dress and veil. But she will always think that she lost a great opportunity that day – and a picturesque one.

By the way, I have a new inmate in my house – a kitten. He was evidently lost during the emigration. Amélie says he is three months old. He arrived at her door crying with hunger the other morning. Amélie loves beasties better than humans. She took him in and fed him. But as she has six cats already, she seemed to think that it was my duty to take this one. She cloaked that idea in the statement that it was 'good for me' to have 'something alive' moving about me in the silent little house. So she put him in my lap. He settled himself down, went to sleep, and showed no inclination to leave me.

At the end of two hours he owned me – the very first cat I ever knew, except by sight.

So you may dismiss that idea which torments you – I am no longer alone.

I am going to send this letter at once to be dropped in the box in front of the post office, where I am very much afraid it may find that of last week, for we have had no letters yet nor have I seen or heard anything of the promised *automobile postale*. However, once a stamped letter is out of my hand, I always feel at least as if it had started, though in all probability this may rest indefinitely in that box in the 'deserted village'.

II

It is over a week since I wrote you. But I have really been very busy, and not had a moment.

To begin with, the very day after I wrote to you, Amélie came down with one of her sick headaches, and she has the most complete sort I ever met.

She crawled upstairs that morning to open my blinds. I gave one look at her, and ordered her back to bed. If there is anything that can make one look worse than a first-class bilious attack I have never met it. One can walk round and do things when one is suffering all sorts of pain, or when one is trembling in every nerve, or when one is dying of consumption, but I defy anyone to be useful when one has an active sick headache.

Amélie protested, of course; 'the work must be done'. I did not see why it had to be. She argued that I was the mistress, 'had a right to be attended to – had a right to expect it'. I did not see that either. I told her that her logic was false. She clinched it, as she thought, by declaring that I looked as if I needed to be taken care of.

I was indignant. I demanded the handglass, gave one look at myself, and I was inclined to let it slide off the bed to the floor, à la Camille, only Amélie would not have seen the joke. I did look old and seedy. But what of that? Of course Amélie does not know yet that I am like the 'Deacon's One Hoss Shay' – I may look dilapidated, but so long as I do not absolutely drop apart, I can go.

So I told Amélie that if I were the mistress, I had a right to be obeyed, and that there were times when there was no question of mistress and maid, that this was one of those times, that she had been a trump and a brick, and other nice things, and that the one thing I needed was to work with my own hands. She finally yielded, but not to my arguments – to Nature.

Perhaps owing to the excitement of three weeks, perhaps to the fact that she had worked too hard in the sun, and also, it may be, owing to the long run she took, of which I wrote you in my letter of last week, it is the worst attack I ever saw. I can tell you I wished for a doctor, and she is even now only a little better.

However, I have had what we used to call 'a real nice time playing house'. Having nothing else to do, I really enjoyed it. I have swept and dusted, and handled all my little treasures, touching everything with a queer sensation – it had all become so very precious. All the time my thoughts flew back to the past. That is the prettiest thing about housework – one can think of such nice things when one is working with one's hands, and is alone. I don't wonder Burns wrote verses as he followed the plough – if he really did.

I think I forgot to tell you in my letter of last week that the people – drummed out of the towns on the other side of the Marne, that is to say, the nearby towns, like those in the plain, and on the hilltops from which the Germans were driven before the 10th – began to return on that night; less than a fortnight after they fled. It was unbelievable to me when I saw them coming back.

When they were drummed out, they took a roundabout route, to leave the main roads free for the army. They came back over the *route nationale*. They fled en masse. They are coming back slowly, in family groups. Day after day, and night after night the flocks of sheep, droves of cattle, carts with pigs in them, people in carts leading now and then a cow, families on foot, carrying cats in baskets, and leading dogs and goats and children, climb the long hill from Couilly, or thread the footpaths on the canal.

They fled in silence. I remember as remarkable that no one talked. I cannot say that they are coming back exactly gaily, but, at any rate, they have found their tongues. The slow procession has been passing for a fortnight now, and at almost any hour of the day, as I sit at my bedroom window, I can hear the distant murmur of their voices as they mount the hill.

I can't help thinking what some of them are going to find out there in the track of the battle. But it is a part of the strange result of war, borne in on me by my own frame of mind, that the very fact that they are going back to their own hearths seems to reconcile them to anything.

Of course these first people to return are mostly the poorer class, who did not go far. Their speedy return is a proof of the morale of the country, because they would surely not have been allowed to come back by the military authorities if the general conviction was not that the German advance had been definitely checked. Isn't it wonderful? I can't get over it.

Even before they began to return, the engineers were at work repairing the bridges as far as Chalons, and the day I wrote to you last week, when Amélie went down the hill to mail your letter, she brought back the news that the English engineers were sitting astride the telegraph poles, pipes in mouth, putting up the wires they cut down a fortnight ago. The next day our post office opened, and then I got newspapers. I can tell you I devoured them. I read Joffre's order of the day. What puzzled me was that it was dated on the morning of September 6, yet we, with our own eyes, saw the battle begin at noon on the 5th – a battle which only stopped at nine that night, to begin again at four the next morning. But I suppose history will sometime explain that.

Brief as the news was in the papers, it was exciting to know that the battle we had seen and heard was really a decisive fight, and that it was considered won by the English and French – in a rainstorm – as long ago as the 10th, and that the fighting to the east of us had been far more terrible than here.

I suppose long before this our myriads of 'special telegraph' men have sent you over details and anecdotes such as we shall never see. We get a meagre '*communiqué* official' and have to be content with that. It is now and then hard for me, who have been accustomed to something different.

None of our shops is open yet. Indeed almost no one has returned to Couilly; and Meaux, they say, is still deserted. Yet I cannot honestly say that I have suffered for anything. I have an abundance of fruit. We have plenty of vegetables in Père's garden. We have milk and eggs. Rabbits and chickens run about in the roads simply asking to be potted. There is no petrol, but I, luckily, had a stock of candles, and I love candlelight – it suits my house better than lamps. It is over a fortnight since we had sugar or butter or coffee. I have tea. I never would have supposed that I could have got along so well and not felt deprived. I suppose we always have too much – I've had the proof. Perhaps had there been anyone with me I should have felt it more. Being alone I did not give it a thought.

Sunday afternoon, the weather being still fine and the distant booming of the cannon making reading or writing impossible – I am not yet habituated to it – I went for a walk. I took the road down the hill in the direction of the Marne. It is a pretty walk – not a house all the way.

It leads along what is called the *Pavé du Roi*, dropping down into the plain of the valley, through the woods, until the wheat fields are reached, and then rising from the plain, gently, to the high suspension bridge which crosses the canal, two minutes beyond which lies the river, here very broad and sluggish.

This part of the canal, which is perfectly straight from Condé to Meaux, is unusually pretty. The banks are steep, and 'tall poplar trees' cast long shadows across grass-edged footpaths, above which the high bridge is swung. There is no bridge here across the Marne; the nearest in one direction is at Isles-lès-Villenoy, and in the other at Meaux. So, as the Germans could not have crossed the Marne here, the canal bridge was not destroyed, though it was mined. The barricades of loose stones which the English built three weeks ago, both at the bridgehead and at a bend in the road just before it is reached, where the road to Mareuil-sur-Marne turns off, were still there.

The road along the canal and through Mareuil is the one over which the German cavalry would have advanced had von Kluck's army succeeded in crossing the Marne at Meaux, and it was patrolled and guarded by the Yorkshire boys on September 2, and the Bedfords from the night of the 3d to the morning of the 5th.

The road from the canal to the river, separated here by only a few yards, leads through a wide avenue, across a private estate belonging to the proprietor of the plaster quarries at Mareuil, to a ferry, beside which was the *lavoir*. There is a sunken and terraced fruit garden below the road, and an extensive enclosure for fancy fowl.

The bank of the river showed me a sad sight. The wash houses were sunk. They lay underwater, with their chimneys sticking out. The little river piers and all the row-boats had been smashed and most of them sunk. A few of them, drawn up on the bank, were splintered into kindling wood. This work of destruction had been done, most effectively, by the English. They had not left a stick anywhere that could have served the invaders. It was an ugly sight, and the only consolation was to say, 'If the Boches had passed, it would have been worse!' This was only ugly. That would have been tragic.

The next day I had my first real news from Meaux. A woman arrived at Amélie's, leading two dogs tied together with rope. She was a music teacher, living at Meaux, and had walked over thirty miles, and arrived exhausted. So they took her in for the night, and the next morning Père harnessed Ninette and took her and her weary dogs to Meaux. It was over two hours each way for Ninette, but it was better than seeing an exhausted woman, almost as old as I am, finishing her pilgrimage on foot. She is the first person returning to Meaux that we have seen. Besides, I imagine Père was glad of the excuse to go across the Marne.

When he came back we knew exactly what had happened at the cathedral city.

The picturesque mill bridges across the Marne have been partly saved. The ends of the bridges on the town side were blown up, and the mills were mined, to be destroyed on the German approach. Père was told that an appeal was made to the English commanders to save the old landmarks if possible, and although at that time it seemed to no one at all likely that they could be saved, this precaution did save them. He tells me that blowing up the bridgeheads smashed all the windows, blew out all the doors, and damaged the walls more or less, but all that is reparable.

Do you remember the last time we were at Meaux, how we leaned on the stone wall on that beautiful Promenade des Trinitaires, and watched the waters of the Marne churned into froth by the huge wheels of the three lines of mills lying from bank to bank? I know you will be glad they are saved. It would have been a pity to destroy that beautiful view. I am afraid that we are in an epoch where we shall have to thank

Fate for every fine thing and every well-loved view which survives this war between the Marne and the frontier, where the ground had been fought over in all the great wars of France since the days of Charlemagne.

It seems that more people stayed at Meaux than I supposed. Monsignor Morbeau stayed there, and they say about a thousand of the poor were hidden carefully in the cellars. It had 14,000 inhabitants. Only about five buildings were reached by bombs, and the damage is not even worth recording.

I am sure you must have seen the Bishop in the days when you lived in Paris, when he was *curé* at Saint-Honoré d'Eylau in the Place Victor Hugo. At that time he was a popular priest – *mondain*, clever and eloquent. At Meaux he is a power. No figure is so familiar in the picturesque old streets, especially on market day, Saturday, as this tall, powerful-looking man in his *soutane* and *barrette*, with his air of authority, familiar yet dignified. He seems to know everyone by name, is all over the market, his keen eyes seeing everything, as influential in the everyday life of his diocese as he is in its spiritual affairs, a model of what a modern archbishop ought to be.

I hear he was on the battlefield from the beginning, and that the first ambulances to reach Meaux found the seminary full of wounded picked up under his direction and cared for as well as his resources permitted. He has written his name in the history of the old town under that of Bossuet – and in the records of such a town that is no small distinction.

The news which is slowly filtering back to us from the plains is another matter.

Some of the families in our *commune* have relatives residing in the little hamlets between Cregy and Monthyon, and have been out to help them re-install themselves. Very little in the way of details of the battle seems to be known. Trees and houses dumbly tell their own tales. The roads are terribly cut up, but road builders are already at work. Huge trees have been broken off like twigs, but even there men are at work, uprooting them and cutting the wood into lengths and piling it neatly along the roadside to be carted away. The dead are buried, and Paris automobiles are rapidly removing all traces of the battles and carrying out of sight such disfigurements as can be removed.

But the details we get regarding the brief German occupation are too disgusting for words. It is not the actual destruction of the battle – for Barcy alone of the towns in sight from here seems to be practically destroyed – which is the most painful, it is the devastation of the German occupation, with its deliberate and filthy defilement of the houses, which defies words, and will leave a blot for all time on the records of the race so vile-minded as to have achieved it. The deliberate ingenuity of the nastiness is its most debasing feature. At Penchard, where the Germans only stayed twenty-four hours, many people were obliged to make bonfires of the bedding and all sorts of other things as the only and quickest way to purge the town of danger in such hot weather.

I am told that Penchard is a fair example of what the Germans did in all these small towns which lay in the line of their hurried retreat.

It is not worthwhile for me to go into detail regarding such disgusting acts.

Your imagination, at its most active, cannot do any wrong to the race which in this war seems determined to offend where it cannot terrorize.

It is wonderfully characteristic of the French that they have accepted this feature of their disaster as they have accepted the rest – with courage, and that they have at once gone to work to remove all the German 'hallmarks' as quickly as possible – and now have gone back to their fields in the same spirit.

It was not until yesterday that I unpacked my little hat-trunk and carefully put its contents back into place.

It has stood all these days under the stairs in the salon – hat, cape, and gloves on it, and shoes beside it, just as I packed it.

I had an odd sensation while I was emptying it. I don't know why I put it off so long. Perhaps I dreaded to find, locked in it, a too vivid recollection of the day I closed it. It may be that I was afraid that, with the perversity of inanimate things, it had the laugh on me.

I don't believe I put it off from fear of having to repack it, for, so far as I can know myself, I cannot find in my mind any signs, even, of a dread that what had happened once could happen again. But I don't know.

I wish I had more newsy things to write you. But nothing is happening here, you see.

III

Well, Amélie came back yesterday, and I can tell you it was a busy day. I assure you that I was glad to see her about the house again. I liked doing the work well enough – for a little while. But I had quite all I wanted of it before the fortnight was over. I felt like 'giving praise' when I saw her coming into the garden, looking just as good as new, and, my word for it, she made things hum yesterday.

The first thing she did, after the house was in order, and lunch out of the way, was to open up the *cave* in which she had stored her household treasures a month ago, and I passed a rare afternoon. I spent a good part of it getting behind something to conceal my silent laughter. If you had been here you would have enjoyed it – and her.

I knew something was as it should not be when I saw her pushing the little wheelbarrow on which were all my waste-baskets – I have needed them. But when I got them back, it about finished my attempts at sobriety. I told her to put them on the dining-room table and I would unpack them and put the contents in place. But before that was done, I had to listen to her 'tale of woe'.

She had hidden practically everything – clocks, bed- and table-linen, all her mattresses, except the ones she and Père slept on, practically all their clothes, except what they had on their backs and one change. I had not given it much thought, though I do remember her saying, when the subterranean passage was sealed up: 'Let the Boches come! They'll find mighty little in my house.'

Well – the clocks are rusted. They are soaking in kerosene now, and I imagine it is little good that will do them. All her linen is damp and smelly, and much of it is mildewed. As for the blankets and flannels – ough!

I felt sympathetic, and tried to appear so. But I was in the condition of '*L'homme qui rit*'. The smallest effort to express an emotion tended to make me grimace horribly. She was so funny. I was glad when she finished saying naughty words about herself, and declaring that '*Madame* was right not to upset her house', and that the next time the Boches thought of coming here they would be welcome to anything she had. 'For,' she ended, 'I'll never get myself into this sort of a mess again, my word of honor!' And she marched out of the house, carrying the bottle of *eau de Javelle* with her. The whole hamlet smells of it this minute.

I had a small-sized fit of hysterics after she had gone, and it was not cured by opening up my wastebaskets and laying out the 'treasures' she had saved for me. I laughed until I cried.

There were my bouillion cups, and no saucers. The saucers were piled in the buffet. There were half a dozen decorated plates which had stood on end in the buffet – just as color notes – no value at all. There were bits of silver, and nearly all the plated stuff. There was an old painted fan, several strings of beads, a rosary which hung on a nail at the head of my bed, a few bits of jewelry – you know how little I care for jewelry – and there were four brass candlesticks.

The only things I had missed at all were the plated things. I had not had teaspoons enough when the English were here – not that they cared. They were quite willing to stir their tea with each other's spoons, since there was plenty of tea – and a 'stick' went with it.

You cannot deny that it had its funny side.

I could not help asking myself, even while I wiped tears of laughter from my eyes, if most of the people I saw flying four weeks ago might not have found themselves in the same fix when it came to taking stock of what was saved and what was lost.

I remember so well being at Aix-les-Bains, in 1899, when the Hotel du Beau-Site was burned, and finding a woman in a wrapper sitting on a bench in the park in front of the burning hotel, with the lace waist of an evening frock in one hand, and a small bottle of alcohol in the other. She explained to me, with some emotion, that she had gone back, at the risk of her life, to get the bottle from her dressing table, 'for fear that it would explode'!

It did not take me half an hour to get my effects in order, but poor Amélie's disgust seems to increase with time. You can't deny that if I had been drummed out and came back to find my house a ruin, my books and pictures destroyed, and only those worthless bits of china and plated ware to 'start housekeeping again', it would have been humorous. Real humor is only exaggeration. That would surely have been a colossal exaggeration.

It is not the first time I have had to ask myself, seriously, 'Why this mania for possession?' The ferryman on the Styx is as likely to take it across as our railroad is to 'handle' it today. Yet nothing seems able to break a person born with that mania for collecting.

I stood looking round at it all when everything was in place, and I realized that if the disaster had come, I should have found it easy to reconcile myself to it in an epoch where millions were facing it with me. It is the law of Nature. Material things, like the friends we have lost, may be eternally regretted. They cannot be eternally grieved for. We must '– be up and doing, With a heart for any fate.'

All the same, it was a queer twist in the order of my life, that, hunting in all directions for a quiet retreat in which to rest my weary spirit, I should have ended by deliberately sitting myself down on the edge of a battlefield – even though it was on the *safe edge* – and stranger still, that there I forgot that my spirit was weary.

We are beginning to pick up all sorts of odd little tales of the adventures of some of the people who had remained at Voisins. One old man there, a mason, who had worked on my house, had a very queer experience. Like all the rest of them, he went on working in the fields all through the menacing days. I can't make out whether he had no realization of actual danger, or whether that was his way of meeting it. Anyway, he disappeared on the morning the battle began, September 5, and did not return for several days. His old wife had made up her mind that the Germans had got him, when one morning he turned up, tired, pale, and hungry, and not in any state to explain his absence.

It was some days before his wife could get the story out of him. He owns a field about halfway between Voisins and Mareuil, close to the *route de Pavé du Roi*, and on the morning that the battle began he was digging potatoes there. Suddenly he saw a small group of horsemen riding down from the canal, and by their spiked helmets he knew them for Germans.

His first idea, naturally, was to escape. He dropped his hoe, but he was too paralyzed with fear to run, and there was nothing to hide behind. So he began walking across the field as well as his trembling old legs would let him, with his hands in his pockets.

Of course the Uhlans overtook him in a few minutes, and called out to him, in French, to stop. He stopped at once, expecting to be shot instantly.

They ordered him to come out into the road. He managed to obey. By the time he got there terror had made him quite speechless.

They began to question him. To all their questions he merely shook his head. He understood well enough, but his tongue refused its office, and by the time he could speak the idea had come to him to pretend that he was not French – that he was a refugee – that he did not know the country – was lost – in fact, that he did not know anything. He managed to carry it off, and finally they gave him up as a bad job, and rode away up the hill towards my house.

Then he had a new panic. He did not dare go home. He was afraid he would find them in the village, and that they would find out he had lied and harm his old wife, or perhaps destroy the town. So he had hidden down by the canal until hunger drove him home. It is a simple tale, but it was a rude experience for the old man, who has not got over it yet.

I am afraid all this seems trivial to you, coming out of the midst of this terrible war. But it is actually our life here. We listen to the cannon in ignorance of what is happening. Where would be the sense of my writing you that the battle-front has settled down to uncomfortable trench work on the Aisne; that Manoury is holding the line in front of us from Compiègne to Soissons, with Castelnau to the north of him, with his left wing resting on the Somme; that Maud'huy was behind Albert; and that Rheims cathedral had been persistently and brutally shelled since September 18? We only get news of that sort intermittently. Our railroad is in the hands of the Minister of War, and every day or two our communications are cut off, from military necessity. You know, I am sure, more about all this than we do, with your cable men filling the newspapers.

But if I am seeing none of that, I am seeing the spirit of these people, so sure of success in the end, and so convinced that, even if it takes the whole world to do it, they will yet see the Hohenzollern dynasty go up in the smoke of the conflagration it has lighted.

Of course, the vicious destruction of the great cathedral sends shivers down my back. Every time I hear the big guns in that direction I think of the last time we were there. Do you remember how we sat, in the twilight of a rainy day, in our top-floor room, at the Lion d'Or, in the wide window seat, which brought us just at a level with that dear tympanum, with its primitive stone carving of David and Goliath, and all those wonderful animals sitting up so bravely on the lacework of the parapet? Such a wave of pity goes over me when I think that not only is it destroyed, but that future generations are deprived of seeing it; that one of the greatest achievements of the hands of man, a work which has withstood so many wars in what we called 'savage times', before any claims were made for 'Kultur', should have been destroyed in our days. Men have come and men have gone (apologies to Tennyson) – it is the law of living. But the wilful, unnecessary destruction of the great works of man, the testimony which one age has left as a heritage to all time – for that loss neither Man nor Time has any consolation. It is a theft from future ages, and for it Germany will merit the hatred of the world through the coming generations.

IV

Amélie and I went up to Paris day before yesterday, for the first time since the battle – you see everything here dates 'before' and 'after' the battle, and will for a long time.

Trains had been running between Paris and Meaux for ten days, and will soon go as far as Chalons, where the Etat-Major was the last time we heard of it. Isn't that pretty quick work? And with three big bridges to build? But the army needed the road, and the engineers were at work five days after the battle.

There are but few trains – none yet on our branch road – so we had to go to Esbly. It took two hours to get to Paris – hardly more than twelve miles. We simply crawled most of the way. We crept through the tunnel this side of Lagny, and then stood on this side of the Marne, and whistled and shrieked a long time before we began to wiggle across the unfinished bridge, with workmen hanging up on the derricks and scaffoldings in all sorts of perilous positions, and all sorts of grotesque attitudes. I was glad when we were over.

I found the town more normal than it was when I was there six weeks ago. If I had not seen it in those first days of the mobilization it would have seemed sadder than it did, and, by contrast, while it was not the Paris that you know, it was quiet and peaceful – no excitement of any sort in the streets, practically no men anywhere. All the department shops were open, but few people were in them, and very little to sell. Many of the small shops were closed, and will be, I imagine, until the end of the war. All the Austrian and German shops, and there were many of them, are, of course, closed for good, making wide spaces of closed shutters in the Avenue de l'Opéra and the rue de la Paix, and the rue Scribe, where so many of the steamship offices are. That, and the lack of omnibuses and tramways and the scarcity of cabs, makes the once brilliant and active quarter look quite unnatural. However, it gives one a chance to see how really handsome it is.

A great many of the most fashionable hotels are turned to hospitals, and everywhere, especially along the Champs-Elysées, the flags of the Red Cross float over once gay resorts, while big white bunting signs extend across almost every other *façade*, carrying the name and number of a hospital.

Every sort of business is running short-handed, and no big office or bank is open between the hours of noon and two o'clock.

I saw no one – there was no one to see. I finished the little business I had to do and then I went back to the station and sat on the terrace of the café opposite, and, for an hour, I watched the soldiers going in at one gate, and the public – Indian file – presenting its papers at another. No carriages can enter the courtyard. No one can carry anything but hand luggage, and porters are not allowed to pass the gates, so one had to carry one's bundles one's self across the wide, paved court. However, it is less trying to do this than it was in other days, as one runs no risk from flying motor-cabs.

We did not leave Paris until six – it was already dark – and there were few lights along the road. The Germans would love to destroy this road, which is on the direct line to the front, but I cannot imagine a bomb from an aeroplane reaching it at night, except by accident.

By the way, the attitude of the public towards these war airships is queer. It seems a great deal more curiosity than fear. I had heard this stated, and I had a chance to see it exemplified. Just as Amélie and I were stumbling in the dusk over the rough pavement of the court, we heard an aeroplane overhead. Everyone stopped short and looked up. Some fool called

'*Une Taube – une Taube*!' People already inside the station turned and ran back to see. Of course, it wasn't a Taube. Still, the fact that someone said it was, and that everyone ran out to look up at it, was significant, as I am sure they would have done just the same if it had really been a German machine.

We came back even more slowly than we had gone up. It took ten minutes by my watch to cross the bridge at Chalifère. We jigged a bit and stopped; staggered a bit, and trembled, and stopped; crawled a bit, and whistled. I had a feeling that if anyone disobeyed the order pasted on every window, and leaned out, we should topple over into the stream. Still, no one seemed to mind. With the curtains drawn, everyone tried to read, by the dim light, a newspaper. It is remarkable how even ordinary people face danger if a panic can be prevented. The really great person is the one who even in a panic does not lose his head, and the next best thing to not being fazed at danger is, I believe, to be literally paralyzed. Total immobility often passes for pluck.

It was nearly half past eight when we reached Esbly; the town was absolutely dark. Père was there with the donkey cart, and it took nearly an hour and a half to climb the hill to Huiry. It was pitch dark, and oh, so cold! Both Condé and Voisins, as well as Esbly, had street lamps – gas – before the war, but it was cut off when mobilization began, and so the road was black. This ordinary voyage seemed like journeying in a wilderness, and I was as tired as if I had been to London, which I take to be the hardest trip for the time it consumes that I know. I used to go to London in seven hours, and this trip to Paris and back had taken four hours and a half by train and three by carriage.

I found your letter dated September 25 – in reply to my first one mailed after the battle. I am shocked to hear that I was spectacular. I did not mean to be. I apologize. Please imagine me very red in the face and feeling a little bit silly. I should not mind your looking on me as a heroine and all those other names you throw at me if I had had time to flee along the roads with all I could save of my home on my back, as I saw thousands doing.

But I cannot pick up your bouquets, considering that all I had to do was 'sit tight' for a few days, and watch – at a safe distance – a battle sweep back. All you must say about that is 'she did have luck'. That's what I say every day.

As our railway communication is to be cut again, I am hurrying this off, not knowing when I can send another. But as you see, I have no news to write – just words to remind you of me, and say that all is well with me in this world where it is so ill for many.

V

It was not until I got out my letter-book this morning that I realized that I had let three weeks go by without writing to you. I have no excuse to offer, unless the suspense of the war may pass as one.

We have settled down to a long war, and though we have settled down with hope, I can tell you every day demands its courage.

The fall of Antwerp was accepted as inevitable, but it gave us all a sad day. It was no use to write you things of that sort. You, I presume, do not need to be told, although you are so far away, that for me, personally, it could only increase the grief I felt that Washington had not made the protest I expected when the Belgian frontier was crossed. It would have been only a moral effort, but it would have been a blow between the eyes for the nervous Germans.

All the words we get from the front tell us that the boys are standing the winter in the trenches very well. They've simply got to – that is all there is to that.

Amélie is more astonished than I am. When she first realized that they had got to stay out there in the rain and the mud and the cold, she just gasped out that they never would stand it.

I asked her what they would do then – lie down and let the Germans ride over them? Her only reply was that they would all die. It is hard for her to realize yet the resistance of her own race.

I am realizing in several ways, in a small sense, what the men are enduring. I take my bit of daily exercise walking round my garden. I always have to carry a trowel in my sweater pocket, and I stop every ten steps to dig the cakes of mud off my sabots. I take up a good bit of my landed property at every step. So I can *guess*, at least, what it must be out in the trenches. This highly cultivated, well-fertilized French soil has its inconveniences in a country where the ground rarely freezes as it does in New England.

Also I am very cold.

When I came out here I found that the coal dealer was willing to deliver coal to me once a week. I had a long, covered box along the wall of the kitchen which held an ample supply of coal for the week. The system had two advantages – it enabled me to do my trading in the *commune*, which I liked, and it relieved Amélie from having to carry heavy hods of coal in all weathers from the grange outside. But, alas, the railroad communications being cut – no coal! I had big wood enough to take me through the first weeks, and have some still, but it will hardly last me to Christmas – nor does the open fire heat the house as the *salamandre* did. But it is wartime, and I must not complain – yet.

You accuse me in your last letter of being flippant in what seems to you tragic circumstances. I am sorry that I make that impression on you. I am not a bit flippant. I can only advise you to come over here, and live a little in this atmosphere, and see how you would feel. I am afraid that no amount of imagining what one will or will not do prepares one to know what one will really do face to face with such actualities as I live amongst. I must confess that had I had anyone dear to me here, anyone for whose safety or moral courage I was – or imagined I was – responsible (for, after all, we are responsible for no one), my frame of mind and perhaps my acts might have been different. I don't know. Why, none of the men that Î see have the air of feeling they are heroes – they just seem to think of it all as if it were merely 'in the day's work'.

For example, do you remember that handsome younger brother of my sculptor friend – the English boy who was in the heavy artillery, and had been in China and North Nigeria with Sir Frederick Ludgard as an aide-de-camp, and finally as assistant governor general? Well, he was with the first division of the British Expedition which landed in France in the middle of August. He made all that long, hard retreat from Belgium to the Marne, and was in the terrible Battle of the Rivers. I am enclosing a letter I have just received from him, because I think it very characteristic. Besides, if you remember him, I am sure that it will interest you. I don't know where it is from – they are not allowed to tell. It came, as army letters do, without any stamp – the carriage is free – with the round red stamp of the censor, a crown in the middle, and the words 'Passed by the Censor', and the number printed around it. Here it is:

My dearest M—

October 30, 1914

Last night I heard your account of your experiences between September 1 and 9, and it made me boil anew with disappointment that my attempts to reach Huiry on September 4 were frustrated. I was disappointed enough at the time, but then my regret was tempered by the thought that you were probably safe in Paris, and I should only find an empty house at La Creste. Now that I know that I should have found you – you!!! – it makes me wild, even after this interval of time, to have missed a sight of you. Now let me tell you how it came about that you nearly received a visit from me.

156

I left England August 17, with the 48th Heavy Battery (3d division). We landed at Rouen, and went by train, via Amiens, to Houtmont, a few kilometres west of Mauberge. There we detrained one morning at two o'clock, marched through Malplaquet into Belgium, and came in contact with the enemy at once.

The story of the English retreat must be familiar to you by now. It was a wonderful experience. I am glad to have gone through it, though I am not anxious to undergo such a time again. We crossed the Marne at Meaux, on September 3, marching due east to Signy-Signets. Funnily enough it was not until I had actually crossed the Marne that I suddenly realized that I was in your vicinity. Our route, unfortunately, led right away from you, and I could not ask to get away while we were actually on the march, and possibly going many miles in another direction. The following day, however – the 4th – we retraced our steps somewhat, and halted to bivouac a short distance west of a village named La Haute Maison – roughly about six miles from you. I immediately asked permission to ride over to Huiry. The Major, with much regret, declined to let me leave, and, since we received orders to march again an hour later, he was right. We marched all that night. I have marked out our road with arrows on the little map enclosed. We reached a place called Fontenay about 8.30 the next morning, by which time I was twenty miles from you, and not in a condition to want anything but sleep and food. That was our farthest point south. But, sad to say, in our advance we went by a road farther east, and

quite out of reach of you, and crossed the Marne at
a place called Nanteuil. I got your first letter about
one day's march south of Mons.

Best love, dearest M—. Write again.

Isn't that a calm way to state such a trying experience as that retreat? It is only a sample of a soldier's letter.

If he were disappointed you can imagine that I was. Luckily I had seen him in June, when he was here on a visit, having just returned from North Nigeria, after five years in the civil service, to take up his grade in the army, little dreaming there was to be a war at once.

If he had come that afternoon imagine what I should have felt to see him ride down by the picket at the gate. He would have found me pouring tea for Captain Edwards of the Bedfords. It would have surely added a touch of reality to the battle of the next days. Of course I knew he was somewhere out there, but to have seen him actually riding away to it would have been different. Yet it might not, for I am sure his conversation would have been as calm as his letters, and they read as much as if he were taking an exciting pleasure trip, with interesting risks thrown in, as anything else. That is so English. On some future day I suppose we shall sit together on the lawn – he will probably lie on it – and swap wonderful stories, for I am going to be one of the veterans of this war.

I must own that when I read the letter I found it suggestive of the days that are gone. Imagine marching through Malplaquet and over all that West Flanders country with its memories of Marlborough, and where, had the Dutch left the Duke a free hand, he would have marched on Paris – with other Allies – as he did on Lille. I must own that history, with its records of bitter enemies yesterday, bosom friends today, does not inspire one with much hope of seeing the dreamer's vision of universal peace realized.

Still, I must confess that the attitude of French and English to one another today is almost thrilling. The English Tommy Atkins and the French *poilu* are delightful together. For that matter, the French peasants love the English. They never saw any before, and their admiration and devotion to 'Tommee', as they call him, is unbounded. They think him so 'chic', and he is.

No one – not even I, who so love them – would ever accuse the *'piou-piou'* of being chic.

The French conscript in his misfits has too long been the object of affectionate sarcasm and the subject of caricature to be unfamiliar to the smiles of the whole world.

You see the army outfits are made in three sizes only. So far as my observation goes none of the three measurements fits anyone today, and as for the man who is a real 'between' – well, he is in a sad box. But what of that? He doesn't seem to care. He is so occupied today fighting, just as he did in the days of the great Napoleon, that no one cares a rap how he looks – and surely he does not.

You might think he would be a bit self-conscious regarding his appearance when he comes in contact with his smarter looking Ally. Not a bit of it. The *poilu* just admires Tommy and is proud of him. I do wish you could see them together. The *poilu* would hug Tommy and plant a kiss on each of his cheeks – if he dared. But, needless to say, that is the last sort of thing Tommy wants. So, *faute de mieux* the *poilu* walks as close to Tommy as he can – when he gets a chance – and the undemonstrative, sure-of-himself Tommy permits it without a smile – which is doing well. Still, in his own way Tommy admires back – it is mutual.

The Englishman may learn to unbend – I don't know. The spirit which has carried him all over the world, rubbed him against all sorts of conditions and so many civilizations without changing his character, and made of him the one race immune to home-sickness, has persisted for centuries, and may be so bred in the bone, fibre, and soul of the race as to persist forever. It may have made his legs and his spine so straight that he can't unbend. He has his own kind of fun, but it's mostly of the sporting sort. He will, I imagine, hardly contract the Frenchman's sort, which is so largely on his lips, and in his mentality, and has given the race the most mobile faces in the world.

I am enclosing a copy of the little map Captain S— sent me. It may give you an idea of the route the English were moving on during the battle, and the long forced march they made after the fighting of the two weeks ending August 30.

I imagine they were all too tired to note how beautiful the country was. It was lovely weather, and coming down the route from Haute Maison, by La Chapelle, to the old moated town of Crécy-en-Brie at sunset, must have been beautiful; and then climbing by Voulangis to the Forest of Crécy on the way to Fontenay by moonlight even more lovely, with the panorama of Villiers and the valley of the Morin seen through the trees of the winding road, with Montbarbin standing, outlined in white light, on the top of a hill, like a fairy town. Tired as they were, I do hope there were some among them who could still look with a dreamer's eyes on these pictures.

Actually the only work I have done of late has been to dig a little in the garden, preparing for winter. I did not take my geraniums up until last week. As for the dahlias I wrote you about, they became almost a scandal in the *commune*. They grew and grew, like Jack's beanstalk – prodigiously. I can't think of any other word to express it. They were eight feet high and full of flowers, which we cut for the *Jour des Morts*. I know you won't believe that, but it is true. A few days later there came a wind-storm, and when it was over, in spite of the heavy poles I put in to hold them up, they were laid as flat as though the German cavalry had passed over them. I was heartbroken, but Père only shrugged his shoulders and remarked: 'If one will live on the top of a hill facing the north what can one expect?' And I had no reply to make. Fortunately the wind can't blow my panorama away, though at present I don't often look out at it. I content myself by playing in the garden on the south side, and, if I go out at all, it is to walk through the orchards and look over the valley of the Morin, towards the south.

My, but I'm cold – too cold to tell you about. The ends of my fingers hurt the keys of my machine.

VI

November 28, 1914

I am sorry that, as you say in your letter of October 16, just received, you are disappointed that I 'do not write you more about the war'. Dear child, I am not seeing any of it. We are settled down here to a life that is nearly normal – much more normal than I dreamed could be possible forty miles from the front. We are still in the zone of military operations, and probably shall be until spring, at least. Our communications with the outside world are frequently cut. We get our mail with great irregularity. Even our local mail goes to Meaux, and is held there five days, as the simplest way of exercising the censorship. It takes nearly ten days to get an answer to a letter to Paris.

All that I see which actually reminds me of the war – now that we are used to the absence of the men – I see on the *route nationale*, when I drive down to Couilly. Across the fields it is a short and pretty walk. Amélie makes it in twenty minutes. I could, if it were not for climbing that terrible hill to get back.

Besides, the mud is inches deep. I have a queer little four-wheeled cart, covered, if I want to unroll the curtains. I call it my perambulator, and really, with Ninette hitched in, I am like an overgrown baby in its baby carriage, and any nurse I ever knew would push a perambulator faster than that donkey drags mine. Yet it just suits my mood. I sit comfortably in it, and travel slowly – time being non-existent – so slowly that I can watch the wheat sprout, and gaze at the birds and the view and the clouds. I do hold on to the reins – just for looks – though I have no need to, and I doubt if Ninette suspects me of doing anything so foolish. On the road I always meet officers riding along, military cars flying along, army couriers spluttering along on motor cycles, heavy motor transports groaning up hill, or thundering down, and now and then a long train of motor-ambulances. Almost any morning, at nine, I can see the long line of *camions* carrying the *revitaillement* towards the front, and the other afternoon, as I was driving up the hill, I met a train of ambulances coming down. The big grey things slid, one after another, around the curve of the Demi-Lune, and simply flew by me, raising such a cloud of dust that after I had counted thirty, I found I could not see them, and the continual tooting of the horns began to make Ninette nervous – she had never seen anything like that before – so, for fear she might do some trick she never had done in her life, like shying, and also for fear that the drivers, who were rushing by exactly in the middle of the road, might not see me in the dust, or a car might skid, I slid out, and led my equipage the rest of the way. I do assure you these are actually all the war signs we see, though, of course, we still hear the cannon.

But, though we don't see it, we feel it in many ways. My neighbors feel it more than I do! For one example – the fruit crop this year has been an absolute loss. Luckily the cassis got away before the war was declared, but we hear it was a loss to the buyers, and it was held in the Channel ports, necessarily, and was spoiled. But apples and pears had no market. In ordinary years purchasers come to buy the trees, and send their own pickers and packers, and what was not sold in that way went to the big Saturday market at Meaux. This year there is no market at Meaux. The town is still partly empty, and the railroad cannot carry produce now. This is a tragic loss to the small cultivator, though, as yet, he is not suffering, and he usually puts all such winnings into his stocking.

We still have no coal to speak of. I am burning wood in the salon – and green wood at that. The big blaze – when I can get it – suits my house better than the *salamandre* did. But I cannot get a temperature above 42 Fahrenheit. I am used to sixty, and I remember you used to find that too low in Paris. I blister my face, and freeze my back, just as we used to in the old days of glorious October at the farm in New Sharon, where my mother was born, and where I spent my summers and part of the autumn in my schooldays.

You might think it would be easy to get wood. It is not. The army takes a lot of it, and those who, in ordinary winters, have wood to sell, have to keep it for themselves this year. Père has cut down all the old trees he could find – old prune trees, old apple trees, old chestnut trees – and it is not the best of firewood. I hated to see even that done, but he claimed that he wanted to clear a couple of pieces of land, and I try to believe him. Did you ever burn green wood? If you have, enough said!

Unluckily – since you expect me to write often – I am a creature of habit. I never could write as you can, with a pad on my knees, huddled over the fire. I suppose that I could have acquired the habit if I had begun my education at the Sorbonne, instead of polishing off there. I remember when I first began to haunt that university, eighteen years ago, how amazed I was to see the students huddled into a small space with overcoats and hats on their knees, a notebook on top of them, an ink-pot in one hand and a pen in the other, and, in spite of obstacles, absorbed in the lecture. I used to wonder if they had ever heard of 'stylos', even while I understood, as I never had done before, the real love of learning that marks the race. Alas! I have to be halfway comfortable before I can half accomplish anything.

I am thankful to say that the temperature has been moderating a little, and life about me has been active. One day it was the big threshing machine, and the work was largely done by women, and the air was full of throbbing and dust. Yesterday it was the cider press, and I stood about, at Amélie's, in the sun, half the afternoon, watching the motor hash the apples, and the press squeeze out the yellow juice, which rushed foaming into big vats. Did you ever drink cider like that?

It is the only way I like it. It carried me back to my girlhood and the summers in the Sandy River valley. I don't know why it is, of late, that my mind turns so often back to those days, and with such affection. Perhaps it is only because I find myself once more living in the country. It may be true that life is a circle, and as one approaches the end the beginning becomes visible, and associated with both the beginning and end of mine there is a war. However it is to be explained, there remains the fact that my middle distances are getting wiped out.

In these still nights, when I cannot sleep, I think more often than of anything else of the road running down the hill by the farm at New Sharon, and of the sounds of the horses and wagons as they came down and crossed the wooden bridge over the brook, and of the voices – so strange in the night – as they passed. There were more night sounds in those memories than I ever hear here – more crickets, more turnings over of Nature, asleep or awake. I rarely hear many night sounds here. From sundown, when people go clattering by in their wooden shoes from the fields, to daylight, when the birds awake, all is silence. I looked out into the moonlight before I closed my shutters last night. I might have been alone in the world. Yet I like it.

The country is lovely here in winter – so different from what I remember of it at home. My lawn is still green, so is the *corbeille d'argent* in the garden border, which is still full of silvery bunches of bloom, and will be all winter. The violets are still in bloom. Even the trees here never get black as they do in New England, for the trunks and branches are always covered with green moss. That is the dampness. Of course, we never have the dry invigorating cold that makes a New England winter so wonderful. I don't say that one is more beautiful than the other, only that each is different in its charm. After all, Life, wherever one sees it, is, if one has eyes, a wonderful pageant, the greatest spectacular melodrama I can imagine. I'm glad to have seen it. I have not always had an orchestra stall, but what of that? One ought to see things at several angles and from several elevations, you know.

VII

We have been having some beautiful weather.

Yesterday Amélie and I took advantage of it to make a pilgrimage across the Marne, to decorate the graves on the battlefield at Chambry. Crowds went out on All Soul's Day, but I never like doing anything, even making a pilgrimage, in a crowd.

You can realize how near it is, and what an easy trip it will be in normal times, when I tell you that we left Esbly for Meaux at half past one – only ten minutes by train – and were back in the station at Meaux at quarter to four, and had visited Monthyon, Villeroy, Neufmontier, Penchard, Chauconin, Barcy, Chambry, and Vareddes.

The authorities are not very anxious to have people go out there. Yet nothing to prevent is really done. It only takes a little diplomacy. If I had gone to ask for a passport, nine chances out of ten it would have been refused me. I happened to know that the wife of the big livery stable man at Meaux, an energetic – and, incidentally, a handsome – woman, who took over the business when her husband joined his regiment, had a couple of automobiles, and would furnish me with all the necessary papers. They are not taxi-cabs, but handsome touring cars. Her chauffeur carries the proper papers. It seemed to me a very loose arrangement, from a military point of view, even although I was assured that she did not send out anyone she did not know. However, I decided to take advantage of it.

While we were waiting at the garage for the car to be got out, and the chauffeur to change his coat, I had a chance to talk with a man who had not left Meaux during the battle, and I learned that there were several important families who had remained with the Archbishop and aided him to organize matters for saving the city, if possible, and protect the property of those who had fled, and that the measures which those sixty citizens, with Archbishop Marbeau at their head, took for the safety of the poor, the care for the wounded and dead, is already one of the proudest documents in the annals of the historic town.

But never mind all these things, which the guides will recite for you, I imagine, when you come over to make the grand tour of Fighting France, for on these plains about Meaux you will have to start your pilgrimage.

I confess that my heart beat a little too rapidly when, as we ran out of Meaux, and took the *route départmentale* of Senlis, a soldier stepped to the middle of the road and held up his gun – *baionette au canon.*

We stopped.

Were we after all going to be turned back? I had the guilty knowledge that there was no reason why we should not be. I tried to look magnificently unconcerned as I leaned forward to smile at the soldier. I might have spared myself the effort. He never even glanced inside the car. The examination of the papers was the most cursory thing imaginable – a mere formality. The chauffeur simply held his stamped paper towards the guard. The guard merely glanced at it, lifted his gun, motioned us to proceed – and we proceeded.

It may amuse you to know that we never even showed the paper again. We did meet two *gendarmes* on bicycles, but they nodded and passed us without stopping.

The air was soft, like an early autumn day, rather than December as you know it. There was a haze in the air, but behind it the sun shone. You know what that French haze is, and what it does to the world, and how, through it, one gets the sort of landscape painters love. With how many of our pilgrimages together it is associated! We have looked through it at the walls of Provins, when the lindens were rosy with the first rising of the sap; we have looked through it at the circular panorama from the top of the ruined tower of Montlhéry; we have looked through it across Jean Jacques Rousseau's country, from the lofty terrace of Montmorency, and from the platform in front of the prison of Philippe Auguste's unhappy Danish wife, at Etampes, across the valley of the Juine; and from how many other beautiful spots, not to forget the view up the Seine from the terrace of the Tuileries.

Sometime, I hope, we shall see these plains of the Marne together. When we do, I trust it will be on just such another atmospheric day as yesterday.

As our road wound up the hill over the big paving stones characteristic of the environs of all the old towns of France, everything looked so peaceful, so pretty, so normal, that it was hard to realize that we were moving towards the front, and were only about three miles from the point where the German invasion was turned back almost three months ago to a day, and it was the more difficult to realize as we have not heard the cannon for days.

A little way out of Meaux, we took a road to the west for Chauconin, the nearest place to us which was bombarded, and from a point in the road I looked back across the valley of the Marne, and I saw a very pretty white town, with red roofs, lying on the hillside. I asked the chauffeur:

'What village is that over there?'

He glanced around and replied: 'Quincy.'

It was my town. I ought not to have been surprised. Of course I knew that if I could see Chauconin so clearly from my garden, why, Chauconin could see me. Only, I had not thought of it.

Amélie and I looked back with great interest. It did look so pretty, and it is not pretty at all – the least pretty village on this side of the hill. 'Distance' does, indeed, 'lend enchantment'. When you come to see me I shall show you Quincy from the other side of the Marne, and never take you into its streets. Then you'll always remember it as a fairy town.

It was not until we were entering into Chauconin that we saw the first signs of war. The approach through the fields, already ploughed, and planted with winter grain, looked the very last thing to be associated with war. Once inside the little village – we always speak of it as '*le petit Chauconin*' – we found destruction enough. One whole street of houses was literally gutted. The walls stand, but the roofs are off and doors and windows gone, while the shells seem burned out. The destruction of the big farms seems to have been pretty complete. There they stood, long walls of rubble and plaster, breeched; ends of farm buildings gone; and many only a heap of rubbish. The surprising thing to me was to see here a house destroyed, and, almost beside it, one not even touched. That seemed to prove that the struggle here was not a long one, and that a comparatively small number of shells had reached it.

Neufmortier was in about the same condition. It was a sad sight, but not at all ugly. Ruins seem to 'go' with the French atmosphere and background. It all looked quite natural, and I had to make an effort to shake myself into a becoming frame of mind. If you had been with me I should have asked you to pinch me, and remind me that 'all this is not yet ancient history', and that a little sentimentality would have become me. But Amélie would never have understood me.

It was not until we were driving east again to approach Penchard that a full realization of it came to me. Penchard crowns the hill just in the center of the line which I see from the garden. It was one of the towns bombarded on the evening of September 5, and, so far as I can guess, the destruction was done by the French guns which drove the Germans out that night.

They say the Germans slept there the night of September 4, and were driven out the next day by the French *soixante-quinze*, which trotted through Chauconin into Penchard by the road we had just come over.

I enclose you a *carte postale* of a battery passing behind the apse of the village church, just as a guarantee of good faith.

But all signs of the horrors of those days have been obliterated. Penchard is the town in which the Germans exercised their taste for wilful nastiness, of which I wrote you weeks ago. It is a pretty little village, beautifully situated, commanding the slopes to the Marne on one side, and the wide plains of Barcy and Chambry on the other. It is prosperous looking, the home of sturdy farmers and the small *rentiers*. It has an air of humble thrift, with now and then a pretty garden, and here and there suggestions of a certain degree of greater prosperity, an air which, in France, often conceals unexpected wealth.

You need not look the places up unless you have a big map. No guidebook ever honored them.

From Penchard we ran a little out to the west at the foot of the hill, on top of which stand the white walls of Montyon, from which, on September 5, we had seen the first smoke of battle.

I am sure that I wrote some weeks ago how puzzled I was when I read Joffre's famous *ordre du jour*, at the beginning of the Marne offensive, to find that it was dated September 6, whereas we had seen the battle begin on the 5th. Here I found what I presume to be the explanation, which proves that the offensive along the rest of the line on the 6th had been a continuation simply of what we saw that Saturday afternoon.

At the foot of the hill crowned by the walls of Montyon lies Villeroy – today the objective point for patriotic pilgrimages. There, on the 5th of September, the 276th Regiment was preparing its soup for lunch, when, suddenly, from the trees on the heights, German shells fell amongst them, and food was forgotten, while the French at Saint-Soupplet on the other side of the hill, as well as those at Villeroy, suddenly found themselves in the thick of a fight – the battle we saw.

They told me at Villeroy that many of the men in the regiments engaged were from this region, and here the civilians dropped their work in the fields and snatched up guns which the dead or wounded soldiers let fall and entered the fight beside their uniformed neighbors. I give you that picturesque and likely detail for what it is worth.

At the foot of the hill between Montyon and Villeroy lies the tomb in which two hundred of the men who fell here are buried together. Among them is Charles Péguy, the poet, who wore a lieutenant's stripes, and was referred to by his companions on that day as *'un glorieux fou dans sa bravoure'*. This long tomb, with its crosses and flags and flowers, was the scene on All Soul's Day of the commemorative ceremony in honor of the victory, and marks not only the beginning of the battle, but the beginning of its triumph.

From this point we drove back to the east, almost along the line of battle, to the hillside hamlet of Barcy, the saddest scene of desolation on this end of the great fight.

It was a humble little village, grouped around a dear old church, with a graceful square tower supporting a spire. The little church faced a small square, from which the principal street runs down the hill to the open country across which the French 'push' advanced. No house on this street escaped. Some of them are absolutely destroyed. The church is a mere shell. Its tower is pierced with huge holes. Its bell

172

lies, a wreck, on the floor beneath its tower. The roof has fallen in, a heaped-up mass of *débris* in the nave beneath. Its windows are gone, and there are gaping wounds in its side walls. Oddly enough, the *Chemin de la Croix* is intact, and some of the peasants look on that as a miracle, in spite of the fact that the High Altar is buried under a mass of tiles and plaster.

The doors being gone, one could look in, over the temporary barrier, to the wreck inside, and by putting a donation into the contribution box for the *restauration* fund it was possible to enter – at one's own risk – by a side door. It was hardly worthwhile, as one could see no more than was visible from the doorways, and it looked as if at any minute the whole edifice would crumble. However, Amélie wanted to go inside, and so we did.

We entered through the *mairie*, which is at one side, into a small courtyard, where the school children were playing under the propped-up walls as gaily as if there had never been a bombardment.

The *mairie* had fared little better than the church, and the schoolroom, which has its home in it, had a temporary roofing, the upper part being wrecked.

The best idea that I got of the destruction was, however, from a house almost opposite the church. It was only a shell, its walls alone standing. As its windows and doors had been blown out, we could look in from the street to the interior of what had evidently been a comfortable country house. It was now like an uncovered box, in the centre of which there was a conical shaped heap of ashes as high as the top of the fireplace. We could see where the stairs had been, but its entire contents had been burned down to a heap of ashes – burned as thoroughly as wood in a fireplace. I could not have believed in such absolute destruction if I had not seen it.

While we were gazing at the wreck I noticed an old woman leaning against the wall and watching us. Out of her weather-beaten, time-furrowed old face looked a pair of dark eyes, red-rimmed and blurred with much weeping. She was rubbing her distorted old hands together nervously as she watched us. It was inevitable that I should get into conversation with her, and discover that this wreck had been, for years, her home, that she had lived there all alone, and that everything she had in the world – her furniture, her clothing, and her *savings* – had been burned in the house.

You can hardly understand that unless you know these people. They keep their savings hidden. It is the well-known old story of the French stocking which paid the war indemnity of 1870. They have no confidence in banks. The State is the only one they will lend to, and the fact is one of the secrets of French success.

If you knew these people as I do, you would understand that an old woman of that peasant type, ignorant of the meaning of war, would hardly be likely to leave her house, no matter how many times she was ordered out, until shells began to fall about her. Even then, as she was rather deaf, she probably did not realize what was happening, and went into the street in such fear that she left everything behind her.

From Barcy we drove out into the plain, and took the direction of Chambry, following the line of the great and decisive fight of September 6 and 7.

We rolled slowly across the beautiful undulating country of grain and beet fields. We had not gone far when, right at the edge of the road, we came upon an isolated mound, with a rude cross at its head, and a tiny *tricolore* at its foot – the first French grave on the plain.

We motioned the chauffeur to stop, and we went on, on foot.

First the graves were scattered, for the boys lie buried just where they fell – cradled in the bosom of the mother country that nourished them, and for whose safety they laid down their lives. As we advanced they became more numerous, until we reached a point where, as far as we could see, in every direction, floated the little *tricolore* flags, like fine flowers in the landscape. They made tiny spots against the far-off horizon line, and groups like beds of flowers in the foreground, and we knew that, behind the skyline, there were more.

Here and there was a haystack with one grave beside it, and again there would be one, usually partly burned, almost encircled with the tiny flags which said: 'Here sleep the heroes'.

It was a disturbing and a thrilling sight. I give you my word, as I stood there, I envied them. It seemed to me a fine thing to lie out there in the open, in the soil of the fields their simple death has made holy, the duty well done, the dread over, each one just where he fell defending his motherland, enshrined forever in the loving memory of the land he had saved, in graves to be watered for years, not only by the tears of those near and dear to them, but by those of the heirs to their glory – the children of the coming generation of free France.

You may know a finer way to go. I do not. Surely, since Death is, it is better than dying of old age between clean sheets. Near the end of the route we came to the little walled cemetery of Chambry, the scene of one of the most desperate struggles of the 6th and 7th of September. You know what the humble village burying-grounds are like. Its wall is about six feet high, of plaster and stone, with an entrance on the road to the village. To the west and northwest the walls are on the top of a bank, high above the crossroads. I do not know the position of the pursuing French army. The chauffeur who drove us could not enlighten us. As near as I could guess, from the condition of the walls, I imagine that the French artillery must have been in the direction of Penchard, on the wooded hills.

The walls are pierced with gun holes, about three feet apart, and those on the west and southwest are breeched by cannon and shell fire. Here, after the position had been several times stormed by artillery, the *Zouaves* made one of the most brilliant bayonet charges of the day, dashing up the steep banks and through the breeched walls. Opposite the gate is another steep bank where can still be seen the improvised gun positions of the French when they pushed the retreat across the plain.

The cemetery is filled with new graves against the wall, for many of the officers are buried here – nearly all of the regiment of *Zouaves*, which was almost wiped out in the charge before the position was finally carried – it was taken and lost several times.

From here we turned east again towards Vareddes, along a fine road lined with enormous old trees, one of the handsomest roads of the department. Many of these huge trees have been snapped off by shells as neatly as if they were mere twigs. Along the road, here and there, were isolated graves.

Vareddes had a tragic experience. The population was shockingly abused by the Germans. Its aged priest and many other old men were carried away, and many were shot, and the town badly damaged.

We had intended to go through Vareddes to the heights beyond, where the heroes of the 133d, 246th, 289th, and of the regiment which began the battle at Villeroy – the 276th – are buried. But the weather had changed, and a cold drizzle began to fall, and I saw no use in going on in a closed car, so we turned back to Meaux.

It was still light when we reached Meaux, so we gave a look at the old mills – and put up a paean of praise that they were not damaged beyond repair – on our way to the station.

As we came back to Esbly I strained my eyes to look across to the hill on which my house stands – I could just see it as we crawled across the bridge at Isles-lès-Villenoy – and felt again the miracle of the battle which swept so near to us. In my innermost heart I had a queer sensation of the absurdity of my relation to life. Fate so often shakes its fist in my face, only to withhold the blow within a millimetre of my nose. Perhaps I am being schooled to meet it yet.

I brought back one fixed impression – how quickly Time had laid its healing hand on this one battlefield. I don't know what will be the effect out there where the terrible trench war is going on. But here, where the fighting turned, never to return – at least we believe it never will – it has left no ugly traces. The fields are cleaned, the roads are repaired. Rain has fallen on ruins and washed off all the marks of smoke. Even on the road to Vareddes the thrifty French have already carried away and fagotted the wrecked trees, and already the huge, broken trunks are being uprooted, cut into proper length, and piled neatly by the roadside to be seasoned before being carted away. There was nothing raw about the scene anywhere. The villages were sad, because so silent and empty.

I had done my best to get a tragic impression. I had not got it. I had brought back instead an impression heroic, uplifting, altogether inspiring.

By the time you come over, and I lead you out on that pilgrimage, it will be even more beautiful. But, alas, I am afraid that day is a long way off.

VIII

December 30, 1914

I would wish above all things, if some fairy gave me the chance, to be a hibernating animal this year, during which the weather has almost called an armistice along our front, locked from the Swiss border to the sea.

There is but one consolation, and that is that, costly and terrible as have been the first four months of the war, three of the great aims of the German strategy have been buried too deep ever to be dug up – their hope of a short war is gone; they did not get to Paris, and now know that they never will; they did not, and never can get to Calais, and, in spite of their remarkable feats, and their mighty strength, in the face of those three facts even their arrogance cannot write 'victory' against their arms.

I have to confess that I am almost as cold as the boys out there in the rain and the mud. I have managed to get a little coal – or what is called coal this year. It is really *charbon de forge* – a lot of damp, black dust with a few big lumps in it, which burns with a heavy, smelly, yellow smoke. In normal times one would never dignify it by the name of coal, but today we are thankful to get it, and pay for it as if it were gold. It will only burn in the kitchen stove, and every time we put any on the fire, my house, seen from the garden, appears like some sort of a factory. Please, therefore, imagine me living in the kitchen. You know the size of a compact French kitchen. It is rather close quarters for a lady of large ideas.

The temperature of the rest of the house is down almost to zero. Luckily it is not a cold winter, but it is very damp, as it rains continually. I have an armchair there, a footstool, and use the kitchen table as a desk; and even then, to keep fairly warm, I almost sit on top of the stove, and I do now and then put my feet in the oven.

I assure you that going to bed is a ceremony. Amélie comes and puts two hot bricks in the foot of the bed. I undress in the kitchen, put on felt shoes, and a big wrap, and, with my hot water bottle in one hand and a book in the other, I make a dash for the arctic regions, and Amélie tidies up the kitchen, locks the doors behind her, and takes the keys away with her.

I am cosy and comfy in bed, and I stay there until Amélie has built the fire and got the house in order in the morning.

My getting up beats the *lever de Marie Antoinette* in some of its details, though she was accustomed to it, and probably minded less than I do. I am not really complaining, you know. But you want to know about my life – so from that you can imagine it. I shall get acclimated, of course. I know that.

I was in Paris for Christmas – not because I wanted to go, but because the few friends I have left there felt that I needed a change, and clinched the matter by thinking that they needed me. Besides I wanted to get packages to the English boys who were here in September, and it was easier to do it from Paris than from here.

While I was waiting for the train at Esbly I had a conversation with a woman who chanced to sit beside me on a bench on the *quai*, which seemed to me significant.

Today everyone talks to everyone. All the barriers seem to be down. We were both reading the morning paper, and so, naturally, got to talking. I happened to have an English paper, in which there was a brief account of the wonderful dash made by the Royal Scots at Petit Bois and the Gordon Highlanders at Maeselsyeed Spur, under cover of the French and British artillery, early in the month, and I translated it for her. It is a moral duty to let the French people get a glimpse of the wonderful fighting quality of the boys under the Union Jack.

In the course of the conversation she said what was self-evident, 'You are not French?' I told her that I was an American. Then she asked me if I had any children, and received a negative reply.

She sighed, and volunteered that she was a widow with an only son who was 'out there', and added: 'We are all of us French women of a certain class so stupid when we are young. I adore children. But I thought I could only afford to have one, as I wanted to do so much for him. Now if I lose that one, what have I to live for? I am not the sort of woman who can marry again. My boy is a brave boy. If he dies he will die like a brave man, and not begrudge the life he gives for his country. I am a French mother and must offer him as becomes his mother. But it was silly of me to have but this one. I know, now that it is too late, that I could have done as well, and it may be better, with several, for I have seen the possibilities demonstrated among my friends who have three or four.'

Of course I did not say that the more she had, the more she might have had to lose, because I thought that if, in the face of a disaster like this, French women were thinking such thoughts – and if one does, hundreds may – it might be significant.

I had a proof of this while in Paris. I went to a house where I have been a visitor for years to get some news of a friend who had an apartment there. I opened the door to the *concierge's loge* to put my question. I stopped short. In the window, at the back of the half dark room, sat the *concierge*, whom I had known for nearly twenty years, a brave, intelligent, fragile woman. She was sitting there in her black frock, gently rocking herself backward and forward in her chair. I did not need to put a question. One knows in these days what the unaccustomed black dress means, and I knew that the one son I had seen grow from childhood, for whom she and the

180

father had sacrificed everything that he might be educated, for whom they had pinched and saved – was gone.

I said the few words one can say – I could not have told five minutes later what they were – and her only reply was like the speech of the woman of another class that I had met at Esbly.

'I had but the one. That was my folly. Now I have nothing – and I have a long time to live alone.'

It would have been easy to weep with her, but they don't weep. I have never seen fewer tears in a great calamity. I have read in newspapers sent me from the States tales of women in hysterics, of women fainting as they bade their men goodbye. I have never seen any of it. Something must be wrong with my vision, or my lines must have fallen in brave places. I can only speak of what I see and hear, and tears and hysterics do not come under my observation.

I did not do anything interesting in Paris. It was cold and grey and sad. I got my packages off to the front. They went through quickly, especially those sent by the English branch post office, near the Etoile, and when I got home, I found the letters of thanks from the boys awaiting me. Among them was one from the little corporal who had pulled down my flags in September, who wrote in the name of the C company, Yorkshire Light Infantry, and at the end of the letter he said: 'I am sorry to tell you that Captain Simpson is dead. He was killed leading his company in a charge, and all his men grieved for him.'

That gave me a deep pang. I remembered his stern, bronzed, but kindly face, which lighted up so with a smile, as he sat with me at tea on that memorable Wednesday afternoon, and of all that he did so simply to relieve the strain on our nerves that trying day. I know nothing about him – who he was – what he had for family – he was just a brave, kindly, human being, who had met me for a few hours, passed on – and passed out. He is only one of thousands, but he is the one whose sympathetic voice I had heard and who, in all the hurry and fatigue of those hard days, had had time to stop and console us here, and whom I had hoped to see again; and I grieved with his men for him.

I could not write last week. I had no heart to send the usual greetings of the season. Words still mean something to me, and when I sat down, from force of habit, to write the letters I have been accustomed to send at this season, I simply could not. It seemed to me too absurd to even celebrate the anniversary of the days when the angel hosts sang in the skies their 'Peace on earth, good will to men' to herald the birth of Him who added to religion the command, 'Love one another' , and man, only forty miles away, occupied in wholesale slaughter. We have a hard time juggling to make our pretensions and our acts fit.

If this cold and lack of coal continues I am not likely to see much or write much until the spring campaign opens. Here we still hear the guns whenever Rheims or Soissons are bombarded, but no one ever, for a minute, dreams that they will ever come nearer.

Though I could not send you any greetings last week, I can say, with all my heart, may 1915 bring us all peace and contentment!

IX

January 21, 1915

I have been trying to feel in a humor to write all this month, but what with the changeable weather, a visit to Paris, and the depression of the terrible battle at Soissons – so near to us – I have not had the courage. All the same, I frankly confess that it has not been as bad as I expected. I begin to think things are never as bad as one expects.

Do you know that it is not until now that I have had a passport from my own country? I have never needed one. No one here has ever asked me for one, and it was only when I was in Paris a week ago that an American friend was so aghast at the idea that I had, in case of accident, no real American protection, that I went to the Embassy, for the first time in my life, and asked for one, and seriously took the oath of allegiance. I took it so very seriously that it was impressed on me how careless we, who live much abroad, get about such things.

I know that many years ago, when I was first leaving the States, it was suggested that such a document might be useful as an identification, and I made out my demand, and it was sent after me to Rome. I must have taken the oath at that time, but it was in days of peace, and it made no impression on me. But this time I got a great big choke in my throat, and looked up at the Stars and Stripes over the desk, and felt more American than I ever felt in my life. It cost me two dollars, and I felt the emotion was well worth the money, even at a high rate of exchange.

I did practically nothing else in Paris, except to go to one or two of the hospitals where I had friends at work.

Paris is practically normal. A great many of the American colony who fled in September to Bordeaux and to London have returned, and the streets are more lively, and the city has settled down to live through the war with outward calm if no gaiety. I would not have believed it would be possible, in less than five months, and with things going none too well at the front, that the city could have achieved this attitude.

When I got back, I found that, at least, our ambulance was open.

It is only a small hospital, and very poor. It is set up in the *salle de récréation* of the *commune*, which is beside the church and opposite the *mairie*, backed up against the wall of the park of the Château de Quincy. It is really a branch of the military hospital at Meaux, and it is under the patronage of the occupant of the Château de Quincy, who supplies such absolute necessities as cannot be provided from the government allowance of two francs a day per bed. There are twenty-eight beds.

Most of the beds and bedding were contributed by the people in the *commune*. The town crier went about, beating his drum, and making his demand at the crossroads, and everyone who could spare a bed or a mattress or a blanket carried his contribution to the *salle*. The wife of the mayor is the directress, the doctor from Crécy-en-Brie cares for the soldiers, with the assistance of Soeur Jules and Soeur Marie, who had charge of the town dispensary, and four girls of the Red Cross Society living in the *commune*.

The installation is pathetically simple, but the room is large and comfortable, with four rows of beds, and extra ones on the stage, and it is heated by a big stove. Naturally it gets more sick and slightly wounded than serious cases, but the boys seem very happy, and they are affectionately cared for. There is a big court for the convalescents, and in the spring they will have the run of the park.

About the twelfth we had a couple of days of the worst cannonading since October. It was very trying. I stood hours on the lawn listening, but it was not for several days that we knew there had been a terrible battle at Soissons, just forty miles north of us.

There is a great difference of opinion as to how far we can hear the big guns, but an officer on the train the other day assured me that they could be heard, the wind being right, about one hundred kilometres – that is to say, eighty miles – so you can judge what it was like here, on the top of the hill, half that distance away by road, and considerably less in a direct line.

Our official *communiqué*, as usual, gave us no details, but one of the boys in our town was wounded, and is in a nearby ambulance, where he has been seen by his mother; she brings back word that it was, as he called it, 'a bloody slaughter in a hand-to-hand fight'. But of course, nothing so far has been comparable to the British stand at Ypres. The little that leaks slowly out regarding that simply makes one's heart ache with the pain of it, only to rebound with the glory.

Human nature is a wonderful thing, and the locking of the gate to Calais, by the English, will, I imagine, be, to the end of time, one of the epics, not of this war alone, but of all war. Talk about the 'thin red line'. The English stood, we are told, like a ribbon to stop the German hordes – and stopped them.

It almost seems a pity that, up to date, so much secrecy has been maintained. I was told last week in Paris that London has as yet no dream of the marvelous feat her volunteer army achieved – a feat that throws into the shade all the heroic defenses sung in the verse of ancient times. Luckily these achievements do not dull with years.

On top of the Soissons affair came its result: the French retreat across the Aisne caused by the rising of the floods which carried away the bridges as fast as the engineers could build them, and cut off part of the French, even an ambulance, and, report says, the men left across the river without ammu-nition fought at the end with the butts of their broken guns, and finally with their fists.

Of course this brings again that awful cry over the lack of preparation, and lack of ammunition.

It is a foolish cry today, since the only nation in the world ready for this war was the nation that planned and began it.

Even this disaster – and there is no denying that it is one – does not daunt these wonderful people. They still see two things, the Germans did not get to Paris, nor have they got to Calais, so, in spite of their real feats of arms – one cannot deny those – an endeavor must be judged by its purpose, and, so judged, the Germans have, thus far, failed. Luckily the French race is big enough to see this and take heart of grace. God knows it needs to, and thank Him it can.

Don't you imagine that I am a bit down. I am not. I am cold. But, when I think of the discomfort in the hurriedly con-structed trenches, where the men are in the water to their ankles, what does my being cold in a house mean? Just a record of discomfort as my part of the war, and it seems, day after day, less important. But oh, the monotony and boredom of it! Do you wonder that I want to hibernate?

X

March 23, 1915

Can it be possible that it is two months since I wrote to you? I could not realize it when I got your reproachful letter this morning. But I looked in my letter-book, and found that it was true.

The truth is – I have nothing to write about. The winter and its discomforts do not inspire me any more than the news from the front does, and no need to tell you that does not make one talkative.

It has been a damp and nasty and changeable winter – one of the most horrid I ever experienced. There has been almost no snow. Almost never has the ground frozen, and not only is there mud, mud everywhere, but freshets also. Today the Marne lies more like an open sea than a river across the fields in the valley. One can imagine what it is like out there in the trenches.

We have occasional lovely sunny days, when it is warmer out-of-doors than in – and when those days came, I dug a bit in the dirt, planted tulips and sweet peas.

Sometimes I have managed to get fuel, and when that happened, I was ever so cosy in the house. Usually, when the weather was at its worst, I had none, and was as nicely uncomfortable as my worst enemy could ask.

As a rule my days have been divided into two parts. In the forenoon I have hovered about the gate watching for the newspaper. In the afternoon I have re-chewed the news in the vain endeavor to extract something encouraging between the lines – and failed. Up to date I have not found anything tangible to account for such hope as continues to 'spring eternal' in all our breasts. It springs, however, the powers be thanked. At present it is as big an asset as France has.

A Zeppelin got to Paris last night. We are sorry, but we'll forget it as soon as the women and children are buried. We are sorry, but it is not important.

Things are a bit livened up here. Day before yesterday a regiment of dragoons arrived. They are billeted for three months. They are men from the *midi*, and, alas! none too popular at this moment. Still, they have been well received, and their presence does liven up the place. This morning, before I was up, I heard the horses trotting by for their morning exercise, and got out of bed to watch them going along the hill. After the deadly tiresome waiting silence that has reigned here all winter, it made the hillside look like another place.

Add to that the fact that the field work has begun, and that, when the sun shines, I can go out on the lawn and watch the ploughs turning up the ground, and see the winter grain making green patches everywhere – and I do not need to tell you that, with the spring, my thoughts will take a livelier turn. The country is beginning to look beautiful. I took my drive along the valley of the Grande Morin in the afternoon yesterday. The wide plains of the valley are being ploughed, and the big horses dragging ploughs across the wide fields did look lovely – just like a Millet or a Daubigny canvas.

Since I wrote you I have been across to the battlefield again, to accompany a friend who came out from Paris. It was all like a new picture. The grain is beginning to sprout in tender green about the graves, which have been put in even better order than when I first saw them. The rude crosses of wood, from which the bark had not even been stripped, have been replaced by tall, carefully made crosses painted white, each marked with a name and number. Each single grave and each group of graves has a narrow footpath about it, and is surrounded by a wire barrier, while tiny approaches are arranged to each. Everywhere military signs are placed, reminding visitors that these fields are private property, that they are all planted, and entreating all politely to conduct themselves accordingly, which means literally, 'keep off the wheat'.

The German graves, which, so far as I remember, were unmarked when I was out there nearly four months ago, have now black disks with the number in white.

You must not mind if I am dull these days. I have been studying a map of the battle-front, which I got by accident. It is not inspiring. It makes one realize what there is ahead of us to do. It will be done – but at what a price!

Still, spring is here, and in spite of one's self, it helps.

XI

All through the month of April I intended to write, but I had not the courage.

All our eyes were turned to the north where, from April 22 to Thursday, May 13 – five days ago – we knew the second awful battle at Ypres was going on. It seems to be over now.

What with the new war deviltry, asphyxiating gas – with which the battle began, and which beat back the line for miles by the terror of its surprise – and the destruction of the *Lusitania* on the 7th, it has been a hard month. It has been a month which has seen a strange change of spirit here.

I have tried to impress on you, from the beginning, that odd sort of optimism which has ruled all the people about me, even under the most trying episodes of the war. Up to now, the hatred of the Germans has been, in a certain sense, impersonal. It has been a racial hatred of a natural foe, an accepted evil, just as the uncalled-for war was. It had wrought a strange, unexpected, altogether remarkable change in the French people. Their faces had become more serious, their bearing more heroic, their laughter less frequent, and their humor more biting. But, on the day, three weeks ago, when the news came of the first gas attack, before which the Zouaves and the Turcos fled with blackened faces and frothing lips, leaving hundreds of their companions dead and disfigured on the road to Langtmarck, there arose the first signs of awful hatred that I had seen.

I frankly acknowledge that, considering the kind of warfare the world is seeing today, I doubt very much if it is worse to be asphyxiated than to be blown to pieces by an *obus*. But this new and devilish arm which Germany has added to the horrors of war seemed the last straw, and within a few weeks, I have seen grow up among these simple people the conviction that the race which planned and launched this great war has lost the very right to live; and that none of the dreams of the world which looked towards happiness can ever be realized while Prussia exists, even if the war lasts twenty years, and even if, before it is over, the whole world has to take a hand in it.

Into this feeling, ten days ago, came the news of the destruction of the *Lusitania*. We got the news here on the 8th. It struck me dumb.

For two or three days I kept quietly in the house. I believe the people about me expected the States to declare war in twenty-four hours. My neighbors who passed the gate looked at me curiously as they greeted me, and with less cordiality as the days went by. It was as if they pitied me, and yet did not want to be hard on me, or hold me responsible.

You know well enough how I feel about these things. I have no sentimentality about the war. A person who had that, and tried to live here so near it, would be on the straight road to madness. If the world cannot stop war, if organized governments cannot arrive at a code of morals which applies to nations the same law of right and wrong which is enforced on individuals, why, the world and humanity must take the consequences, and must reconcile themselves to the belief that such wars as this are as necessary as surgical operations. If one accepts that point of view – and I am ready to do so – then every diabolical act of Germany will rebound to the future good of the race, as it, from every point of view, justifies the hatred which is growing up against Germany. We are taught that it is right, moral, and, from every point of view, necessary to hate evil, and, in this twentieth century, Germany is the most absolute synonym of evil that history has ever seen.

Having stated that fact, it does not seem to me that I need say anything further on the subject.

In the meantime, I have gone on imitating the people about me. They are industriously tilling their fields. I continue cutting my lawn, planting my dahlias, pruning my roses, tying up my flowering peas, and watching my California poppies grow like the weeds in the fields.

When I am not doing that, with a pot in one hand, and the tongs in the other, I am picking slugs out of the flowerbeds and giving them a dose of boiling water, or lugging about a watering pot. I do it energetically, but my heart is not in it, though the garden is grateful all the same, and is as nice a symbol of the French people as I can imagine.

We have the dragoons still with us. They don't interest me hugely – not as the English did when they retreated here last September, nor as the French infantry did on their way to the battlefield. These men have never been in action yet. Still they lend a picturesqueness to the countryside, though to me it is, as so much of the war has been, too much like the decor of a drama. Every morning they ride by the gate, two abreast, to exercise their lovely horses, and just before noon they come back. All the afternoon they are passing in groups, smoking, chatting, and laughing, and, except for their uniforms, they do not suggest war, of which they actually know as little as I do.

After dinner, in the twilight, for the days are getting long, and the moon is full, I sit on the lawn and listen to them singing in the street at Voisins, and they sing wonderfully well, and they sing good music. The other evening they sang choruses from 'Louise' and 'Faust', and a wonderful baritone sang '*Vision Fugitive*'. The air was so still and clear that I hardly missed a note.

A week ago tonight we were aroused late in the evening, it must have been nearly midnight, by an *alerte* announcing the passing of a Zeppelin. I got up and went out-of-doors, but neither heard nor saw anything, except a bicycle going over the hill, and a voice calling 'Lights out'. Evidently it did not get to Paris, as the papers have been absolutely dumb.

One thing I have done this week. When the war began I bought, as did nearly everyone else, a big map of Germany and the battle-fronts surrounding it, and little envelopes of tiny British, Belgian, French, Montenegrin, Servian, Russian, German, and Austrian flags, mounted on pins. Every day, until the end of last week, I used to put the flags in place as well as I could after studying the day's *communiqué*.

I began to get discouraged in the hard days of last month, when day after day I was obliged to retreat the Allied flags on the frontier, and when the Russian offensive fell down, I simply tore the map off the wall, and burned it, flags and all.

Of course I said to myself, in the spirit I have caught from the army, 'All these things are but incidents, and will have no effect on the final result. A nation is not defeated while its army is still standing up in its boots, so it is folly to bother over details.'

Do you ever wonder what the poets of the future will do with this war? Is it too stupendous for them, or, when they get it in perspective, can they find the inspiration for words where now we have only tightened throats and a great pride that, in an age set down as commercial, such deeds of heroism could be?

Who will sing the dirge of General Hamilton in the little cemetery of Lacouture last October, when the farewell salute over his grave was turned to repel a German attack, while the voice of the priest kept on, calm and clear, to the end of the service? Who will sing the destruction of the Royal Scots, two weeks later, in the battle of Ypres? Who will sing the arrival of General Moussy, and of the French corps on the last day of that first battle of Ypres, when a motley gathering of cooks and laborers with staff officers and dismounted cavalry, in shining helmets, flung themselves pell-mell into a bayonet charge with no bayonets, to relieve the hard-pressed English division under General Bulfin? And did it. Who will sing the great chant in honor of the 100,000 who held Ypres against half a million, and locked the door to the Channel? Who will sing the bulldog fighting qualities of Rawlinson's 7th division, which held the line in those October days until reinforcements came, and which, at the end of the fight, mustered 44 officers out of 400, and only 2,336 men out of 23,000? Who will sing the stirring scene of the French *Chasseurs*, advancing with bugles and shouting the 'Marseillaise', to storm and take the *col de Bonhomme* in a style of warfare as old as French history? And these are but single exploits in a war now settled down to sullen, dull trench work, a war only in the early months of what looks like years of duration.

Doesn't it all make your blood flow fast? You see it tempts me to make an oration. You must overlook my eloquence! One does – over here, in the midst of it – feel such a reverence for human nature today. The spirit of heroism and self-sacrifice lives still amongst us. A world of machinery has not yet made a race incapable of greatness. I have a feeling that from the soil to which so many thousands of men have voluntarily returned to save their country's honor must spring up a France greater than ever. It is the old story of Atlas. Besides, 'What more can a man do' – you know the rest. It is one of the things that make me sorry to feel that our own country is evidently going to avoid a movement which might have been at once healthy and uplifting. I know that you don't like me to say that, but I'll let it go.

XII

June 1, 1915

Well, I have really had a very exciting time since I last wrote you. I have even had a caller. Also my neighbor at Voulangis, on the top of the hill, on the other side of the Morin, has returned from the States, to which she fled just before the Battle of the Marne. I even went to Paris to meet her. To tell you the actual truth, for a few days, I behaved exactly as if there were no war. I had to pinch myself now and then to remind myself that whatever else might be real or unreal, the war was very actual.

I must own that Paris seems to get farther and farther from it every day. From daybreak to sunset I found it hard to realize that it was the capital of an invaded country fighting for its very existence, and the invader no farther from the Boulevards than Noyon, Soissons, and Rheims – on a battlefront that has not changed more than an inch or two – and often an inch or two in the wrong direction – since last October.

I could not help thinking, as I rode up the Champs-Elysées in the sun – it was Sunday – how humiliated the Kaiser, that crowned head of Terrorizers, would be if he could have seen Paris that day.

Children were playing under the trees of the broad mall; automobiles were rushing up and down the avenue; crowds were sitting all along the way, watching the passers and chatting; all the big hotels, turned into ambulances, had their windows open to the glorious sunny warmth, and the balconies were crowded with invalid soldiers and white-garbed nurses; not even arms in slings or heads in bandages looked sad, for everyone seemed to be laughing; nor did the crippled soldiers, walking slowly along, add a tragic note to the wonderful scene.

It was strange – it was more than strange. It seemed to me almost unbelievable.

I could not help asking myself if it could last.

Every automobile which passed had at least one soldier in it. Almost every well-dressed woman had a soldier beside her. Those who did not, looked sympathetically at every soldier who passed, and now and then stopped to chat with the groups – soldiers on crutches, soldiers with canes, soldiers with an arm in a sling, or an empty sleeve, leading the blind, and soldiers with nothing of their faces visible but the eyes.

By every law I knew the scene should have been sad. But some law of love and sunshine had decreed that it should not be, and it was not.

It was not the Paris you saw, even last summer, but it was Paris with a soul, and I know no better prayer to put up than the cry that the wave of love which seemed to throb everywhere about the soldier boys, and which they seemed to feel and respond to, might not – with time – die down. I knew it was too much to ask of human nature. I was glad I had seen it.

In this atmosphere of love Paris looked more beautiful to me than ever. The fountains were playing in the Place de la Concorde, in the Tuileries gardens, at the Rond Point, and the gardens, the Avenue and the ambulances were bright with flowers. I just felt, as I always do when the sun shines on that wonderful vista from the Arc de Triomphe to the Louvre, that nowhere in the world was there another such picture, unless it be the vista from the Louvre to the Arc de Triomphe. When I drove back up the hill at sunset, with a light mist veiling the sun through the arch, I felt so grateful to the fate which had decreed that never again should the German army look on that scene, and that a nation which had a capital that could smile in the face of fate as Paris smiled that day, must not, cannot, be conquered.

Of course after dark it is all different. It is then that one realizes that Paris is changed. The streets are no longer brilliantly lighted. There are no social functions. The city seems almost deserted. One misses the brightness and the activity. I really found it hard to find my way about and recognize familiar street corners in the dark. A few days of it were enough for me, and I was glad enough to come back to my quiet hilltop. At my age habits are strong.

Also let me tell you things are slowly changing here. Little by little I can feel conditions closing up about me, and I can see 'coming events' casting 'their shadows before'.

Let me give you a little example.

A week ago today my New York doctor came down to spend a few days with me. It was a great event for a lady who had not had a visitor for months. He wanted to go out to the battlefield, so I arranged to meet his train at Esbly, go on with him to Meaux, and drive back by road.

I started for Esbly in my usual *sans gêne* manner, and was disgusted with myself on arriving to discover that I had left all my papers at home. However, as I had never had to show them, I imagined it would make no difference.

I presented myself at the ticket-office to buy a ticket for Meaux, and you can imagine my chagrin when I was asked for my papers. I explained to the station-master, who knows me, that I had left them at home. He was very much distressed – said he would take the responsibility of selling me a ticket if I wanted to risk it – but the new orders were strict, and he was certain I would not be allowed to leave the station at Meaux.

Naturally, I did not want to take such a risk, or to appear, in any way, not to be *en règle*. So I took the doctor off the train, and drove back here for my papers, and then we went on to Meaux by road.

197

It was lucky I did, for I found everything changed at Meaux. In the first place, we could not have an automobile, as General Joffre had issued an order forbidding the circulation inside of the military zone of all automobiles except those connected with the army. We could have a little victoria and a horse, but before taking that, we had to go to the *préfet de police* and exhibit our papers and get a special *sauf-conduit* – and we had to be diplomatic to get that.

Once started, instead of sliding out of the town past a guard who merely went through the formality of looking at the driver's papers, we found, on arriving at the entrance into the route de Senlis, that the road was closed with a barricade, and only one carriage could pass at a time. In the opening stood a soldier barring the way with his gun, and an officer came to the carriage and examined all our papers before the sentinel shouldered his musket and let us pass. We were stopped at all the crossroads, and at that between Barcy and Chambry – where the pedestal of the monument to mark the limit of the battle in the direction of Paris is already in place – we found a group of a dozen officers – not non-commissioned officers, if you please, but captains and majors. There our papers, including American passports, were not only examined, but signatures and seals verified.

This did not trouble me a bit. Indeed I felt it well, and high time, and that it should have been done ten months ago.

It was a perfect day, and the battlefield was simply beautiful, with the grain well up, and people moving across it in all directions. These were mostly people walking out from Meaux, and soldiers from the big hospital there making a pilgrimage to the graves of their comrades. What made the scene particularly touching was the number of children, and the nurses pushing babies in their carriages. It seemed to me such a pretty idea to think of little children roaming about this battlefield as if it were a garden. I could not help wishing the nation was rich enough to make this place a public park.

In spite of only having a horse we made the trip easily, and got back here by dinner-time.

Two days later we had an exciting five minutes.

It was breakfast time. The doctor and I were taking our coffee out-of-doors, on the north side of the house, in the shade of the ivy-clad wall of the old grange. There the solitude is perfect. No one could see us there. We could only see the roofs of the few houses at Joncheroy, and beyond them the wide amphitheater-like panorama, with the square towers of the cathedral of Meaux at the east and Esbly at the west, and Mareuil-lès-Meaux nestled on the river in the foreground.

You see I am looking at my panorama again. One can get used to anything, I find.

It was about nine o'clock.

Suddenly there was a terrible explosion, which brought both of us to our feet, for it shook the very ground beneath us. We looked in the direction from which it seemed to come – Meaux – and we saw a column of smoke rising in the vicinity of Mareuil – only two miles away. Before we had time to say a word we saw a second puff, and then came a second explosion, then a third and a fourth. I was just rooted to my spot, until Amélie dashed out of the kitchen, and then we all ran to the hedge – it was only a hundred feet or so nearer the smoke, and we could see women running in the fields – that was all.

But Amélie could not remain long in ignorance like that. There was a staff officer cantoned at Voisins and he had telephonic communication with Meaux, so down the hill she went in search of news, and fifteen minutes later we knew that a number of Taubes had tried to reach Paris in the night, that there had been a battle in the air at Crépy-les-Valois, and one of these machines had dropped four bombs, evidently meant for Meaux, near Mareuil, where they had fallen in the fields and harmed no one.

We never got any explanation of how it happened that a Taube should be flying over us at that hour, in broad daylight, or what became of it afterward. Probably someone knows. If someone does, he is evidently not telling us.

Amélie's remark, as she returned to her kitchen, was: 'Well, it was nearer than the battle. Perhaps next time –' She shrugged her shoulders, and we all laughed, and life went on as usual. Well, I've heard the whirr of a German bomb, even if I did not see the machine that threw it.

The doctor did not get over laughing until he went back to Paris. I am afraid he never will get over guying me about the shows I get up to amuse my visitors. I expect that I must keep a controlling influence over him, or, before he is done joking, the invisible Taube will turn into a Zeppelin, or perhaps a fleet of airships.

XIII

Having an American neighbor nearby again has changed life more than you would imagine.

She is only five miles away. She can come over on horseback in half an hour, and she often arrives for coffee, which is really jolly. Now and then she drives over unexpectedly, and carries me back with her for the night. I never feel like staying longer, but it changes the complexion of life. Besides, we can talk about our native land – in English – and that is a change.

Now don't imagine that I have been lonely. I have not. I was quite contented before she returned, but I have never concealed from you that the war is trying. I needed, now and then, to exchange words with one of my own race, and to say things about my own country which I'd be burned at the stake before I'd say before a French person.

Beside, the drive from here to Voulangis is beautiful. We have three or four ways to go, and each one is prettier than the other. Sometimes we go through Quincy, by the Château de Moulignon, to Pont aux Dames, and through the old moated town of Crécy-en-Brie. Sometimes we go down the valley of the Mesnil, a hilly path along the edge of a tiny river, down which we dash at a breakneck speed, only possible to an expert driver. Indeed Père never believes we do it. He could not. Since he could not, to him it is impossible to anyone.

Just now the most interesting way is through Couilly and Saint-Germain, by the Bois de Misère, to Villiers-sur-Morin, whence we climb the hill to Voulangis, with the valley dropping away on one side. It is one of the loveliest drives I know, along the Morin, by the mills, through the almost virgin forest.

The artillery – territorials – is cantoned all along here, at Villiers, at Crecy, and at Voulangis. The road is lined with grey cannon and ammunition wagons. Every little way there is a sentinel in his box, and horses are everywhere.

Some of the sentinel boxes are, as we used to say in the States, 'too cute for words'. The prettiest one in the *Département* is right here, at the corner of the *route Madame*, which crosses my hill, and whence the road leads from the Demi-Lune right down to the canal. It is woven of straw, has a nice floor, a Gothic roof, a Gothic door, and the tiniest Gothic window, and a little flag floating from its peak.

It is a little *bijou*, and I did hope that I could beg, borrow, steal, or buy it from the dragoon who made it. But I can't. The lieutenant is attached to it, and is going to take it with him, alas!

I happened to be at Voulangis when the territorials left – quite unexpectedly, as usual. They never get much notice of a *relève*.

We were sitting in the garden at tea when the assemblage general was sounded, and the order read to march at four next morning.

You never saw such a bustle – such a cleaning of boots, such a packing of sacks, such a getting together of the officers' canteens – orderlies getting about quickly, and trying to give demonstrations of 'efficiency' (how I detest the very word!), and such a rounding up of last things for the commissary department, including a mobilization of Brie cheese (this is its home), and such a pulling into position of cannon – all the inevitable activity of a regiment preparing to take the road, after a two months' *cantonnement*, in absolute ignorance of the direction they were to take, or their destination.

The last thing I saw that night was the light of their lanterns, and the last thing I heard was the march of their hob-nailed boots. The first thing I heard in the morning, just as day broke, was the neighing of the horses, and the subdued voices of the men as the teams were harnessed.

We had all agreed to get up to see them start. It seemed the least we could do. So, well wrapped up in our big coats, against the chill of four o'clock, we went to the little square in front of the church, from which they were to start, and where the long line of grey cannon, grey ammunition, cami-ons, grey commissary wagons were ready, and the men, *sac au dos*, already climbing into place – one mounted on each team of four horses, three on each gun-carriage, facing the horses, with three behind, with their backs to the team. The horses of the officers were waiting in front of the little inn opposite, from which the officers emerged one by one, mounted and rode to a place in front of the church. We were a little group of about twenty women and children standing on one side of the square, and a dead silence hung over the scene. The men, even, spoke in whispers.

The commander, in front of his staff, ran his eyes slowly over the line, until a *sous-officier* approached, saluted, and announced, 'All ready', when the commander rode to the head of the line, raised one hand above his head, and with it made a sharp forward gesture – the unspoken order '*en avant*' – and backed his horse, and the long grey line began to move slowly towards the Forêt de Crécy, the officers falling into place as it passed.

Some of the men leaned down to shake hands as they went by, some of the men saluted, not a word was spoken, and the silence was only broken by the tramp of the horses, the strain-ing of the harnesses, and rumble of the wheels.

It was all so different – as everything in this war has been – from anything I had ever dreamed when I imagined war. Yet I suppose that the future dramatist who uses this period as a background can get his effects just the same, without greatly falsifying the truth. You know I am like Uncle Sarcey – a really model theater audience. No effect, halfway good, passes me by. So, as I turned back at the garden gate to watch the long grey line winding slowly into the forest, I found that I had the same chill down my back and the same tightness over my eyes and in my throat, which, in the real theater-goers, announce that an effect has 'gone home'.

The only other thing I have done this month which could interest you was to have a little tea party on the lawn for the convalescent boys of our ambulance, who were 'personally conducted' by one of their nurses.

Of course they were all sorts and all classes. When I got them grouped round the table, in the shade of the big clump of lilac bushes, I was impressed, as I always am when I see a number of common soldiers together, with the fact that no other race has such intelligent, such really well-modelled faces, as the French. It is rare to see a fat face among them. There were farmers, blacksmiths, casters, workmen of all sorts, and there was one young law student, and the mixed group seemed to have a real sentiment of fraternity.

Of course, the law student was more accustomed to society than the others, and became, naturally, a sort of leader. He knew just what to do, and just how to do it – how to get into the salon when he arrived, and how to greet his hostess. But the rest knew how to follow suit, and did it, and, though some of them were a little shy at first, not one was confused, and in a few minutes they were all quite at their ease. By the time the brief formality of being received was over, and they were all gathered round the tea table, the atmosphere had become comfortable and friendly, and, though they let the law student lead the conversation, they were all alert and interested, and when one of them did speak, it was to the point.

When tea was over and we walked out on the lawn on the north side of the house to look over the field of the battle in which most of them had taken part, they were all ready to talk – they were on ground they knew. One of them asked me if I could see any of the movements of the armies, and I told him that I could not, that I could only see the smoke, and hear the artillery fire, and now and then, when the wind was right, the sharp repeating fire of rifles as well as *mitrailleuses*, and that I ended by distinguishing the *soixante-quinze* from other artillery guns.

'Look down there, in the wide plain below Montyon,' said the law student. I looked, and he added, 'As nearly as I can judge the ground from here, if you had been looking there at eleven o'clock in the morning, you would have seen a big movement of troops.'

Of course I explained to him that I had not expected any movement in that direction, and had only watched the approach from Meaux.

Beyond that one incident, these wounded soldiers said no word about battles. Most of the conversation was political.

When the nurse looked at her watch and said it was time to return to the hospital, as they must not be late for dinner, they all rose. The law student came, cap in hand, made me a low bow, and thanked me for a pleasant afternoon, and every man imitated his manner – with varying degrees of success – and made his little speech and bow, and then they marched up the road, turning back, as the English soldiers had done – how long ago it seems – to wave their caps as they went round the corner.

I did wish that you could have been there. You always used to love the French. You would have loved them more that afternoon.

It is wonderful how these people keep up their courage. To me it seems like the uplift of a Holy Cause. They did expect a big summer offensive. But it does not come, and we hear it rumored that, while we have men enough, the Germans have worked so hard, while the English were recruiting, that they are almost impregnably entrenched, and that while their ammunition surpasses anything we can have for months yet, it would be military suicide to throw our infantry against their superior guns. In the meantime, while the Allies are working like mad to increase their artillery equipments, the Germans are working just as hard, and Time serves one party as well as the other. I suppose it will only be after the war that we shall really know to what our disappointment was due, and, as usual, the same cry consoles us all: 'None of these things will change the final result!' and most people keep silent under the growing conviction that this 'may go on for years'.

One thing I really must tell you – not a person mentioned the *Lusitania* at the tea party, which was, I suppose, a handsome effort at reticence, since the lady of the house was an American, and the Stars and Stripes, in little, were fluttering over the chimney.

I take note of one remark in your last letter, in reply to mine of May 18. You twit me with 'rounding off my periods'. I apologize. You must remember that I earned my bread and salt doing that for years, and habit is strong. I no longer do it with my tongue in my cheek. My word for that.

XIV

August 1, 1915

Well, dear girl, not a bit of news to tell you. I have really done nothing this last month but look at my flowers, superintend the gathering of my plums, put up a few pots of *confiture*, mow the lawn, and listen to the guns, now and then, read the *communiqués*, and sigh over the disasters in the east and the deadlock at Gallipoli.

At the end of the first year of the war the scene has stretched out so tremendously that my poor tired brain can hardly take it in. I suppose it is all clear to the general staff, but I don't know. To me it all looks like a great labyrinth – and the Germans are at the gates of Warsaw. Of course this does not 'alter the final result' – when that comes – but it means more destruction, more land to win back, and, I imagine, such desolation in Poland as makes even the Belgian disaster look, by comparison, small.

Oddly enough, while we know that this will brace up the Germans, fighting all about their borders on invaded territory, it does not effect the faith of the people here, who have even the courage to turn aside from their own grief, with tears in their eyes, to pity Poland. What a price Belgium pays for her courage to be honorable, and at what a price Poland must accept her independence! Everyone is philosophical here, but one does not have to be heartless to be that.

I find it ironical that my flowers bloom, that gay hummingbirds hover over my *Mas de Perse*, that I have enough to eat, that sleep comes to me, and that the country is so beautiful.

Our dragoons have ridden away – on to the front, I am told, and silence has settled down on us.

I am well – there ends the history of a month, and I am not the only one in France leading a life like that – and still the cannon are pounding on in the distance.

XV

Well, the *sans gêne* days seem to be passed.

Up to now, as I have told you, the *sauf-conduit* matter, except on the last day I was at Meaux, was the thinnest sort of formality. I had to have one to leave the *commune*, but the blank forms were lying around everywhere. I had only to stop at the hotel at Couilly, step into the café, pick up a form and ask the proprietor to fill it out, and that was all that was necessary. I might have passed it on to anyone, for, although my name was written on it, no one ever took the trouble to fill out the description. The ticket seller at the station merely glanced at the paper in my hand when I bought a ticket, and the *gendarmes* at the ticket window in Paris, when there were any – often there were none – did no more. Of course, the possession of a *sauf-conduit* presupposes all one's papers *en règle*, but I never saw anyone examining to make sure of that.

All this is ended. We are evidently under a new *régime*.

I had my first intimation yesterday, when I had a domiciliary visit from the *gendarmes* at Esbly. It was a very formal, thorough affair, the two officers treating me, at the beginning of the interview, as if I were a very guilty person.

I was upstairs when I saw them arrive on their wheels. I put down my sewing, and went down to be ready to open the door when they knocked. They didn't knock. I waited a bit, then opened the door. There was no one on the terrace, but I heard their voices from the other side of the house. I went in search of them. They were examining the back of the house as if they had never seen one like it before. When they saw me, one of them said sharply, without the slightest salute: 'There is no bell?'

I acknowledged the self-evident fact.

'How does one get in, since you keep your door locked?' he added.

'Well,' I replied, with a smile, 'as a rule, one knocks.'

To that his only reply was: 'Your name?'

I gave it to him.

He looked on his paper, repeated it – mispronouncing it, of course, and evidently sure that I did not know how to pronounce it myself.

'Foreigner,' he stated.

I could not deny the charge. I merely volunteered '*Américaine*'.

Then the inquiry continued like this. 'Live here?'

'Evidently.'

'How long have you lived here?'

'Since June, 1914.'

That seemed to strike him as a very suspicious date, and he stared at me hard for a moment before he went on: 'What for?'

'Principally because I leased the house.'

'Why do you remain here in war-time?'

'Because I have nowhere else to go,' and I tried not to smile.

'Why don't you go home?'

'This is my home.'

'Haven't you any home in America?'

I resisted telling him that it was none of his business, and did my best to look pathetic – it was that, or laugh – as I answered: 'Alas! I have not.'

This seemed to strike both of them as unbelievable, and they only stared at me as if trying to put me out of countenance.

In the meantime, some of the people of Huiry, interested always in *gendarmes*, were standing at the top of the hill watching the scene, so I said: 'Suppose you come inside and

I will answer your questions there,' and I opened the door of the salon, and went in.

They hesitated a moment, but decided to follow me. They stood, very stiffly, just inside the door, looking about with curiosity. I sat down at my desk, and made a motion to them to be seated. I did not know whether or not it was correct to ask *gendarmes* to sit down, but I ventured it. Evidently it was not correct, for they paid no attention to my gesture.

When they were done looking about, they asked me for my papers.

I produced my American passport. They looked at the huge steel-engraved document with great seriousness. I am sure they had never seen one before. It impressed them – as well it might, in comparison with the civil papers of the French government.

They satisfied themselves that the picture affixed was really I – that the name agreed with that on their books. Of course, they could not read a word of it, but they looked wise. Then they asked me for my French papers. I produced my *permis de séjour* – permitting me to stay in France provided I did not change my residence, and to which was affixed the same photograph as that on my passport; my declaration of my civil situation, duly stamped; and my '*immatriculation*', a leaf from the register on which all foreigners are written down, just as we would be if admitted to a hospital or an insane asylum.

The two men put their heads together over these documents – examined the signatures and the seals with great gravity – with evident regret to find that I was quite *en règle*.

Finally they permitted me to put the documents all back in the case in which I carry them.

I thought the scene was over. Not at all. They waited until I shut the case, and replaced it in my bag – and then:

'You live alone?' one asked.

I owned that I did.

'But why?'

'Well,' I replied, 'because I have no family here.'

'You have no domestic?'

I explained that I had a *femme de ménage*.

'Where is she?'

I said that at that moment she was probably at Couilly, but that ordinarily when she was not here, she was at her own home.

'Where is that?' was the next question.

So I took them out on to the terrace again, and showed them Amélie's house.

They stared solemnly at it, as if they had never seen it before, and then one of them turned on me quickly, as if to startle me. '*Vous êtes une femme de lettres?*'

'It is so written down in my papers,' I replied.

'*Journaliste?*'

I denied my old calling without the quiver of an eyelash. I hadn't a scruple. Besides, my old profession many a time failed me, and it might have been dangerous to have been known as even an ex-journalist today within the zone of military operations.

Upon that followed a series of the most intimate questions anyone ever dared put to me – my income, my resources, my expectations, my plans, etc. – and all sorts of questions I too rarely put to myself even, and never answer to myself. Practically the only question they did not ask was if I ever intended to marry. I was tempted to volunteer that information, but, as neither man had the smallest sense of humor, I decided it was wiser to let well enough alone.

It was only when they were stumped for another single question that they decided to go. They saluted me politely this time, a tribute I imagine to my having kept my temper under great provocation to lose it, went out of the gate, stood whispering together a few minutes, and gazing back at the house, as if afraid they would forget it, looked up at the plaque on the gatepost, made a note, mounted their wheels, and sprinted down the hill, still in earnest conversation.

I wondered what they were saying to one another. Whatever it was, I got an order early the next morning to present myself at the *gendarmerie* at Esbly before eleven o'clock.

Père was angry. He seemed to feel, that, for some reason, I was under suspicion, and that it was a man's business to defend me. So, when Ninette brought my perambulator to the gate, there was Père, in his *veston* and *casquette*, determined to go with me and see me through.

At Esbly I found a different sort of person – a gentleman – he told me he was not a *gendarme* by *métier*, but a volunteer – and, although he put me through practically the same paces, it was different. He was sympathetic, not averse to a joke, and, when it was over, he went out to help me into my baby cart, thanked me for troubling myself, assured me that I was absolutely *en règle*, and even went so very far as to say that he was pleased to have met me. So I suppose, until the commander at Esbly is changed, I shall be left in peace.

This will give you a little idea of what it is like here. I suppose I needed to be shaken up a bit to make me realize that I was near the war. It is easy to forget it sometimes.

Amélie came this morning with the tale that it was rumored that all foreigners were to be 'expelled from the *zone des armées*'. It might be. Still, I am not worrying. 'Sufficient to the day', you know.

XVI

September 8, 1915

You have the date quite right.

It is a year ago today – this very 8th of September – since I saw the French soldiers march away across the hill, over what we call the 'Champs Madame' – no one knows why – on their way to the battle behind Meaux.

By chance – you could not have planned it, since the time it takes a letter to reach me depends on how interesting the censor finds it – your celebration of that event reached me on its anniversary.

You are absolutely wrong, however, to pull such a long face over my situation. You write as if I had passed through a year of misery. I have not. I am sure you never got that impression from my letters, and I assure you that I am writing exactly as I feel – I have no *façade* up for you.

I own it has been a year of tension. It has been 365 days and a fourth, not one of which has been free from anxiety of some sort or other. Sometimes I have been cold. Sometimes I have been nervous. But all the same, it has been fifty-two weeks of growing respect for the people among whom I live, and of ever-mounting love of life, and never-failing conviction that the sum of it is beauty. I have had to fight for the faith in that, but I have kept it. Always 'In the midst of life we are in Death', but not always is death so fine and beautiful a thing as in these days. No one would choose that such things as have come to pass in the last year should be, but since they are, don't be so foolish as to pity me, who have the chance to look on, near enough to feel and to understand, even though I am far enough off to be absolutely safe – alas! eternally a mere spectator. And speaking of having been cold reminds me that it is beginning

214

to get cold again. We have had heavy hailstorms already, hail as big and hard as dried peas, and I have not as yet been able to get fuel. So I am looking forward to another trying winter. In the spring my coal-dealer assured me that last winter's situation would not be repeated, and I told him that I would take all the coal he could get me. Having said that, I took no further thought of the matter. Up to date he has not been able to get any. The railroad is too busy carrying war material.

I was pained by the tone of your last letter. Evidently mine of the Fourth of July did not please you. Evidently you don't like my politics or my philosophy, or my 'deadly parallels', or any of my thoughts about the present and future of my native land. Destroy the letter. Forget it, and we'll talk of other things, and, to take a big jump –

Did you ever keep cats?

There is a subject in which you can find no offence, and if it does not appeal to you it is your own fault.

If you never have kept cats, you have missed lots of fun, you are not half educated, you have not been disciplined at all. A cat is a wonderful animal, but he is not a bit like what, on first making his acquaintance, you think he is going to be, and he never becomes it.

Now I have been living a year this September with one cat, and part of the time, with two. I am wiser than I used to be. By fits and starts I am more modest.

I used to think that a cat was a tame animal, who lapped milk, slept, rolled up ornamentally on a rug, now and then chased his tail, and now and then played gracefully with a ball, came and sat on your knee when you invited him, and caught mice, if mice came where he was.

All the cats I had seen in the homes of my friends surely did those things. I thought them 'so pretty', 'so graceful', 'so soft', and I always said they 'gave a cosy look to a room'.

But I had never been intimate with a cat.

When the English soldiers were here a year ago, Amélie came one morning bringing a kitten in her apron. You remember I told you of this. He was probably three months old – so Amélie says, and she knows all about cats. She said offhand: '*C'est un chat du mois de juin.*' She seems to know what month well-behaved cats ought to be born. So far as I know, they might be born in any old month. He was like a little tiger, with a white face and shirt-front, white paws and lovely green eyes.

He had to have a name, so, as he had a lot of brown, the color of the English uniform, and came to me while the soldiers were here, I named him Khaki. He accepted it, and answered to his name at once. He got well rapidly. His fur began to grow, and so did he.

At first he lived up to my idea of what a kitten should be. He was always ready to play, but he had much more originality than I knew cats to have. He was so amusing that I gave lots of time to him. I had corks, tied to strings, hanging to all the door knobs and posts in the house, and, for hours at a time, he amused himself playing games like basketball and football with these corks. I lost hours of my life watching him, and calling Amélie to 'come quick' and see him. His ingenuity was remarkable. He would take the cork in his front paws, turn over on his back, and try to rip it open with his hind paws. I suppose that was the way his tiger ancestors ripped open their prey. He would carry the cork, attached to the post at the foot of the staircase, as far up the stairs as the string would allow him, lay it down and touch it gently to make it roll down the stairs so that he could spring after it and catch it before it reached the bottom. All this was most satisfactory. That was what I expected a cat to do.

He lapped his milk all right. I did not know what else to give him. I asked Amélie what she gave hers. She said 'soup made out of bread and drippings'. That was a new idea. But Amélie's cats looked all right. So I made the same kind of soup for Khaki. Not he! He turned his back on it. Then Amélie suggested bread in his milk. I tried that. He lapped the milk, but left the bread. I was rather in despair. He looked too thin. Amélie suggested that he was a thin kind of a cat. I did not want a thin kind of a cat. I wanted a roly-poly cat.

One day I was eating a dry biscuit at tea time. He came and stood beside me, and I offered him a piece. He accepted it. So, after that, I gave him biscuit and milk. He used to sit beside his saucer, lap up his milk, and then pick up the pieces of biscuit with his paw and eat them. This got to be his first show trick. Everyone came to see Khaki eat 'with his fingers'.

All Amélie's efforts to induce him to adopt the diet of all the other cats in Huiry failed. Finally I said: 'What does he want, Amélie? What do cats, who will not eat soup, eat?'

Reluctantly I got it – 'Liver.'

Well, I should think he did. He eats it twice a day.

Up to that time he had never talked even cat language. He had never meowed since the day he presented himself at Amélie's and asked for sanctuary.

But we have had, from the beginning, a few collisions of willpower. The first few weeks that he was a guest in my house, I was terribly flattered because he never wanted to sleep anywhere but on my knees. He did not squirm round as Amélie said kittens usually did. He never climbed on my shoulders and rubbed against my face. He simply jumped up in my lap, turned round once, lay down, and lay perfectly still. If I got up, I had to put him in my chair, soothe him a bit, as you would a baby, if I expected him to stay, but, even then, nine times out of ten, as soon as I was settled in another chair, he followed, and climbed into my lap.

Now things that are flattering finally pall. I began to guess that it was his comfort, not his love for me, that controlled him. Well – it is the old story.

But the night question was the hardest. He had a basket. He had a cushion. I have the country habit of going to bed with the chickens. The cat came near changing all that. I used to let him go to sleep in my lap. I used to put him in his basket by the table with all the care that you would put a baby. Then I made a dash for upstairs and closed the doors. Ha! ha! In two minutes he was scratching at the door. I let him scratch. 'He must be disciplined,' I said. There was a cushion at the door, and finally he would settle down and in the morning he was there when I woke. 'He will learn,' I said. H'm!

One night, while I was in my dressing room, I neglected to latch the bedroom door. When I was ready to get into bed, lo! there was Khaki on the foot of the bed, close against the foot-board, fast asleep. Not only was he asleep, but he was lying on his back, with his two white paws folded over his eyes as if to keep the lamplight out of them. Well – I had not the heart to drive him away. He had won. He slept there. He never budged until I was dressed in the morning, when he got up, as if it were the usual thing, and followed, in his most dignified manner, down to breakfast.

Well, that was struggle number one. Khaki had scored.

But, no sooner had I got myself reconciled – I felt pretty shamefaced – when he changed his plans. The very moment I was ready for bed he wanted to go out. He never meowed. He just tapped at the door, and if that did not succeed, he scratched on the window, and he was so one-idea-ed that nothing turned him from his purpose until he was let out.

For a time I used to sit up for him to come in. I was ashamed to let Amélie know. But, one night, after I had been out in the garden with a lantern hunting for him at midnight, I heard a

218

gentle purring sound, and, after looking in every direction, I finally located him on the roof of the kitchen. Being a bit dull, I imagined that he could not get down. I stood up on a bench under the kitchen window, and called him. He came to the eaves, and I could just reach him, but, as I was about to take him by a leg and haul him down, he retreated just out of my reach, and said what I imagined to be a pathetic 'meow'. I talked to him. I tried to coax him to come within reach again, but he only went up the roof to the ridgepole and looked down the other side and said 'meow'. I was in despair, when it occurred to me to get the stepladder. You may think me impossibly silly, but I never supposed that he could get down.

I went for the key to the grange, pulled out the ladder, and hauled it along the terrace, and was just putting it up, when the little devil leaped from the roof into the lilac bush, swayed there a minute, ran down, scampered across the garden, and dashed up a pear tree, and – well, I think he laughed at me.

Anyway, I was mad. I went in and told him that he might stop out all night for all I cared. Still, I could not sleep for thinking of him – used to comfort – out in the night, and it was chilly. But he had to be disciplined.

I had to laugh in the morning, for he was playing on the terrace when I opened the door, and he had a line of three first-class mice laid out for me. I said: 'Why, good morning, Khaki, did mother make him stay out all night? Well, you know he was a naughty cat!'

He gave me a look – I fancied it was quizzical – rolled over, and showed his pretty white belly, then jumped up, gave one look up at the bedroom window, scampered up the salon shutter, crouched on the top, and, with one leap, was through the bedroom window. When I rushed upstairs – to see if he had hurt himself, I suppose, – he was sitting on the foot of the bed, and I think he was grinning.

So much for disciplining a cat.

However, I had learned something – and, evidently, he had also. I had learned that a cat can take care of himself, and has a right to live a cat's life, and he learned that I was dull. We treat each other accordingly. The truth is – he owns me, and the house, and he knows it.

Since then he asks for the door, and gets it when he asks. He goes and comes at his own sweet will. When he wants to come in, in the daytime, he looks in at all the windows until he finds me. Then he stands on his hind legs and beats the window with his paws until I open it for him. In the night, he climbs to the bedroom window, and taps until he wakens me. You see, it is his house, not mine, and he knows it. What is the drollest of all – he is never one minute late to his meals.

He is familiarly known to all my neighbors as 'the Grand Duc de Huiry' and he looks the part. Still, from my point of view, he is not an ideal cat. He is not a bit caressing. He never fails to purr politely when he comes in. But he is no longer playful. He never climbs up to my shoulder and rubs against my face as some of Amélie's commoner cats will do. He is intelligent and handsome – just a miniature tiger, and growls like a new arrival from the jungle when he is displeased – and he is a great ratter. Moreover Amélie has decided that he is an '*intellectuel*'.

One morning, when he had been out all night, and did not return until almost breakfast-time, he was sitting on my knee, making his toilette, while I argued the matter with him. Amélie was dusting. I reproached him with becoming a *rôdeur*, and I told him that I should be happier about him if I knew where he was every night, and what he did.

He yawned as if bored, jumped off my knees and began walking round the library, and examining the books.

'Well,' remarked Amélie, 'I can tell you where he goes. He has a class in Maria's grange, where the wheat is stored – a class of mice. He goes every evening to give conferences on history and the war, and he eats up all the stupid pupils.'

I had to laugh, but before I could ask her how she knew, Khaki jumped up on top of the lowest line of books, and disappeared behind.

Amélie shrugged her shoulders, and said: '*Voila*! He has gone to prepare his next conference.' And he really had chosen a line of books on history.

You see Amélie knows beasties better than I do. There really is a sort of freemasonry between certain people and dumb animals. I have not a bit of it, though I love them. You would adore to see Amélie play with cats. She knows how. And as for her conversation with them, it is wonderful. I remarked the fact to her one day, when her morning salutations with the cats had been unusual. She replied, with her customary shrug: '*Eh bien, Madame, toujours, entre eux, les bêtes se comprennent.*'

So much in brief for cat number one. Number two is a different matter.

In the spring, four kittens were born at Amélie's. They were all sorts of mongrels. There was a dear little fluffy, half angora, which I named Garibaldi, and Amélie, as usual, vulgarized it at once into 'Didine'. There was a long-legged blue kitten which I dubbed Roi Albert. There was a short-legged, sturdy little energetic striped one which I called General Joffre, and a yellow and black fellow, who was, of course, Nicolas. I regretted there weren't two more, or three.

Garibaldi was about the dearest kitten I ever saw. He attached himself to me at once. When he was only a round fluffy ball he would try to climb into my lap whenever I went to see the kittens. The result was that when he was still very young, he came to live with me, and I never saw so altogether loveable an animal. He has all the cat qualities I ever dreamed of. As Amélie says: '*Il a tout pour lui, et il ne manque que la parole.*' And it is true. He crawls up my back. He will lie for hours on my shoulder purring his little soft song into my ear. He will sit beside me on my desk, looking at me with his pretty yellow eyes, as if he and I were the whole of his world. If I walk in the garden, he is under my feet. If I go up to Amélie's he goes too.

His attachment has its drawbacks. He tries to sit on my book when I am reading, and longs to lie on the keyboard of my machine when I am writing. If I try to read a paper when he is on my lap he immediately crawls under it, and gets between my eyes and the print. I am terribly flattered, but his affection has its inconveniences. Needless to say, Khaki hates him, and never passes him without growling. Luckily Didine is not a bit afraid of him. Up to date they have never fought. Didine has a great admiration for Khaki, and *will* tag him. The difference in their characters is too funny. For example, if Didine brings a mouse into the garden Khaki never attempts to touch it. He will sit apart, indulgently watching Didine play with his prey, torment it, and finally kill it, and never offer to join in the sport. On the contrary, if Khaki brings in a mouse, Didine wants to join in the fun at once. Result – Khaki gives one fierce growl, abandons his catch and goes out of the garden. Difference, I suppose, between a thoroughbred sport and, well, a common cat.

I could fill a volume with stories about these cats. Don't worry. I shall not.

You ask me if I have a dog. Yes, a big black *caniche* named Dick, a good watch-dog, but too fond of playing. I call him an 'india-rubber dog', because when he is demanding a frolic, or asking to have a stone thrown for him – his idea of happiness – he jumps up and down on his four stiff legs exactly like a toy woolly dog on an elastic.

He is a good dog to walk with, and loves to 'go'. He is very obedient on the road for that reason – knows if he is naughty he can't go next time.

So now you have the household complete. I'll warrant you won't be content. If you are not, there is no satisfying you. When I pour all my political dreams on paper, and shout on to my machine all my disappointments over the attitude of Washington, you take offence. So what can I do? I cannot send you letters full of stirring adventures. I don't have any. I can't write you dramatic things about the war. It is not dramatic here, and that is as strange to me as it seems to be to you.

XVII

October 3, 1915

We have been as near to getting enthusiastically excited as we have since the war began.

Just when everyone had a mind made up that the Allies could not be ready to make their first offensive movement until next spring – resigned to know that it would not be until after a year and a half, and more, of war that we could see our armies in a position to do more than continue to repel the attacks of the enemy – we all waked up on September 27 to the unexpected news that an offensive movement of the French in Champagne had actually begun on the 25th, and was successful.

For three or four days the suspense and the hope alternated. Every day there was an advance, an advance that seemed to be supported by the English about Loos, and all the time we heard at intervals the far-off pounding of the artillery.

For several days our hearts were high. Then there began to creep into the papers hints that it had been a gallant advance, but not a great victory, and far too costly, and that there had been blunders, and we all settled back with the usual philosophy, studied the map of our first-line trenches on September 25, when the attack began – running through Souain and Perthes, Mesnil, Massiges, and Ville-sur-Tourbe. We compared it with the line on the night of September 29, when the battle practically ended, running from the outskirts of Auderive in the west to behind Cernay in the east, and took what comfort we could in the twenty-five kilometres of advance, and three hilltops gained. It looked but a few steps on the map, but it was a few steps nearer the frontier.

Long before you get this, you will have read, in the American papers, details hidden from us, though we know more about this event than about most battles.

You remember the tea-party I had for the boys in our ambulance in June? Well, among the soldiers here that day was a chap named Litigue. He was wounded – his second time – on September 25, the first day of the battle. He was nursed in our ambulance the first time by Mlle. Henriette, and yesterday she had a letter from him, which she lets me translate for you, because it will give you some idea of the battle, of the spirit of the *poilus*, and also because it contains a bit of news and answers a question you asked me several weeks ago, after the first use of gas attacks in the north.

A l'hôpital Saint-André de Luhzac,

September 30, 1915

Mademoiselle,

I am writing you tonight a little more at length than I was able to do this morning – then I had not the time, as my nurse was waiting beside my bed to take the card to the post. I wrote it the moment I was able, at the same time that I wrote to my family. I hope it reached you.

I am going to tell you in as few words as possible, how the day passed. The attack began the 25th, at exactly quarter past nine in the morning. The preparatory bombardment had been going on since the 22d. All the regiments had been assembled the night before in their shelters, ready to leap forward.

At daybreak the bombardment recommenced – a terrible storm of shells of every calibre – bombs, torpedoes – flew overhead to salute the Boches, and to complete the destruction which had been going on for three days.

Without paying attention to the few obus *which the Boches sent over in reply to our storm, we all mounted the parapets to get a view of the scene. All along our front, in both directions, all we could see was a thick cloud of dust and smoke. For four hours we stood there, without saying a word, waiting the order to advance; officers, common soldiers, young and old, had but one thought – to get into it and be done with it as quickly as possible. It was just nine o'clock when the officers ordered us into line, ready to advance – sac au dos, bayonets fixed, musettes full of grenades and asphyxiating bombs. Everyone of us knew that he was facing death out there, but I saw nowhere the smallest sign of shrinking, and at quarter past nine, when we got the signal to start, one cry: 'En avant, et vive la France!' burst from thousands and thousands of throats, as we leaped out of the trenches, and it seemed to me that it was but one bound before we were on them.*

Once there I seem to remember nothing in detail. It was as if, by enchantment, that I found myself in the midst of the struggle, in heaps of dead and dying. When I fell, and found myself useless in the fight, I dragged myself, on my stomach, towards our trenches. I met stretcher-bearers who were willing to carry me, but I was able to crawl, and so many of my comrades were worse off, that I refused. I crept two kilometres like that until I found a dressing

station. I was suffering terribly with the bullet in
my ankle. They extracted it there and dressed the
ankle, but I remained, stretched on the ground, two
days before I was removed, and I had nothing to
eat until I reached here yesterday – four days after
I fell. But that could not be helped. There were so
many to attend to.

I will let you know how I get on, and I hope for
news from you. In the meantime I send you my
kindest regards, and my deep gratitude.

Your big friend,

Litigue, A.

I thought you might be interested to see what sort of a letter
a real *poilu* writes, and Litigue is just a big workman, young
and energetic.

You remember you asked me if the Allies would ever bring
themselves to replying in sort to the gas attacks. You see what
Litigue says so simply. They *did* have asphyxiating bombs.
Naturally the most honorable army in the world cannot
neglect to reply in sort to a weapon like that. When the Boches
have taken some of their own medicine the weapon will be
less freely used. Besides, today our men are all protected
against gas.

I had hardly settled down to the feeling that the offensive
was over and that there was another long winter of inaction
– a winter of the same physical and material discomforts as
the first – lack of fuel, suspense – when the news came which
makes my feeling very personal. The British offensive in the
north has cost me a dear friend. You remember the young
English officer who had marched around me in September of

last year, during the days preceding the battle of the Marne? He was killed in Belgium on the morning of September 26 – the second day of the offensive. He was in command of an anti-aeroplane battery advanced in the night to what was considered a well-concealed position. The German guns, however, got the range. Shrapnel nearly wiped out the command, and the Captain was wounded in the head. He died at the hospital at Etaples half an hour after he arrived, and lies buried in the English cemetery on the dunes, with his face towards the country for which he gave his young life.

I know one must not today regret such sacrifices. Death is – and no one can die better than actively for a great cause. But, when a loved one goes out in youth; when a career of achievement before which a really brilliant future opened, is snapped, one can still be proud, but it is through a veil of tears.

I remember so well that Sunday morning, the 26th of September. It was a beautiful day. The air was clear. The sun shone. I sat all the morning on the lawn watching the clouds, so small and fleecy, and listening to the far-off cannon, not knowing then that it meant the 'big offensive'. Oddly enough we spoke of him, for Amélie was examining the cherry tree, which she imagined had some sort of malady, and she said: 'Do you remember when Captain Noel was here last year how he climbed the tree to pick the cherries?' And I replied that the tree hardly looked solid enough now to bear his weight. I sat thinking of him, and his life of movement and activity under so many climes, and wondered where he was, little thinking that already, that very morning, the sun of his dear life was told, and that we should never, as I had dreamed, talk over his adventures in France as we had so often talked over those in India, in China, and in Africa.

It is odd, but when a friend so dear as he was, yet whom one only saw rarely, in the étapes of his active career, goes out across the great *bourne*, into the silence and the invisible, it takes time to realize it. It is only after a long waiting, when not even a message comes back, that one comprehends that there are to be no more meetings at the crossroads. I moved one more portrait into the line under the flags tied with black – that was all.

You hardly knew him, I know, but no one ever saw his upright figure, his thin, clear-cut features, bronzed by tropic suns, and his direct gaze, and forgot him.

XVIII

December 6, 1915

It is two months since I wrote – I know it. But you really must not reproach me so violently as you do in yours of the 21st of November, just received.

To begin with, there is no occasion for you to worry. I may be uncomfortable. I am in no danger. As for the discomforts – well, I am used to them. I cannot get coal very often, and when I do I pay twenty-six dollars a ton for it, and it is only imitation coal, at that. I cannot get washing done oftener than once in six weeks. Nothing dries out-of-doors in this country of damp winters. I am often forced to live my evenings by candlelight, which is pretty extravagant, as candles are costly, and it takes a good many to get through an evening. They burn down like paper tapers in these days.

When I don't write it is simply because I have nothing more interesting than things like that to tell you. The situation is chronic, and, like chronic diseases, much more likely to get worse than to get better. You should be grateful to me for sparing you, instead of blaming me.

I might not have found the inspiration to write today if something had not happened.

This morning the town crier beat his drum all over the hill, and read a proclamation forbidding all foreigners to leave the *commune* during the next thirty days without a special *permis* from the general in command of the 5th Army Corps.

No one knows what this means. I have been to the *mairie* to enquire simply because I had promised to spend Christmas at Voulangis, and, if this order is formal, I may have difficulty in going. I have no desire to celebrate, only there is a child there, and the lives of little children ought not to

230

be too much saddened by the times and events they do not understand.

I was told at the *mairie* that they had no power, and that I would have to address myself to Monsieur le General. They could not even tell me what form the request ought to take. So I came home, and wrote the letter as well as I could.

In the meantime, I am distinctly informed that until I get a reply from headquarters I cannot go out of the *commune* of Quincy-Segy.

If I really obey the letter of this order I cannot even go to Amélie's. Her house is in the *commune* of Couilly, and mine in Quincy, and the boundary line between the two *communes* is the path beside my garden, on the south side, and runs up the middle of my road from that point.

It is annoying, as I hardly know Quincy, and don't care for it, and never go there except to present myself at the *mairie*. It is further off the railroad line than I am here. Couilly I know and like. It is a pretty prosperous village. It has better shops than Quincy, which has not even a *pharmacie*, and I have always done my shopping there. My mail comes there, and the railway station is there, and everyone knows me.

The idea that I can't go there gives me, for the first time since the battle, a shut-in feeling. I talked to the *garde champê-tre*, whom I met on the road, as I returned from the *mairie*, and I asked him what he thought about the risk of my going to Couilly. He looked properly grave, and said:

'I would not, if I were in your place. Better run no risks until we understand what this is to lead to.'

I thanked him, with an expression just as serious and important as his. 'I'll obey,' I said to myself, 'though to obey will be comic.'

So I turned the corner on top of the hill. I drove close to the east side of the road, which was the Quincy side, and as I passed the entrance to Amélie's court I called to Père to come out and get Ninette and the cart. I then climbed out and left the turn-out there.

I did not look back, but I knew Père was standing in the road looking after me in amazement, and not understanding a bit that I had left my cart on the Quincy side of the road for him to drive it into Couilly, where I could not go.

'I'll obey,' I repeated to myself, viciously, as I strolled down the Quincy side of the road and crossed in front of the gate where the whole width of the road is in my *commune*.

I hadn't been in the house five minutes before Amélie arrived.

'What's the matter?' she demanded, breathlessly.

'Nothing.'

'Why didn't you drive into the stable as usual?'

'I couldn't.'

'Why couldn't you?'

'Because I am forbidden to go to Couilly.'

I thought she was going to see the joke and laugh. She didn't. She was angry, and I had a hard time to make her see that it was funny. In fact, I did not really make her see it at all, for an hour later, wanting her, I went up to the Quincy side of the road, leaned against the wall, opposite her entrance, and blew my big whistle for ten minutes without attracting her attention.

That attempt at renewing the joke had two results. I must tell you that one of the few friends who has ever been out here felt that the only annoying thing about my being so absolutely alone was that, if anything happened and I needed help, I had no way of letting anyone know. So I promised, and it was agreed with Amélie, that, in need, I should blow my big whistle – it can be heard half a mile. But that was over two years ago. I have never needed help. I have used the whistle to call Dick.

I whistled and whistled and whistled until I was good and mad. Then I began to yell: 'Amélie – Mélie – Père!' and they came running out, looking frightened to death, to find me, red in the face, leaning against the wall – on the Quincy side of the road.

'What's the matter?' cried Amélie.

'Didn't you hear my whistle?' I asked.

'We thought you were calling Dick.'

The joke was on me.

When I explained that I wanted some fresh bread to toast and was not allowed to go to their house in Couilly for it, it ceased to be a joke at all.

It was useless for me to laugh, and to explain that an order was an order, and that Couilly was Couilly, whether it was at my gate or down the hill.

Père's anger was funnier than my joke. He saw nothing comic in the situation. To him it was absurd. Monsieur le Général, *commandant de la cinquième armée,* ought to know that I was all right. If he didn't know it, it was high time someone told him.

In his gentle old voice he made quite a harangue.

All Frenchmen can make harangues.

It was difficult for me to convince him that I was not in the slightest degree annoyed; that I thought it was amusing; that there was nothing personally directed against me in the order; that I was only one of many foreigners inside the *zone des armées*; that the only way to catch the dangerous ones was to forbid us all to circulate.

I might have spared myself the breath it took to argue with him. If I ever thought I could change the conviction of a French peasant, I don't think so since I have lived among them. I spent several days last summer trying to convince Père that the sun did not go round the earth. I drew charts of the heavens – you should have seen them – and explained the solar system. He listened attentively – one has to listen when the *patronne* talks, you know – and I thought he understood. When it was all over – it took me three days – he said to me:

'*Bien*. All the same, look at the sun. This morning it was behind Maria's house over there. I saw it. At noon it was right over my orchard. I saw it there. At five o'clock it will be behind the hill at Esbly. You tell me it does not move! Why, I see it move every day. *Alors* – it moves.'

I gave it up. All my lovely exposition of us rolling through space had missed. So there is no hope of my convincing him that this new regulation regarding foreigners is not designed expressly to annoy me.

I often wonder exactly what all this war means to him. He reads his newspaper religiously. He seems to understand. He talks very well about it. But he is detached in a way. He hates it. It has aged him terribly. But just what it means to him I can't know.

XIX

Christmas Day, 1915

Well, here I am, alone, on my second war Christmas! All my efforts to get a *permis de sortir* failed.

Ten days after I wrote you last, there was a rumor that all foreigners were to be expelled from the zone of military operations. My friends in Paris began to urge me to close up the house and go into town, where I could at least be comfortable.

I simply cannot. I am accustomed now to living alone. I am not fit to live among active people. If I leave my house, which needs constant care, it will get into a terrible condition, and, once out of it, there is no knowing what difficulty I might have to get back. The future is all so uncertain. Besides, I really want to see the thing out right here.

I made two efforts to get a permission to go to Voulangis. It is only five miles away. I wrote to the commander of the 5th Army Corps twice. I got no answer. Then I was told that I could not hope to reach him with a personal letter – that I must communicate with him through the civil authorities. I made a desperate effort. I decided to dare the regulations and appeal to the commander of the *gendarmes* at Esbly.

There I had a queer interview – at first very discreet and very misleading, so far as they were concerned. In the end, however, I had the pleasure of seeing my two letters to Monsieur le General attached to a long sheet of paper, full of writing – my dossier, they called it. They did not deign to tell me why my letters, sent to the army headquarters, had been filed at the *gendarmerie*. I suppose that was none of my business. Nor did they let me see what was written on the long sheet to which the letters were attached. Finally, they did stoop to tell me that a *gendarme* had been to the *mairie* regarding my case, and that if I would present myself at Quincy the next morning, I would find a petition covering my demand awaiting my signature. It will be too late to serve the purpose for which it was asked, but I'll take it for Paris, if I can get it.

For lack of other company I invited Khaki to breakfast with me today. He didn't promise formally to come – but he was there. By devoting myself to him he behaved very well indeed, and did not disturb the table decorations. Luckily, they were not good to eat. He sat in a chair beside me, and now and then I had to pardon him for putting his elbow on the table. I did that the more graciously as I was surprised that he did not sit on it. He had his own fork, and except that, now and then, he got impatient and reached out a white paw to take a bit of chicken from my fork just before it reached my mouth, he committed no grave breach of table manners. He did refuse to keep his bib on, and he ate more than I did, and enjoyed the meal better. In fact, I should not have enjoyed it at all but for him. He had a gorgeous time.

I did not invite Garibaldi. He did not know anything about it. He is too young to enjoy a 'function'. He played in the garden during the meal, happy and content to have a huge breakfast of bread and gravy; he is a bread eater – thoroughly French.

I even went so far as to dress for Khaki, and put a Christmas rose in my hair. Alas! It was all wasted on him.

This is all the news I have to send you, and I cannot even send a hopeful message for 1916. The end looks farther off for me than it did at the beginning of the year. It seems to me that the world is only now beginning to realize what it is up against.

XX

Well, I have really been to Paris, and it was so difficult that I ask myself why I troubled.

I had to await the pleasure of the commander of the *Cinquième Armée*, as the Embassy was powerless to help me, although they did their best with great good will. I enclose you my *sauf-conduit* that you may see what so important a document is like. Then I want to tell you the funny thing – I never had to show it once. I was very curious to know just how important it was. I went by the way of Esbly. On buying my ticket I expected to be asked for it, as there was a printed notice beside the window to the ticket office announcing that all purchasers of tickets must be furnished with a *sauf-conduit*. No one cared to see mine. No one asked for it on the train. No one demanded it at the exit in Paris. Nor, when I returned, did anyone ask for it either at the ticket office in Paris or at the entrance to the train. Considering that I had waited weeks for it, had to ask for it three times, had to explain what I was going to do in Paris, where I was going to stay, how long, etc., I had to be amused.

I was really terribly disappointed. I had longed to show it. It seemed so *chic* to travel with the consent of a big general.

Of course, if I had attempted to go without it, I should have risked getting caught, as, at any time, the train was liable to be boarded and all papers examined.

I learned at the Embassy, where the military attaché had consulted the Ministry of War, that an arrangement was to be made later regarding foreigners, and that we were to be provided with a special book which, while it would not allow us to circulate freely, would give us the right to demand a permission – and get it if the military authorities chose. No great change that.

The visit served little purpose except to show me a sad-looking Paris and make me rejoice to get back.

Now that the days are so short, and it is dark at four o'clock, Paris is almost unrecognizable. With shop-shutters closed, tramway windows curtained, very few street-lights – none at all on short streets – no visible lights in houses, the city looks dead. You'd have to see it to realize what it is like.

The weather was dull, damp, the cold penetrating, and the atmosphere depressing, and so was the conversation. It is better here on the hilltop, even though, now and then, we hear the guns.

Coming back from Paris there were almost no lights on the platforms at the railway stations, and all the coaches had their curtains drawn. At the station at Esbly the same situation – a few lights, very low, on the main platform, and absolutely none on the platform where I took the narrow-gauge for Couilly. I went stumbling, in absolute blackness, across the main track, and literally felt my way along the little train to find a door to my coach. If it had not been for the one lamp on my little cart waiting in the road, I could not have seen where the exit at Couilly was. It was not gay, and it was far from gay climbing the long hill, with the feeble rays of that one lamp to light the blackness. Luckily Ninette knows the road in the dark.

In the early days of the war it used to be amusing in the train, as everyone talked, and the talk was good. Those days are passed. With the now famous order pasted on every window: *Taisez-vous! Méfiez-vous / Les oreilles ennemies vous écoutent* no one says a word. I came back from Paris with half a dozen officers in the compartment. Each one, as he entered, brought his hand to salute, and sat down, without a word. They did not even look at one another. It is one of the most marked changes in attitude that I have seen since the war. It is right. We were all getting too talkative, but it takes away the one charm there was in going to Paris. I've had no adventures since I wrote to you Christmas Day, although we did have, a few days after that, five minutes of excitement.

One day I was walking in the garden. It was a fairly bright day, and the sun was shining through the winter haze. I had been counting my tulips, which were coming up bravely, admiring my yellow crocuses, already in flower, and hoping the sap would not begin to rise in the rose bushes, and watching the Marne, once more lying like a sea rather than a river over the fields, and wondering how that awful winter freshet was going to affect the battle-front, when, suddenly, there was a terrible explosion. It nearly shook me off my feet.

The letter carrier from Quincy was just mounting the hill on his wheel, and he promptly tumbled off it. I happened to be standing where I could see over the hedge, but before I could get out the stupid question, 'What was that?' there came a second explosion, then a third and a fourth.

They sounded in the direction of Paris.

'Zeppelins,' was my first thought, but that was hardly the hour for them.

I stood rooted to the spot. I could hear voices at Voisins, as if all the world had rushed into the street. Then I saw Amélie running down the hill. She said nothing as she passed. The postman picked himself up, passed me a letter, shrugged his shoulders, and pushed his wheel up the hill.

I patiently waited until the voices ceased in Voisins. I could see no smoke anywhere. Amélie came back at once, but she brought no explanation. She only brought a funny story.

There is an old woman in Voisins, well on to ninety, called Mère R—. The war is too tremendous for her localized mind to grasp. Out of the confusion she picks and clings to certain isolated facts. At the first explosion, she rushed, terrorized, into the street, gazing up to the heavens, and shaking her withered old fists above her head, she cried in her shrill, quavering voice: 'Now look at that! They told us the Kaiser was dying. It's a lie. It's a lie, you see, for here he comes throwing his cursed bombs down on us.'

You know all this month the papers have had Guillaume dying of that ever-recurring cancer of the throat. I suppose the old woman thinks Guillaume is carrying all this war on in person. In a certain sense she is not very far wrong.

For a whole week we got no explanation of that five minutes' excitement. Then it leaked out that the officer of the General Staff, who has been stationed at the Chateau de Condé, halfway between here and Esbly, was about to change his section. He had, in the park there, four German shells from the Marne battlefield, which had not been exploded. He did not want to take them with him, and it was equally dangerous to leave them in the park, so he decided to explode them, and had not thought it necessary to warn anybody but the railroad people.

It is a proof of how simple our life is that such an event made conversation for weeks.

XXI

Well, we are beginning to get a little light – we foreigners – on our situation. On February 2, I was ordered to present myself again at the *mairie*. I obeyed the summons the next morning, and was told that the military authorities were to provide all foreigners inside the *zone des armées*, and all foreigners outside, who, for any reason, needed to enter the zone, with what is called a '*carnet d'*étrangère', and that, once I got that, I would have the privilege of asking for a permission to circulate, but, until that document was ready, I must be content not to leave my *commune*, nor to ask for any sort of a *sauf-conduit*.

I understand that this regulation applies even to the doctors and *infirmières*, and ambulance drivers of all the American units at work in France. I naturally imagine that some temporary provision must be made for them in the interim.

I had to make a formal petition for this famous carnet, and to furnish the military authorities with two photographs – front view – size and form prescribed.

I looked at the mayor's secretary and asked him how the Old Scratch – I said frankly *diable* – I was to get photographed when he had forbidden me to leave my *commune*, and knew as well as I that there was no photographer here.

Quite seriously he wrote me a special *permit* to go to Couilly where there is a man who can photograph. He wrote on it that it was good for one day, and the purpose of the trip 'to be photographed by the order of the mayor in order to get my *carnet d'étrangère*', and he solemnly presented it to me, without the faintest suspicion that it was humorous.

Between you and me, I did not even use it. I had still one of the photographs made for my passport and other papers.

Amélie carried it to Couilly and had it copied. Very few people would recognize me by it. It is the counterfeit presentment of a smiling, fat old lady, but it is absolutely *réglementaire* in size and form, and so will pass muster. I have seen some pretty queer portraits on civil papers.

We are promised these carnets in the course of 'a few weeks', so, until then, you can think of me as, to all intents and purposes, really interned.

It may interest you to know that on the 9th – just a week ago – a Zeppelin nearly got to Meaux. It was about half past eleven in the evening when the drums beat 'lights out', along the hillside. There weren't many to put out, for everyone is in bed at that hour, and we have no streetlights, but an order is an order. The only result of the drum was to call everyone out of bed, in the hope 'to see a Zeppelin'. We neither heard nor saw anything.

Amélie said with a grin next morning, '*Eh bien*, only one thing is needed to complete our experiences – that a bomb should fall shy of its aim – the railroad down there – and wipe Huiry off the map, and write it in history.'

I am sorry that you find holes in my letters. It is your own fault. You do not see this war from my point of view yet – alas! But you will. Make a note of that. The thing that you will not understand, living, as you do, in a world going about its daily routine, out of sight, out of hearing of all this horror, is that Germany's wilful destruction is on a preconceived plan – a racial principle. The more races she can reduce and enfeeble the more room there will be for her. Germany wants Belgium – but she wants as few Belgians as possible. So with Poland, and Servia, and northeast France. She wants them to die out as fast as possible. It is a part of the programme of a people calling themselves the elect of the world – the only race, in their opinion, which ought to survive.

She had a forty-four years' start of the rest of the world in preparing her programme. It is not in two years, or in three, that the rest of the world can overtake her. That advantage is going to carry her a long way. Some people still believe that advantage will exist to the end. I don't. Still, one of the overwhelming facts of this war is to me that: Germany held Belgium and northeast France at the end of 1914, and yet, all along the Allied fronts, with Germany fighting on invaded territory, they cried: 'She is beaten!' So, indeed, her strategy was. At the end of 1915 she had two new allies, and held all of Servia, Montenegro, and Russian Poland, and still the Allies persisted: 'She is licked, but she does not know it yet.' It is one of the finest proofs of the world's faith in the triumph of the Right that so many believe this to be true.

You are going to come some day to the opinion I hold – that if we want universal peace we must first get rid of the race that does not want it or believe in it. Forbidden subject? I know. But when I resist temptation you find holes in my letters, and seem to imagine that I am taking no notice of things that happen. I notice fast enough, and I am so interested that I hope to see the condemnation, already passed in England, against Kaiser, Kronprinz and Company, for 'wilful murder', executed, even if I cannot live to see Germany invaded.

This is what you get for saying, 'You make no comment on the overrunning of Servia or the murder of Edith Cavell, or the failure of the Gallipoli adventure.' After all, these are only details in the great undertaking. As we say of every disaster, 'They will not affect the final result.' It is getting to be a catchword, but it is true.

Germany is absolutely right in considering Great Britain her greatest enemy. She knows today that, even if she could get to Paris or Petrograd, it would not help her. She would still have Britain to settle with. I wonder if the Kaiser has yet waked up to a realization of his one very great achievement – the reawakening of Greater Britain? He dreamed of dealing his mother's country a mortal blow.

The blow landed, but it healed instead of killing.

This war is infernal, diabolical – and farcical – if we look at the deeds that are done every day. Luckily we don't and mustn't, for we all know that there are things in the world a million times worse than death, and that there are future results to be aimed at which make death gloriously worthwhile. Those are the things we *must* look at.

I have always told you that I did not find the balance of things much changed, and I don't. I am afraid that you cannot cultivate, civilize, humanize – choose your word – man to such a point that, so long as he is not emasculated, his final argument in the cause of honor and justice will not be his fists – with or without a weapon in them – which is equivalent to saying, I am afraid, that so long as there are two men on earth there will always be the chance of a fight.

Thus far February has been a droll month. I have seen Februaries in France which have been spring-like, with the chestnut trees in bud, and the primroses in flower, and lilacs in leaf. This February has been a strange mixture of spring awkwardly slipping out of the lap of winter and climbing back again. There have been days when the sun was so warm that I could drive without a rug, and found furs a burden; there have been wonderful moonlit nights; but the most of the time, so far, it has been nasty. On warm days flowers began to sprout and the buds on the fruit trees to swell. That made Père sigh and talk about the *lune rousse*. We have had days of wind and rain which belonged in a correct March. I am beginning to realize that the life of a farmer is a life of anxiety. If I can take Père's word for it, it is always cold when it should not be; the hot wave never arrives at the right moment; when it should be dry it rains; and when the earth needs water the rain refuses to fall. In fact, on his testimony, I am convinced that the weather is never just right, except to the mere lover of nature, who has nothing to lose and nothing to gain by its caprices.

The strange thing is that we all stand it so well. If anyone had told me that I could have put up with the life I have been living for two winters and be none the worse for it, I should have thought him heartless. Yet, like the army, I am surely none the worse for it, and, in the army, many of the men are better for it. The youngsters who come home on leave are as rugged as possible. They have straightened up and broadened their chests. Even the middle-aged are stronger. There is a man here who is a master mason, a hard-working, ambitious, honest chap, very much loved in the *commune*. He worked on my house, so I know him well. Before the war he was very delicate. He had chronic indigestion, and constantly recurring sore throats. He was pale, and his back was beginning to get round. As he has five children, he is in an ammunition factory. He was home the other day. I asked him about his health, he looked so rosy, so erect, and strong. He laughed, and replied: 'Never so well in my life. I haven't had a cold this winter, and I sleep in a board shanty and have no fire, and I eat in a place so cold my food is chilled before I can swallow it. My indigestion is a thing of the past. I could digest nails!'

You see I am always looking for consolations in the disaster. One must, you know.

XXII

March 2, 1916

We are living these days in the atmosphere of the great battle of Verdun. We talk Verdun all day, dream Verdun all night – in fact, the thought of that great attack in the east absorbs every other idea. Not in the days of the Marne, nor in the trying days of Ypres or the Aisne was the tension so terrible as it is now. No one believes that Verdun can be taken, but the anxiety is dreadful, and the idea of what the defence is costing is never absent from the minds even of those who are firmly convinced of what the end must be.

I am sending you a Forain cartoon from the *Figaro*, which exactly expresses the feeling of the army and the nation.

You have only to look on a map to know how important the position is at Verdun, the supposed-to-be-strongest of the four great fortresses – Verdun, Toul, Epinay, and Belfort – which protect the only frontier by which the Kaiser has a military right to try to enter France, and which he avoided on account of its strength.

Verdun itself is only one day's march from Metz. If you study it up on a map you will learn that, within a circuit of thirty miles, Verdun is protected by thirty-six redoubts. But what you will not learn is that this great fortification is not yet connected with its outer redoubts by the subterranean passages which were a part of the original scheme. It is that fact which is disturbing. Every engineer in the French army knows that the citadel at Metz has underground communications with all its circle of outer ramparts. Probably every German engineer knows that Verdun's communication passages were never made. Isn't it strange (when we remember that, even in the days of walled cities, there were always subterraneans leading out of the fortified towns beyond the walls – wonderful works of masonry, intact today, like those of Provins, and even here on this hill) that a nation which did not want war should have left unfinished the protection of such a costly fortress?

You probably knew, as usual, before we did, that the battle had begun. We knew nothing of it here until February 23, three days after the bombardment began, with the French outer lines nine miles outside the city, although only twenty-four hours after was the full force of the German artillery let loose, with fourteen German divisions waiting to march against the three French divisions holding the position. Can you wonder we are anxious?

We have been buoyed up for weeks by the hope of an Allied offensive – and instead came this!

The first day's news was bad, so was that of the 24th. I have never since the war began felt such a vibrant spirit of anxiety about me. To add to it, just before midnight on the 24th snow began to fall. In the morning there was more snow on the ground than I had ever seen in France. It was a foot deep in front of the house, and on the north side, where it had drifted, it was twice that depth. This was so unusual that no one seemed to know what to do. Amélie could not get to me. No one is furnished with foot-gear to walk in snow, except men who happen to have high galoshes. I looked out of the window, and saw Père shovelling away to make a path to the gate, but with an iron shovel it was a long passage. It was nine o'clock before he got the gate open, and then Amélie came slipping down. Père was busy all day keeping that path open, for the snow continued to fall.

This meant that communications were all stopped. Trains ran slowly on the main lines, but our little road was blocked. It continued to snow for two days, and for two days we had no news from the outside world.

On the morning of the 27th one of our old men went to the Demi-Lune and watched for a military car coming in from Meaux. After hours of waiting, one finally appeared. He ran into the road and hailed it, and as the chauffeur put on his brakes, he called:

'*Et Verdun?*'

'*Elle tient,*' was the reply, and the auto rushed on.

That was all the news we had in those days.

When communications were opened the news we got was not consoling. First phase of the battle closed six days ago – with the Germans in Douaumont, and the fighting still going on – but the spirit of the French not a jot changed. Here, among the civilians, they say: 'Verdun will never fall,' and out at the front, they tell us that the *poilus* simply hiss through their clenched teeth, as they fight and fall, 'They shall not pass.' And all the time we sit inactive on the hilltop holding that thought. It's all we can do.

We were livened up a bit last week because the village clown was on his home leave. He is a lad of twenty-three with a young wife and a little three-year-old girl, who has learned to talk since 'dada' saw her, and is her father right over – full of fun, good-humor, and laughter.

I have told you that we almost never hear war talk. We did hear some while our local clown was home, but how much was true and how much his imagination I don't know. Anyway, his drollery made us all laugh. His mother-in-law had died since he left, and when his wife wept on his shoulder, he patted her on the back, and winked over his shoulder at his admiring friends, as he said: '*Chut, ma fille,* if you are going to cry in these days because someone dies, you'll have no time to sleep. Only think of it, the old lady died in bed, and that is everything which is most aristocratic in these days.'

I regret to say that this did not console wife one bit.

As he never can tell anything without acting it out, he was very comic when he told about the battle in which the Prussian Guard was wiped out. He is in the artillery, and he acted out the whole battle. When he got to the point where the artillery was ordered to advance, he gave an imitation of himself scrambling on to his gun, and swaying there, as the horses struggled to advance over the rough road ploughed with shell, until they reached the field where the Guard had fallen. Then he imitated the gesture of the officer riding beside the guns, and stopping to look off at the field, as, with a shrug, he said: '*Ah, les beaux gars*' then swung his sabre and shouted: '*En avant!*'

Then came the imitation of a gunner hanging on his gun as the gun-carriage went bumping over the dead, the sappers and *pétrole* brigade coming on behind, ready to spray and fire the field, shouting: '*Allez aux enfers, beaux gars de Prusse, et y attendre votre kaiser!*'

It was all so humorous that one was shocked into laughter by the meeting of the comic and the awful. I laughed first and shuddered afterward. But we do that a great deal these days.

I don't think I told you that I had found a wonderful woman to help me one day in the week in the garden. Her name is Louise, and she was born in the *commune*, and has worked in the fields since she was nine years old. She is a great character, and she is handsome – very tall and so straight – thirty-three, married, with three children – never been sick in her life. She is a brave, gay thing, and I simply love to see her striding along the garden paths, with her head in the air, walking on her long legs and carrying her body as steadily as though she had a bucket of water on her head. It is beautiful.

Well, Louise has a brother named Joseph, as handsome as she is, and bigger. Joseph is in the heavy artillery, holding a mountain-top in Alsace, and, would you believe it, he has been there twenty months, and has never seen a German.

Of course, when you think of it, it is not so queer, really. The heavy artillery is miles behind the infantry, and of course the gunners can't see what they are firing at – that is the business of the officers and the eyes of the artillery – the aeroplanes. Still, it is queer to think of firing big guns twenty months and never seeing the targets. Odder still, Joseph tells me he has never seen a wounded or a dead soldier since the war began. Put these little facts away to ponder on. It is a war of strange facts.

XXIII

April 28, 1916

I have lived through such nerve-trying days lately that I rarely feel in the humor to write a letter.

Nothing happens here.

The spring has been as changeable as even that which New England knows. We had four fairly heavy snowstorms in the first fortnight of the awful fighting of Verdun. Then we had wet, and then unexpected heat – the sort of weather in which everyone takes cold. I get up in the morning and dress like a polar bear for a drive, and before I get back the sun is so hot I feel like stripping.

There is nothing for anyone to do but wait for news from the front. It is the same old story – they are seesawing at Verdun, with the Germans much nearer than at the beginning – and still we have the firm faith that they will never get there. Doesn't it seem to prove that had Germany fought an honest war she could never have invaded France?

Now, in addition, we've all this strain of waiting for news from Dublin. The affairs of the whole world are in a mess.

There are many aspects of the war which would interest you if you were sitting down on my hilltop with me – conditions which may seem more significant than they are. For example, the Government has sent back from the front a certain number of men to aid in the farm work until the planting is done. Our *commune* does not get many of these. Our old men and boys and women do the work fairly well, with the aid of a few territorials, who guard the railway two hours each night and work in the fields in the daytime. The women here are used to doing field work, and don't mind doing more than their usual stunt.

I often wonder if some of the women are not better off than in the days before the war. They do about the same work, only they are not bothered by their men.

In the days before the war the men worked in the fields in the summer, and in the *carrière de plâtre*, at Mareuil-lès-Meaux, in the winter. It was a hard life, and most of them drank a little. It is never the kind of drunkenness you know in America, however. Most of them were radical Socialists in politics – which as a rule meant 'ag'in' the government'. Of course, being Socialists and French, they simply had to talk it all over. The café was the proper place to do that – the provincial café being the working-man's club. Of course, the man never dreamed of quitting until legal closing hour, and when he got home, if wife objected, why he just hit her a clip – it was, of course, for her good – 'a woman, a dog, and a walnut tree' – you know the adage.

Almost always in these provincial towns it is the woman who is thrifty, and often she sees but too little of her man's earnings. Still, she is, in her way, fond of him, tenacious in her possession of him, and Sundays and fête days they get on together very handsomely.

All the women here, married or not, have always worked, and worked hard. The habit has settled on them. Few of them actually expect their husbands to support them, and they do not feel degraded because their labor helps, and they are wonderfully saving. They spend almost nothing on their clothes, never wear a hat, and usually treasure, for years, one black dress to wear to funerals. The children go to school bareheaded, in black pinafores. It is rare that the humblest of these women has not money put aside.

You don't have to look very deep into the present situation to discover that, psychologically, it is queer. Marriage is, after all, in so many classes, a habit. Here are the women of the class to which I refer working very little harder than in the days before the war. Only, for nearly two years they have had no drinking man to come home at midnight either quarrelsome or sulky; no man's big appetite to cook for; no man to wash for or to mend for. They have lived in absolute peace, gone to bed early to a long, unbroken sleep, and get twenty-five cents a day government aid, plus ten cents for each child. As they all raise their own vegetables, keep chickens and rabbits, and often a goat, manage to have a little to take to market, and a little time every week to work for other people, and get war prices for their time – well, I imagine you can work out the problem yourself.

Mind you, there is not one of these women, who, in her way, will not assure you that she loves her husband. She would be drawn and quartered before she would harm him. If anything happens to him she will weep bitterly. But, under my breath, I can assure you that there is many a woman of that class a widow today who is better off for it, and so are her children. The husband who died 'en hero', the father dead for his country, is a finer figure in the family life than the living man ever was or could have been.

Of course, it is in the middle classes, where the wives have to be kept, where marriage is less a partnership than in the working classes and among the humbler commercial classes, that there is so much suffering. But that is the class which invariably suffers most in any disaster.

I do not know how characteristic of the race the qualities I find among these people are, nor can I, for lack of experience, be sure in what degree they are absolutely different from those of any class in the States. For example – this craving to own one's home. Almost no one here pays rent. There is a lad at the foot of the hill, in Voisins, who was married just before the war. He has a tiny house of two rooms and kitchen which he bought just before his marriage for the sum of one hundred and fifty francs – less than thirty dollars. He paid a small sum down, and the rest at the rate of twenty cents a week. There is a small piece of land with it, on which he does about as intensive farming as I ever saw. But it is his own.

The woman who works in my garden owns her place. She has been paying for it almost ever since she was married – sixteen years ago – and has still forty dollars to pay. She cultivates her own garden, raises her own chickens and rabbits, and always has some to sell. Her husband works in the fields for other people, or in the quarries, and she considers herself prosperous, as she has been able to keep her children in school, and owes no one a penny, except, of course, the sum due on her little place. She has worked since she was nine, but her children have not, and, when she dies, there will be something for them, if it is no more than the little place. In all probability, before that time comes, she will have bought more land – to own ground is the dream of these people, and they do it in such a strange way.

I remember in my girlhood, when I knew the Sandy River Valley country so well, that when a farmer wanted to buy more land he always tried, at no matter what sacrifice, to get a piece adjoining what he already owned, and put a fence around it. It is different here. People own a piece of land here, and a piece there, and another piece miles away, and there are no fences.

For example, around Père Abelard's house there is a fruit garden and a kitchen garden. The rest of his land is all over the place. He has a big piece of woodland at Pont aux Dames, where he was born, and another on the *route de Mareuil*. He has a field on the *route de Couilly*, and another on the side of the hill on the *route de Meaux*, and he has a small patch of fruit trees and a potato field on the *chemin Madame*, and another big piece of grassland running down the hill from Huiry to Condé.

Almost nothing is fenced in. Grain fields, potato patches, beet fields belonging to different people touch each other without any other barrier than the white stones, almost level with the soil, put in by the surveyors.

Of course they are always in litigation, but, as I told you, a lawsuit is a *cachet* of respectability in France.

As for separating a French man or woman from the land – it is almost impossible. The piece of woodland that Abelard owns at Pont aux Dames is called 'Le Paradis'. It is a part of his mother's estate, and his sister, who lives across the Morin, owns the adjoining lot. It is of no use to anyone. They neither of them ever dream of cutting the wood. Now and then, when we drive, we go and look at it, and Père tells funny stories of the things he did there when he was a lad. It is full of game, and not long ago he had an offer for it. The sum was not big, but invested would have added five hundred francs a year to his income. But no one could make either him or his sister resolve to part with it. So there it lies idle, and the only thing it serves for is to add to the tax bill every year. But they would rather own land than have money in the bank. Land can't run away. They can go and look at it, press their feet on it, and realize that it is theirs.

I am afraid the next generation is going to be different, and the disturbing thing is that it is the women who are changing. So many of them, who never left the country before, are working in the ammunition factories and earning unheard-of money, and spending it, which is a radical and alarming feature of the situation.

You spoke in one of your recent letters of the awful cost of this war in money. But you must remember that the money is not lost. It is only redistributed. Whether or not the redistribution is a danger is something none of us can know yet; that is a thing only the future can show. One thing is certain, it has forcibly liberated women.

You ask how the cats are. They are remarkable. Khaki gets more savage every day, and less like what I imagined a house cat ought to be. He has thrashed every cat in the *commune* except Didine, and never got a scratch to show for it. But he has never scratched me. I slapped him the other day. He slapped back – but with a velvet paw, never even showed a claw.

Didn't you always think a cat hated water? I am sure I did. He goes out in all weathers. Last winter he played in the snow like a child, and rolled in it, and no rainstorm can keep him in the house. The other day he insisted on going out in a pouring rain, and I got anxious about him. Finally I went to the door and called him, and, after a while, he walked out of the dog's kennel, gave me a reproachful look as if to say, 'Can't you leave a chap in peace?' and returned to the kennel. The one thing he really hates is to have me leave the house. He goes where his sweet will leads him, but he seems to think that I should be always on the spot.

XXIV

May 23, 1916

I begin to believe that we shall have no normal settled weather until all this cannon play is over. We've had most unseasonable hailstorms which have knocked all the buds off the fruit trees, so, in addition to other annoyances, we shall have no fruit this year.

There is nothing new here except that General Foch is in the ambulance at Meaux. No one knows it; not a word has appeared in the newspapers. It was the result of a stupid, but unavoidable, automobile accident. To avoid running over a woman and child on a road near here, the automobile, in which he was traveling rapidly in company with his son-in-law, ran against a tree and smashed. Luckily he was not seriously hurt, though his head got damaged.

On Thursday Poincaré passed over our hill, with Briand, en route to meet Joffre at the General's bedside. I did not see them, but some of the people at Quincy did. It was a lucky escape for Foch. He would have hated to die during this war of a simple, unmilitary automobile accident, and the army could ill afford just now to lose one of the heroes of the Marne. Carefully as the fact has been concealed, we knew it here through our ambulance, which is a branch of that at Meaux, where he is being nursed.

Three months since the battle at Verdun began, and it is still going on, with the Germans hardly more than four miles from the city, and yet it begins to look as if they knew themselves that the battle – the most terrible the world has ever seen – was a failure. Still, I have changed my mind. I begin to believe that had Germany centred all her forces on that frontier in August, 1914, when her first-line troops were available, and their hopes high, she would probably have passed. No one can know that, but it is likely, and many military men think so. Isn't it a sort of poetic justice to think that it is even possible that had Germany fought an honorable war she might have got to Paris? 'Whom the gods destroy, they first make mad.'

I do nothing but work in the garden on rare days when it does not rain, and listen to the cannon. That can't be very interesting stuff to make a letter of. The silence here, which was so dear to me in the days when I was preparing the place, still hangs over it. But, oh, the difference! Now and then, in spite of one's self, the very thought of all that is going on so very near us refuses to take its place and keep in the perspective, it simply jumps out of the frame of patriotism and the welfare of the future. Then the only thing to do is to hunt for the visible consolations – and one always finds them.

For example – wouldn't it seem logical that such a warfare would brutalize the men who are actually in it? It doesn't. It seems to have just the contrary effect. I can't tell you how good the men are to one another, or how gentle they are to the children. It is strange that it should be so, but it is. I don't try to understand it, I merely set it down for you.

XXV

June 16, 1916

You can imagine how trying and unseasonable the weather is when I tell you that I not only had a fire yesterday, but that I went to bed with a hot water bottle. Imagine it! I have only been able to eat out-of-doors once so far.

This is not a letter – just a line, lest you worry if you do not hear that I am well. I am too anxiously watching that seesaw at Verdun, with the German army only four miles from the city, at the end of the fourth month, to talk about myself, and in no position to write about things which you know. One gets dumb, though not hopeless. To add to our anxieties the crops are not going to be good. It was continually wet at planting time, and so cold, and there has been so little sun that potatoes are rotting in the fields already, and the harvest will be meagre. The grain, especially that planted last fall, is fairly good, but, as I told you, after the tempest we had, there is to be no fruit. When I say none, I absolutely mean none. I have not one cherry. Louise counted six prunes on my eight trees, and I have just four pears and not a single apple. Père's big orchard is in the same condition. In addition, owing to the terrible dampness – the ground is wet all the time – the slugs eat up all the salad, spoil all the strawberries, and chew off every young green thing that puts its head above the ground, and that in spite of very hard work on my part. Every morning early, and every afternoon, at sundown, I put in an hour's hard work – hard, disgusting work – picking them up with the tongs and dropping them into boiling water. So you see every kind of war is going on at the same time. Where is the good of wishing a bad harvest on Germany, when we get it ourselves at the same time?

However, I suppose that you in the States can help us out, and England has jolly well fixed it so that no one can easily help Germany out.

XXVI

August 4, 1916

Well, here we are in the third year of the war, as Kitchener foresaw, and still with a long way to go to the frontier.

Thanks, by the way, for the article about Kitchener. After all, what can one say of such an end for such a man, after such a career, in which so many times he might have found a soldier's death – then to be drowned like a rat, doing his duty? It leaves one simply speechless. I was, you see. I hadn't a comment to throw at you.

It's hot at last, I'm thankful to say, and equally thankful that the news from the front is good. It is nothing to throw one's hat in the air about, but every inch in the right direction is at least prophetic.

Nothing to tell you about. Not the smallest thing happens here. I do nothing but read my paper, fuss in the garden, which looks very pretty, do up a bundle for my *filleul* once in a while, write a few letters, and drive about, at sundown, in my perambulator. If that is not an absurd life for a lady in the war zone in these days, I'd like to know what it is.

I hope this weather will last. It is good for the war and good for the crops. But I am afraid I shall hope in vain.

XXVII

September 30, 1916

This has been the strangest summer I ever knew. There have been so few really summer days. I could count the hot days on my fingers. None of the things have happened on which I counted.

What a disappointment poor Russia has been to the big world, which knew nothing about her except that she could put fifteen millions of men in the field. However, as we say, 'all that is only a detail'. We are learning things every day. Nothing has opened our eyes more than seeing set at naught our conviction that, once the Rumanian frontier was opened to the Russians, they would be on the Danube in no time.

Do you remember how glibly we talked of the 'Russian steamroller', in September, 1914? I remember that, at that time, I had a letter from a very clever chap who told me that 'expert military men' looked to see the final battle on our front, somewhere near Waterloo, before the end of October, and that even 'before that, the Russian steamroller would be crushing its way to Berlin'. How much expert military men have learned since then!

Still, wasn't it, in a certain sense, lucky that, in spite of the warning of Kitchener, we did not, in the beginning, realize the road we had to travel? As I look back on the two years, it all looks to me more and more remarkable, seen even at this short perspective, that the Allied armies, and most of all, the civilians behind the lines have, in the face of the hard happenings of each day, stood up, and taken it as they have, and hoped on.

I have got into a mood where it seems simply stupid to talk about it, since I am, as usual, only eternally a spectator. I only long to keep my eyes raised in a wide arc towards the end, to live each day as I can, and wait. So why should I try to write to you of things which I do not see, and of which only the last, faint, dying ripples reach us here?

You really must not pity me, as you insist upon doing, because military restrictions draw a line about me, which I may not cross at my own sweet will. I am used to it. It is not hard. For that matter, it is much more trying to my French neighbors than it is to me.

I seem never to have told you that even they may not leave the *commune* without a *sauf-conduit*. To be sure, they have only to go to the *mairie*, and ask for it, to get it.

For months now the bridge over the Marne, at Meaux, has been guarded, and even those going to market cannot cross without showing their papers. The formality is very trying to them, for the reason that the *mairie* opens at eight, and closes at twelve not to reopen again until three and close at six. You see those hours are when everyone is busiest in the fields. The man or woman who has to go to market on Saturday must leave work standing and make a long trip into Quincy – and often they have three or four miles to go on foot to do it – just at the hour when it is least easy to spare the time.

To make it harder still, a new order went out a few weeks ago. Every man, woman, and child (over fifteen) in the war zone has to have, after October 1, a *carte d'identité*, to which must be affixed a photograph.

This regulation has resulted in the queerest of embarrassments. A great number of these old peasants – and young ones too – never had a photograph taken. There is no photographer. The photographer at Esbly and the two at Meaux could not possibly get the people all photographed, and, in this uncertain weather, the prints made, in the delay allowed by the military authorities. A great cry of protestation went up. Photographers of all sorts were sent into the *commune*.

The town crier beat his drum like mad, and announced the places where the photographers would be on certain days and hours, and ordered the people to assemble and be snapped.

One of the places chosen was the courtyard at Amélie's, and you would have loved seeing these bronzed old peasants facing a camera for the first time. Some of the results were funny, especially when the hurried and overworked operator got two faces on the same negative, as happened several times.

Real autumn weather is here, but, for that matter, it has been more like autumn than summer since last spring. The fields are lovely to see on days when the sun shines. I drove the other day just for the pleasure of sitting in my perambulator, on the hillside, and looking over the slope of the wide wheat fields, where the women, in their cotton jackets and their wide hats, were reaping. The harvesting never looked so picturesque. I could pick out, in the distance, the tall figure of my Louise, with a sheaf on her head and a sickle in her hand, striding across the fields, and I thought how a painter would have loved the scene, with the long rays of the late September sunset illuminating the yellow stretch.

Last Wednesday we had a little excitement here, because sixteen German prisoners, who were working on a farm at Vareddes, escaped – some of them disguised as women.

I wasn't a bit alarmed, as it hardly seemed possible that they would venture near houses in this district, but Père was very nervous, and every time the dog barked he was out in the road to make sure that I was all right.

Oddly enough, it happened on the very day when 200 arrived at Meaux to work in the sugar refinery. The next day there was a regular *battue*, as the *gendarmes* beat up the fields and woods in search of the fugitives.

If they caught them, they don't tell, but we have been ordered to harbor no strangers under a severe penalty. But that condition has really existed since the war broke out, as no one is even allowed to engage a workman whose papers have not been *visé* at the *mairie*.

I have had to have a wood fire today – it is alarming, with winter ahead, and so little fuel, to have to begin heating up at the end of September – three weeks or a month earlier than usual.

XXVIII

November 25, 1916

It is raining – a cold and steady downpour. I don't feel in the least like writing a letter. This is only to tell you that I have got enough anthracite coal to go to the end of February, and that the house is warm and cosy, and I am duly thankful to face this third war-winter free from fear of freezing. It cost thirty-two dollars a ton. How does that sound to you?

I have planted my tulip bulbs, cleaned up the garden for winter and settled down to life inside my walls, with my courage in both hands, and the hope that next spring's offensive will not be a great disappointment.

In the meantime I am sorry that Franz Josef did not live to see this war of his out and take his punishment. I used to be so sorry for him in the old days, when it seemed as if Fate showered disasters on the heads of the Hapsburgs. I wasted my pity. The blows killed everyone in the family *but* father. The way he stood it and never learned to be kind or wise proved how little he needed pity.

All the signs say a cold winter. How I envy hibernating animals! I want to live to see this thing out, but it would be nice to crawl into a hole, like a bear, and sleep comfortably until the sun came out in the spring, and the seeds began to sprout, and the army was thawed out, and could move. In the silence on this hilltop, where nothing happens but dishwashing and bedmaking and darning stockings, it is a long way to springtime, even if it comes early.

I amused myself last week by defying the consign. I had not seen a *gendarme* on the road for weeks. I had driven to Couilly once or twice, though to do it I had to cross 'the dead line'. I had met the *garde champêtre* there, and even talked to him, and he had said nothing. So, hearing one day that my friend from Voulangis had a permission to drive to the train at Esbly, and that she was returning about nine in the morning, I determined to meet her on the road, and at least see how she was looking and have a little chat. I felt a longing to hear someone say: 'Hulloa, you,' – just a few words in English.

So if you could have seen the road, just outside of Couilly, Thursday morning, just after nine, you would have seen a Southern girl sitting in a high cart facing east, and an elderly lady in a donkey cart facing west, and the two of them watching the road ahead for the coming of a bicycle pedalled by a *gendarme* with a gun on his back, as they talked like magpies. It was all so funny that I was convulsed with laughter. There we were, two innocent, harmless American women, talking of our family affairs and our gardens, our fuel, our health, and behaving like a pair of conspirators. We didn't dare to get out to embrace each other, for fear – in case we saw a challenge coming – that I could not scramble back and get away quickly enough, and we only stayed a quarter of an hour. We might just as well have carried our lunch and spent the day so far as I could see – only *if* anyone had passed and had asked for our papers there would have been trouble. However, we had our laugh, and decided that it was not worthwhile to risk it again. But I could not help asking myself how, with all their red tape, they ever caught any real suspect.

Do you remember that I told you some time ago about Louise's brother, Joseph, in the heavy artillery, who had never seen a Boche? Well, he is at home again for his eight days. He came to see me yesterday. I said to him: 'Well, Joseph, where did you come from this time?'

'From the same place – the mountains in Alsace. We've not budged for nearly two years.'

'How long are you going to stay there?'

'To the end of the war, I imagine.'

'But why?' I asked.

'What can we do, *madame*?' he replied. 'There we are, on the top of a mountain. We can't get down. The Germans can't get up. They are across the valley on the top of a hill in the same fix.'

'But what do you do up there?' I demanded.

'Well,' he replied, 'we watch the Germans, or at least the aeroplanes do – we can't see them. They work on their defenses. They pull up new guns and shift their emplacements. We let them work. Then our big guns destroy their work.'

'But what do they do, Joseph?'

'Well, they fire a few shots, and go to work again. But I'll tell you something, *madame*, as sure as that we are both living, they would not do a thing if we would only leave them in peace – but we don't.'

'Well, Joseph,' I asked, 'have you seen a Boche yet?'

'Oh, yes, *madame*, I've seen them. I see them, with a glass, working in the fields, ploughing, and getting ready to plant them.'

'And you don't do anything to prevent them?'

'Well, no. We can't very well. They always have a group of women and children with every gang of workmen. They know, only too well, that French guns will not fire at that kind of target. It is just the same with their commissary trains – always women at the head, in the middle, and in the rear.'

Comment is unnecessary!

XXIX

December 6, 1916

Well, at last, the atmosphere on the hilltop is all changed. We have a *cantonnement de régiment* again, and this time the most interesting that we have ever had – the 23d Dragoons, men on active service, who are doing infantry work in the trenches at Tracy-le-Val, in the Forêt de Laigue, the nearest point to Paris, in the battle-front.

It is, as usual, only the decorative and picturesque side of war, but it is tremendously interesting, more so than anything which has happened since the Battle of the Marne.

As you never had soldiers quartered on you – and perhaps you never will have – I wish you were here now.

It was just after lunch on Sunday – a grey, cold day, which had dawned on a world covered with frost – that there came a knock at the salon door. I opened it, and there stood a soldier, with his heels together, and his hand at salute, who said: '*Bonjour, madame, avez-vous un lit pour un soldat?*'

Of course I had a bed for a soldier, and said so at once.

You see it is all polite and formal, but if there is a corner in the house which can serve the army the army has a right to it. Everyone is offered the privilege of being prettily gracious about it, and of letting it appear as if a favor were being extended to the army, but, in case one does not yield willingly, along comes a superior officer and imposes a guest on the house.

However, that sort of thing never happens here. In our *commune* the soldiers are loved. The army is, for that matter, loved all over France. No matter what else may be *conspué*, the crowd never fails to cry '*Vive l'Armée!*' although there are places where the soldier is not loved as a visitor.

I asked the adjutant in, and showed him the room. He wrote it down in his book, saluted me again with a smiling, '*Merci bien, madame*', and went on to make the rounds of the hamlet, and examine the resources of Voisins, Joncheroy, and Quincy.

The non-commissioned officers, who arrange the *cantonne-ments*, are very clever about it. They seem to know, by instinct, just what sort of a man to put in each house, and they rarely blunder.

All that Sunday afternoon they were running around in the mud and the cold drizzle that was beginning to fall, arrang-ing, not only quarters for the men, but finding shelter for three times as many horses, and that was not easy, although every old grange on the hilltop was cleaned out and put in order.

For half an hour the adjutant tried to convince himself that he could put four horses in the old grange on the north side of my house. I was perfectly willing, only I knew that if one horse kicked once, the floor of the loft would fall on him, and that if four horses kicked once, at least three walls would fall in on them. That would not be so very important to me, but I'd hate to have handsome army horses killed like that on my premises.

He finally decided that I was right, and then I went with him up to Amélie's to see what we could do. I never realized what a ruin of a hamlet this is until that afternoon. By putting seven horses in the old grange at Père's – a tumble-down old shack, where he keeps lumber and dead farm wagons – he never throws away or destroys anything – we finally found places for all the horses. There were eleven at Père's, and it took Amélie and Père all the rest of the afternoon to run the stuff out of the old grange, which stands just at the turn of the road, and has a huge broken door facing down the hill.

I often mean to send you a picture of that group of ruins – there are five buildings in it. They were originally all joined together, but some of them have had to be pulled down because they got too dangerous to stand, and in the open spaces there is, in one place, a pavement of red tiles, and in another the roof to a cellar, with stone steps leading up to it. Not a bit of it is of any use to anyone, though the cellars under them are used to store vegetables, and Amélie keeps rabbits in one.

It was while we were arranging all this, and Amélie was assuring them that they were welcome, but that she would not guarantee that the whole group of ruins would not fall on their heads (and everything was as gay as if we were arranging a weekend picnic rather than a shelter for soldiers right out of the trenches), that the adjutant explained how it happened that, in the third year of the war, the fighting regiments were, for the first time, retiring as far as our hill for their *repos*.

He told us that almost all the cavalry had been dismounted to do infantry work in the trenches, but their horses were stalled in the rear. It had been found that the horses were an embarrassment so near to the battle-front, and so it had been decided to retire them further behind the line, and send out part of the men to keep them exercised and in condition, giving the men in turn three weeks in the trenches and three weeks out.

They had first withdrawn the horses to Nanteuil-le-Haudrouin a little northwest of us, about halfway between us and the trenches in the Forêt de Laigue. But that *cantonnement* had not been satisfactory, so they had retired here.

By sundown everything was arranged – 400 horses along the hilltop, and, they tell us, over 15,000 along the valley. We were told that the men were leaving Nanteuil the next morning, and would arrive during the afternoon.

It was just dusk on Monday when they began riding up the hill, each mounted man leading two riderless horses.

It was just after they passed that there came a knock at the *salon* door.

I opened it with some curiosity. When you are to lodge a soldier in a house as intimately arranged as this one is, I defy anyone not to be curious as to what the lodger is to be like.

There stood a tall, straight lad, booted and spurred, with a crop in one gloved hand, and the other raised to his fatigue cap in salute, and a smile on his bonny face – as trig in his leather belted *bleu de ciel* tunic as if ready for parade, and not a sign of war about him but his uniform.

'*Bonjour, madame*,' he said. 'Permit me to introduce myself. Aspirant B—, 23d Dragoons.'

'Regular army?' I said, for I knew by the look of him that this was a professional soldier.

'Saint-Cyr,' he replied. That is the same as our West Point.

'You are welcome, Aspirant,' I said. 'Let me show you to your room.'

'Thank you,' he smiled. 'Not yet. I only came to present myself, and thank you in advance for your courtesy. I am in command of the squad on your hill, replacing an officer who is not yet out of the hospital. I must see my men housed and the horses under shelter. May I ask you, if my orderly comes with my kit, to show him where to put it, and explain to him how he may best get in and out of the house, when necessary, without disturbing your habits?'

I had to laugh as I explained to him that locking up, when soldiers were in the hamlet, was hardly even a formality, and that the orderly could come and go at his will.

'Good,' he replied. 'Then I'll give myself the pleasure of seeing you after dinner. I hope I shall in no way disturb you. I am always in before nine,' and he saluted again, backed away from the door, and marched up the hill. He literally neither walked nor ran, he marched.

I wish I could give you an idea of what he looks like. At first sight I gave him nineteen years at the outside, in spite of his height and his soldierly bearing and his dignity.

Before he came in at half past eight his orderly had brought his kit, unpacked and made himself familiar with the lay of the house, and made friends with Amélie. So the Aspirant settled into an armchair in front of the fire – having asked my permission – to chat a bit, and account for himself, and it was evident to me that he had already been asking questions regarding me – spurred, as usual, by the surprise of finding an American here. As the officers' mess is at the foot of the hill, at Voisins, that had been easy.

So, knowing intuitively, just by his manner and his words, that he had asked questions about me – he even knew that I had been here from the beginning of the war – I, with the privilege of my white hairs, asked him even how old he was. He told me he was twenty – a year older than I thought – that he was an only son, that his father was an officer in the reserves and they lived about forty-five miles the other side of Rheims, that his home was in the hands of the Germans, and the house, which had been literally stripped of everything of value, was the headquarters of a staff officer. And it was all told so quietly, so simply, with no sign of emotion of any sort.

At exactly nine o'clock he rose to his feet, clicked his heels together, made me a drawing-room bow, of the best form, as he said: '*Eh bien, madame, je vous quitte. Bonsoir et bonne nuit.*' Then he backed to the foot of the stairs, bowed again, turned and went up lightly on the toes of his heavy boots, and I never heard another sound of him.

Of course in twenty-four hours he became the child of the house. I feel like a grandmother to him. As for Amélie, she falls over herself trying to spoil him, and before the second day he became 'Monsieur André' to her. Catch her giving a boy like that his military title, though he takes his duties most seriously.

The weather is dreadful – cold, damp, drizzly, but he is in and out, and the busiest person you can imagine. There isn't a horse that has to have his feet washed that he isn't on the spot to see it done properly. There isn't a man who has a pain that he isn't after him to see if he needs the doctor – and I don't need to tell you that his men love him, and so do the horses.

I am taking a full course in military habits, military duties, and military etiquette. I smile inside myself sometimes and wonder how they can keep it up during these war times. But they do.

This morning he came down at half past seven ready to lead his squad on an exercise ride. I must tell you that the soldier who comes downstairs in the morning, in his big coat and kepi, ready to mount his horse, is a different person from the smiling boy who makes me a ballroom bow at the foot of the stairs in the evening. He comes down the stairs as stiff as a ramrod, lifts his gloved hand to his kepi, as he says, '*Bonjour, madame, vous allez bien ce matin?*'

This morning I remarked to him as he was ready to mount: 'Well, young man, I advise you to turn up your collar; the air is biting.'

He gave me a queer look as he replied: '*Merci, – pas régle-mentaire,*' – but he had to laugh, as he shook his head at me, and marched out to his horse.

You do not need to be told how all this changes our life here, and yet it does not bring into it the sort of emotion I anticipated. Thus far I have not heard the war mentioned. The tramping of horses, the moving crowd of men, simply give a new look to our quiet hamlet.

This *cantonnement* is officially called a '*repos*' but seems little like that to me. It seems simply a change of work. Every man has three horses to groom, to feed, to exercise, three sets of harness to keep in order, stables to clean. But they are all so gay and happy, and as this is the first time in eighteen months that any of them have slept in beds they are enjoying it.

Of course, I have little privacy. You know how my house is laid out – the front door opens into the *salon*, and the staircase is there also. When the Aspirant is not on duty outside he has to be here where he can be found, so he sits at the *salon* desk to do his writing and fix up his papers and reports, and when he is not going up and down stairs his orderly is. There seems always to be a cleaning of boots, brushing of coats, and polishing of spurs and rubbing up of leather going on somewhere.

It did not take the men long to discover that there was always hot water in my kitchen, and that they were welcome to it if they would keep the kettles filled, and that I did not mind their coming and going – and I don't, for a nicer crowd of men I never saw. They are not only ready, they are anxious, to do all sorts of odd jobs, from hauling coal and putting it in, to cleaning the chimneys and sweeping the terrace. When they groom the horses they always groom Gamin, our dapple-grey pony, and Ninette, which were never so well taken care of in their lives – so brushed and clipped that they are both handsomer than I knew. Though the regiment has only been here three days every day has had its special excitement.

The morning after they got here we had a royal ten minutes of laughter and movement.

In the old grange at the top of the hill, where they stabled seven horses, there had been a long bar across the back wall, fixed with cement into the side walls, and used to fasten the wagons. They found it just right to tie the horses. It was a fine morning, for a wonder. The sun was shining, and all the barn doors were open to it. The Aspirant and I were standing on the lawn just before noon – he had returned from his morning ride – looking across the Marne at the battlefield. The regiment had been in the battle – but he was, at that time, still at Saint-Cyr. Suddenly we heard a great rumpus behind us, and turned just in season to see all the horses trotting out of the grange. They wheeled out of the wide door in a line headed down the hill, the last two carrying the bar to which they had been attached, like the pole of a carriage, between them. They were all 'feeling their oats', and they thundered down the hill by us, like a cavalry charge, and behind them came half a dozen men simply splitting with laughter.

Amélie had been perfectly right. The old grange was not solid, but they had not pulled the walls down on themselves, they had simply pulled the pole to which they were attached out of its bed.

The Aspirant tried not to smile – an officer in command must not, I suppose, even if he is only twenty. He whistled gently, put up his hand to stop the men from running, and walked quietly into the road, still whistling. Five of the horses, tossing their heads, were thundering on towards the canal. The span, dragging the long pole, swerved on the turn, and swung the pole, which was so long that it caught on the bank. I expected to see them tangle themselves all up, what with the pole and the halters. Not a bit of it. They stopped, panting, and still trying to toss their heads, and the Aspirant quietly picked up a halter, and passed the horses over to the men, saying, in a most nonchalant manner: 'Fasten that pole more securely. Some of you go quietly down the hill. You'll meet them coming back,' and he returned to the garden, and resumed the conversation just where it had been interrupted.

It had been a lively picture to me, but to the soldiers, I suppose, it had only been an every day's occurrence.

My only fear had been that there might be children or a wagon on the winding road. Luckily the way was clear.

An hour later, the men returned, leading the horses. They had galloped down to the river, and returned by way of Voisins, where they had stopped right in front of the house where the Captain was quartered, and the Captain had been in the garden and seen them.

This time the Aspirant had to laugh. He slapped one of the horses caressingly on the nose as he said: 'You devils! Couldn't you go on a lark without telling the Captain about it, and getting us all into trouble?'

To make this all the funnier, that very night three horses stabled in a rickety barn at Voisins, kicked their door down, and pranced and neighed under the Captain's bedroom window.

The Captain is a nice chap, but he is not in his first youth, and he is tired, and, well – he is a bit nervous. He said little, but that was to the point. It was only: 'You boys will see that these things don't happen, or you will sleep in the straw behind your horses.'

This is the first time that I have seen anything of the military organization, and I am filled with admiration for it. I don't know how it works behind the trenches, but here, in the *cantonnement*, I could set my clocks by the soup wagon – a neat little cart, drawn by two sturdy little horses, which takes the hill at a fine gallop, and passes my gate at exactly twenty-five minutes past eleven, and twenty-five minutes past five every day. The men wait, with their *gamelles*, at the top of the hill. The soup looks good and smells delicious. Amélie says that it tastes good. She has five soldiers in her house, and she and Père often eat with them, so she knows.

From all this you can guess what my life is like, and probably will be like until the impatiently awaited spring offensive. But what you will find it hard to imagine is the spirit and gaiety of these men. It is hard to believe that they have been supporting the monotony of trench life for so long, and living under bombardment – and cavalry at that, trained and hoping for another kind of warfare. There is no sign of it on them.

XXX

Well, we did not keep our first division of dragoons as long as we expected. They had passed part of their three weeks out of the trenches at Nanteuil, and on the journey, so it seemed to us as though they were hardly settled down when the order came for them to return. They were here only a little over a week.

I had hardly got accustomed to seeing the Aspirant about the house, either writing, with the cat on his knees, or reading, with Dick sitting beside him, begging to have his head patted, when one evening he came in, and said quietly: 'Well, *madame*, we are leaving you in a day or two. The order for the *relève* has come, but the day and hour are not yet fixed.'

But during the week he was here I got accustomed to seeing him sit before the fire every evening after dinner for a little chat before turning in. He was more ready to talk politics than war, and full of curiosity about 'your Mr Wilson', as he called him. Now and then he talked military matters, but it was technique, and the strategy of war, not the events. He is an enthusiastic soldier, and to him, of course, the cavalry is still '*la plus belle arme de France*'. He loved to explain the use of cavalry in modern warfare, of what it was yet to do in the offensive, armed as it is today with the same weapons as the infantry, carrying carbines, having its hand-grenade divisions, its *mitrailleuses*, ready to go into action as cavalry, arriving like a flash *au galop*, over ground where the infantry must move slowly, and with difficulty, and ready at any time to dismount and fight on foot, to finish a pursuit begun as cavalry. It all sounded very logical as he described it.

He had been under bombardment, been on dangerous scouting expeditions, but never yet in a charge, which is, of course, his ambitious dream. There was an expression of real regret in his voice when he said one evening: '*Hélas*! I have not yet had the smallest real opportunity to distinguish myself.'

I reminded him that he was still very young.

He looked at me quite indignantly as he replied: '*Madame* forgets that there are Aspirants no older than I whose names are already inscribed on the roll of honor.'

You see an elderly lady, unused to a soldier's point of view, may be very sympathetic, and yet blunder as a comforter.

The *relève* passed off quietly. It was all in the routine of the soldiers' lives. They did not even know that it was picturesque. It was late last Friday night that an orderly brought the news that the order had come to move on the morning of the eleventh – three days later – and it was not until the night of the fifteenth that we were again settled down to quiet.

The squad we had here moved in two divisions. Early Monday morning – the eleventh – the horses were being saddled, and at ten o'clock they began to move. One half of them were in full equipment. The other half acted as an escort as far as Meaux, from which place they led back the riderless horses.

The officers explained it all to me. The division starting that day for the trenches dismounted at Meaux, and took a train for the station nearest to the Forêt de Laigue. There they had their hot soup and waited for night, to march into the trenches under cover of the darkness. They told me that it was not a long march, but it was a hard one, as it was up hill, over wet and clayey ground, where it was difficult not to slip back as fast as they advanced.

On arriving at the trenches they would find the men they were to relieve ready to march out, to slip and slide down the hill to the railway, where they would have their morning coffee, and await the train for Meaux, where they were due at noon next day – barring delays.

So, on the afternoon of the twelfth, the men who had acted as escort the day before led the horses to Meaux, and just before four o'clock the whole body arrived on the hill.

This time I saw men right out of the trenches. They were a sorry sight, in spite of their high spirits. The clayey yellow mud of three weeks' exposure in the trenches was plastered on them so thick that I wondered how they managed to mount their horses. I never saw a dirtier crowd. Their faces even looked stiff.

They simply tumbled off their horses, left the escort to stable them, and made a dash for the bath-house, which is at the foot of the hill, at Joncheroy. If they can't get bathed, disinfected, and changed before dark, they have to sleep their first night in the straw with the horses, as they are unfit, in more ways than I like to tell you, to go into anyone's house until that is done, and they are not allowed.

These new arrivals had twenty-four hours' rest, and then, on Thursday, they acted as escort to the second division, and with that division went the Aspirant, and the men they relieved arrived Friday afternoon, and now we are settled down for three weeks.

Before the Aspirant left he introduced into the house the senior lieutenant, whom he had been replacing in the command on my hill, a man a little over thirty – a business man in private life and altogether charming, very cultivated, a book-lover and an art connoisseur. He is a nephew of Lêpine, so many years *préfet de police* at Paris, and a cousin of Senator Reynault, who was killed in his aeroplane at Toule, famous not only as a brave patriot, but as a volunteer for three reasons exempt from active service – a senator, a doctor, and past the age.

I begin to believe, on the testimony of my personal experiences, that all the officers in the cavalry are perfect gentlemen.

The lieutenant settled into his place at once. He puts the coal on the fire at night. He plays with the animals. He locks up, and is as quiet as a mouse and as busy as a bee.

This is all my news, except that I am hoping to go to Paris for Christmas, and to go by the way of Voulangis. It is all very uncertain. My permission has not come yet.

It is over a year since we were shut in. My friends in Paris call me their *permissionaire*, when I go to town. In the few shops where I am known everyone laughs when I make my rare appearances and greets me with: 'Ah, so they've let you out again!' as if it were a huge joke, and I assure you that it does seem like that to me.

The soldiers in the trenches get eight days' permission every four months. I don't seem to get much more – if as much.

XXXI

I went to Paris, as I told you I hoped to do. Nothing new there. In spite of the fact that, in many ways, they are beginning to feel the war, and there is altogether too much talk about things no one can really know anything about, I was still amazed at the gaiety. In a way it is just now largely due to the great number of men *en permission*. The streets, the restaurants, the tea-rooms are full of them, and so, they tell me, are the theaters.

Do you know what struck me most forcibly? You'll never guess. It was that men in long trousers look perfectly absurd. I am so used to seeing the *culotte* and gaiters that the best-looking pantaloons I saw on the boulevards looked ugly and ridiculous.

I left the officer billeted in my house to take care of it. The last I saw of him he was sitting at the desk in the *salon*, his pipe in his mouth, looking comfortable and cosy, and as if settled for life. I only stayed a few days, and came home, on New Year's Eve, to find that he had left the night before, having been suddenly transferred to the staff of the commander of the first army, as *officier de la liaison*, and I had in his place a young *sous-officier* of twenty-two, who proves to be a cousin of the famous French spy, Captain Luxe, who made that sensational escape, in 1910, from a supposed-to-be-impregnable German military prison. I am sure you remember the incident, as the American papers devoted columns to his unprecedented feat. The hero of that sensational episode is still in the army. I wonder what the Germans will do with him if they catch him again? They are hardly likely to get him alive a second time.

I wonder if the German books on military tactics use that escape as a model in their military schools? Do you know that in every French military school the reconnaissance which Count Zeppelin made in Alsace, in the days of 1870, when he was a cavalry officer, is given as a model reconnaissance both for strategy and pluck? I did not, until I was told. Oddly enough, not all that Zeppelin has done since to offend French ideas of decency in war can dull the admiration felt by every cavalry officer for his clever feat in 1870.

Last Thursday – that was the 4th – we had our second *relève*.

The night before they left some of the officers came to say *au revoir*, and to tell me that the Aspirant, who had been with me in December, would be quartered on me again – if I wanted him. Of course I did.

Then the senior lieutenant told me that the regiment had suffered somewhat from a serious bombardment the days after Christmas, that the Aspirant had not only shown wonderful courage, but had had a narrow escape, and had been *cité à l'ordre du jour*, and was to have his first decoration.

We all felt as proud of him as if he belonged to us. I was told that he had been sent into the first-line trenches – only 200 yards from the German front – during the bombardment, 'to encourage and comfort his men' (I quote), and that a bomb had exploded over the trench and knocked a hole in his steel helmet.

I don't know which impressed me most—the idea of a lad of twenty having so established the faith in his courage amongst his superior officers as to be safe as a comfort and encouragement for the men, or the fact that, if the army had had those steel *casques* at the beginning of the war, many lives would have been saved.

The Aspirant came in with the second detachment the night before last – the eighth. The regiment was in and all quartered before he appeared.

We had begun to fear something had happened to him, when he turned up, freshly shaved and clean, but with a tattered overcoat on his arm, and a battered helmet in his hand.

Amélie greeted him with: 'Well, young man, we thought you were lost!'

He laughed, as he explained that he had been to make a toilet, see the regimental tailor, and order a new topcoat.

'I would not, for anything in the world, have had *madame* see me in the state I was in an hour ago. She has to see my rags, but I spared her the dirt,' and he held up the coat to show its rudely sewed-up rents, and turned over his helmet to show the hole in the top.

'And here is what hit me,' and he took out of his pocket a rough piece of a shell, and held it up, as if it were very precious. Indeed, he had it wrapped in a clean envelope, all ready to take up to Paris and show his mother, as he is to have his leave of a week while he is here.

I felt like saying 'Don't', but I didn't. I suppose it is hard for an ambitious soldier of twenty to realize that the mother of an only son, and that son such a boy as this, must have some feeling besides pride in her heart as she looks at him.

So now we are settled again, and used to the trotting of horses, the banging of grenades and splitting of *mitrailleuses*. From the window as I write – I am up in the attic, which Amélie calls the 'atelier', because it is in the top of the house and has a tiny north light in the roof – that being the only place where I am sure of being undisturbed – I can see horses being trained in the wide field on the side of the hill between here and Quincy. They are manoeuvring with all sorts of noises about them – even racing in a circle while grenades and guns are fired.

In spite of all that, there came near being a lovely accident right in front of the gate half an hour ago.

The threshing-machine is at work in front of the old grange on the other side of the road, just above my house. The men had come back from breakfast, and were starting the machine up just as two mounted soldiers, each leading two horses, rode out of the grange at Amélie's, and started down the hill at a trot. The very moment the horses were turning out to pass the machine – and the space was barely sufficient between the machine and the bank – a heedless man blew three awful blasts on his steam whistle to call his aids. The cavalry horses were used to guns, and the shrill mouth whistles of the officers, but that did not make them immune to a steam siren, and in a moment there was the most dangerous mix-up I ever saw. I expected to see both riders killed, and I don't know now why they were not, but neither man was thrown, even in spite of having three frightened horses to master.

It was a stupid thing for the man on the machine to do. He would have only had to wait one minute and the horses would have been by with a clear road before them if they shied. But he 'didn't think'. The odd thing was that the soldiers did not say an ugly word. I suppose they are used to worse.

You have been reproaching me for over a year that I did not write enough about the war. I do hope that all this movement about me interests you. It is not war by any means, but the nearest relation to it that I have seen in that time. It is its movements, its noise, its clothes. It is gay and brave, and these men are no 'chocolate soldiers'.

XXXII

January 30, 1917

My, but it is cold here! Wednesday the 24th it was 13 below zero, and this morning at ten o'clock it was 6 below. Of course this is in Centigrade and not Fahrenheit, but it is a cold from which I suffer more – it is so damp – than I ever did from the dry, sunny, below zero as you know it in the States. Not since 1899 have I seen such cold as this in France. I have seen many a winter here when the ground has hardly frozen at all. This year it began to freeze a fortnight ago. It began to snow on the 17th, a fine dry snow, and as the ground was frozen it promises to stay on. It has so far, in spite of the fact that once or twice since it fell the sun has shone. It looks very pretty, quite unnatural, very reminiscent of New England.

It makes life hard for us as well as the soldiers, but they laugh and say, 'We have seen worse.' They prefer it to rain and mud. But it makes roading hard; everything is so slippery, and if you ever happened to see a French horse or a French person 'walking on ice' I don't need to say more.

Well, the unexpected has happened – the cavalry has moved on. They expected – as much as a soldier ever expects anything – to have divided their time until March between our hill and the trenches in the Forêt de Laigue. But on the twenty-second orders began to rush in from headquarters, announcing a change of plan; a move was ordered and counter-ordered every few hours for three days, until Thursday afternoon, the twenty-fifth, the final order came – the whole division to be ready to mount at seven-thirty the next morning, orders for the direction to come during the night.

You never saw such a rushing about to collect clothes and get them dried. You see it has been very hard to get washing done. The Morin, where the wash houses are, is frozen, and even when things are washed, they won't dry in this air, and there is no coal to heat the drying houses.

However, it was done after a fashion. Everyone who had wood kept a fire up all night.

On Wednesday afternoon I had a little tea-party for some of the *sous-officiers* – mere boys – a simple goodbye spread of bread and butter and dry cookies – nothing else to be had. I could not even make cake, as we have had no fine sugar for months. However, the tea was extra good – sent me from California for Christmas – and I set the table with all my prettiest things, and the boys seemed to enjoy themselves.

They told me before leaving that never since they were at the front had they been anywhere so well received or so comfortable as they have been here, and that it would be a long time before they 'forgot Huiry'. Well, we on our side can say that we never dreamed that a conscript army could have a whole regiment of such fine men. So you see we are all very much pleased with each other, and if the 23d Dragoons are not going to forget us, we are as little likely to forget them.

Thursday evening, before going to bed, the Aspirant and I sat at the kitchen table and made a lot of sandwiches, as they are carrying three days' provisions. They expected a five hours' march on the first day, and a night under the tents, then another day's march, during which they would receive their orders for their destination. When the sandwiches were done, and wrapped up ready for his orderly to put in the saddlebags, with his other provisions, he said: 'Well, I am going to say goodbye to you tonight, and thank you for all your kindness.'

'Not at all,' I answered. 'I shall be up in the morning to see you start.'

He protested. It was so cold, so early, etc. But my mind was made up.

I assure you that it was cold – 18 below – but I got up when I heard the orderly arrive in the morning. I had been awake for hours, for at three o'clock the horses were being prepared. Every man had three to feed and saddle, and pack. Orderlies were running about doing the last packing for the officers, and carrying kits to the baggage-wagons. Amélie came at six. When I got downstairs I found the house warm and coffee ready. The Aspirant was taking his standing. It was more convenient than sitting in a chair. Indeed, I doubt if he could have sat.

I had to laugh at the picture he made. I never regretted so much that I have not indulged in a camera. He was top-booted and spurred. He had on his new topcoat and his mended helmet – catch a young soldier who has been hit on the head by his first *obus* having a new and unscarred one. He was hung over with his outfit like a Santa Claus. I swore he could never get into the saddle, but he scorned my doubts.

To the leather belt about his waist, supported by two straps over his shoulders, were attached his revolver, in its case with twenty rounds of cartridges; his field glasses; his map-case; his *bidon* – for his wine; square document case; his mask against asphyxiating gas; and, if you please, his kodak! Over one shoulder hung a flat, half-circular bag, with his toilet articles, over the other its mate, with a change, and a few necessary articles.

He looked to me as if he would ride two hundred pounds heavy, and he hasn't an ounce of extra flesh on him.

I laughed even harder when I saw him mounted. In one side of the holster was his *gamelle*; in the other, ammunition. The saddlebags contained on one side twenty pounds of oats for the horse; on the other three days' provisions for himself. I knew partly what was in that bag, and it was every bit as heavy as the horse's fodder, for there were sandwiches, sugar, coffee, chocolate, tinned meat, peas, corn, fruit, etc. Behind the saddle was rolled his blanket, inside his section of tent cover – it takes six of them to make a real tent. They are arranged to button together.

I was sitting in the bedroom window when he rode on to the terrace. I had to laugh as I looked down at him.

'And why does *madame* laugh?' he asked, trying to keep a sober face himself.

'Well,' I replied, 'I am only wondering if that is your battle array?'

'Certainly,' he answered. 'Why does it surprise you?'

I looked as serious as I could, as I explained that I had supposed, naturally, that the cavalry went into action as lightly equipped as possible.

He looked really indignant, as he snapped: 'That would be quite unnatural. What do you suppose that Peppino and I are going to do after a battle? Wait for the commissary department to find us? No, *madame*, after a battle it will not be of my mother nor home, nor even of you, that we will be thinking. We shall think of something to eat and drink.' Then he added, with a laugh, 'Alas! We shan't have all these nice things you have given us. They will have been eaten by tomorrow.'

I apologized, and said I'd know better another time, and he patted his horse, as he backed away, and said to him: 'Salute the lady, Peppino, and tell her prettily that you had the honor of carrying Teddy Roosevelt the day he went to the review.' And the horse pawed and bowed and neighed, and his rider wheeled him carefully as he saluted and said: '*Au revoir*, I shall write, and, after the war, I shall give myself the pleasure of seeing you,' and he rode carefully out of the gate – a very delicate operation, as only half of it was open. Laden as the horse was, he just made it, and away he galloped down the hill to Voisins, where the cavalry was assembling.

I stayed in the window a few minutes to wave a goodbye to the men as they led each their three horses down the hill. Then I put on my heaviest coat, a polo cap, all my furs and mittens, thrust my felt shoes into my sabots, and with one hand in my muff, I took the big French flag in the other and went through the snow down to the hedge to watch the regiment pass, on the road to Esbly.

Even before I got out of the house the news came that the 118th Regiment of infantry, the boys who retook Vaux in the great battle at Verdun, had been marching in from Meaux, and were camped, waiting to take up the billets the 23d Dragoons were vacating.

I stood in the snow for nearly half an hour, holding up the heavy flag, which flapped bravely in the icy wind, and watching the long grey line moving slowly along the road below. I could see half a mile of the line – grey, steel-helmeted men, packed horses, grey wagons – winding down the hill in the winter landscape, so different from the France I had always known. Hardly a sound came back – no music, no colors – the long, grey column moved in a silent, almost colorless world. I shifted the heavy flag from one hand to the other as my fingers got stiff, but, alas! I could not shift my feet. Long before the line had passed I was forced to fasten the flag to a post in the hedge and leave it to float by itself, and limp into the house. As a volunteer color-bearer I was a failure. I had to let Amélie take off my shoes and rub my feet, and I had hard work not to cry while she was doing it. I was humiliated, especially as I remembered that the boys had a five hours' march as their first étape, and a bivouac at the end of it.

I had intended to go out later on the *route Madame* to watch the cavalry coming down from the hills on the other side of the Morin, but I could not face the cold. There is nothing heroic about me. So I contented myself with helping Amélie set the house in order.

Needless to tell you that no one knows what this unexpected big movement of troops means.

It is inevitable that we should all imagine that it concerns the coming spring offensive. At any rate, the cavalry is being put back into its saddles, and the crack regiments are coming out of Verdun – the famous corps which has won immortal fame there, and written the name of Verdun in letters of flame in the list of the world's great battles, and enshrined French soldiers in the love of all who can be stirred by courage in a noble cause, or know what it means to have the heart swell at the thought of the 'sacred love of home and country'.

Although I have sworn – and more than once – that I will not talk politics with you again, or discuss any subject which can be considered as its most distant blood relation, yet every time you reiterate 'Aren't the French wonderfully changed? Aren't you more and more surprised at them?' it goes against the grain.

Does it never occur to you that France held her head up wonderfully after the terrible humiliation of 1870? Does it never occur to you what it meant to a great nation, so long a center of civilization, and a great race, so long a leader in thought, to have found herself without a friend, and to have had to face such a defeat – a defeat followed by a shocking treaty which kept that disaster forever before her? Do you never think of the hidden shame, the cankering mortification of the consciousness of that nation across the frontier, which had battened on its victory, and was so strong in brute force, that, however brave a face one might put on, there was behind that smiling front always a hidden fear of Germany – an eternal foe, ever gaining in numbers and eternally shaking her mailed fist.

No nation so humiliated ever rose out of her humiliation as France did, but the hidden memory, the daily consciousness of it, set its outward mark on the race. It bred that sort of bravado which was eternally accusing itself, in the consciousness that it had taken a thrashing it could never hope to avenge. Count up the past dares that France has had to take from Germany, so strong in mere numbers and physical strength that to attempt to fight her alone, as she did in 1870, meant simply to court annihilation, and fruitlessly. That does not mean that France was really afraid, but only that she was too wise to dare attempt to prove that she was not afraid. So many things in the French that the world has not understood were the result of the cankering wound of 1870. This war has healed that wound. Germany is not invincible, and the chivalrous, loving aid that rallied to help France is nonetheless comforting simply because since 1914 all nations have learned that the trend of Germany's ambition was a menace to them as well as to France.

XXXIII

February 2, 1917

I had hardly sent my last letter to the post when news came that the 23d Dragoons had arrived safely at their new *cantonnement*, but here is the letter, which will tell the story. Sorry that you insist on having these things in English – they are so very much prettier in French.

With the Army, January 29

Dear Madame,

Bravo for the pretty idea you had in flinging to the winter breezes the tri-colored flag in honor of our departure. All the soldiers marching out of Voisins saw the colors and were deeply touched. Let me bear witness to their gratitude.

How I regret La Creste. One never knows how happy he is until afterward. I am far from comfortably installed here. I am lodged in an old deserted château. There are no fires, and we are literally refrigerated. However, we shall not stay long, as I am returning to the trenches in a day or two. It will hardly be warm there, but I shall have less time to remember how much more than comfortable I was at Huiry.

We made a fairly decent trip to this place, but I assure you that, in spite of my 'extreme youth', I was near to being frozen en route. We were so cold that finally the whole regiment had to dismount and proceed on foot in the hope of warming up a bit.

*We were all, in the end, sad, cross, and grumbly. You
had spoiled us all at Huiry and Voisins. For my part
I longed to curse someone for having ordered such a
change of base as this, in such weather. Wasn't I well
enough off where I was, toasting myself before your
nice fire, and drinking my tea comfortably every
afternoon?*

*However, we are working tremendously for the
coming offensive. And I hope it will be the final
one, for the Germans are beginning to show signs
of fatigue. News comes to us from the interior, from
a reliable source, which indicates that the situation
on the other side of the Rhine is anything but calm.
More than ever now must we hang on, for the victory is almost within our clutch.*

Accept, madame, *the assurance of my most respectful homage,*

A— B—

So you see, we were all too previous in expecting the offensive.
The cavalry is not yet really mounted for action. But we hope
all the same.

The 118th is slowly settling down, but I'll tell you about
that later.

XXXIV

February 10, 1917

Well, the 118th has settled down to what looks like a long *cantonnement*. It is surely the liveliest as well as the biggest we ever had here, and every little town and village is crowded between here and Coulommier. Not only are there 5,000 infantry billeted along the hills and in the valleys, but there are big divisions of artillery also. The little square in front of our railway station at Couilly is full of grey cannon and ammunition wagons, and there are military kitchens and all sorts of commissary wagons along all the roadsides between here and Crécy-en-Brie, which is the distributing headquarters for all sorts of material.

As the weather has been intolerably cold, though it is dry and often sunny, the soldiers are billeted in big groups of fifty or sixty in a room or grange, where they sleep in straw, rolled in their blankets, packed like sardines to keep warm.

They came in nearly frozen, but they thawed out quickly, and now they don't mind the weather at all.

Hardly had they got thawed out when an epidemic of mumps broke out. They made quick work of evacuating those who had it, and stop its spreading, to the regret, I am afraid, of a good many of the boys. One of them said to me the day after the mumpy ones were taken over to Meaux: 'Lucky fellows. I wish I had the mumps. After Verdun it must be jolly to be in the hospital with nothing more dangerous than mumps, and a nice, pretty girl, in a white cap, to pet you. I can't think of a handsomer way to spend a *repos* than that.'

When I tell you that these soldiers say, 'Men who have not been at Verdun have not seen the war yet,' and then add that the life of the 118th here looks like a long picnic, and that they make play of their work, play of their grenade practice, which they vary with football, play of their twenty miles hikes, I give you leave to laugh at my way of seeing the war, and I'll even laugh with you.

That reminds me that I never see a thousand or so of these boys on the big plain playing what they call football that I don't wish some American chaps were here to teach them the game. All they do here is to throw off their coats and kick the ball as far, and as high, as possible, and run like racers after it, while the crowd, massed on the edge of the field, yells like mad. The yelling they do very well indeed, and they kick well, and run well. But, if they only knew the game – active, and agile, and light as they are – they would enjoy it, and play it well.

I had one of the nicest thrills I have had for many a day soon after the 118th arrived.

It was a sunny afternoon. I was walking in the road, when, just at the turn above my house, two officers rode round the corner, saluted me, and asked if the road led to Quincy. I told them the road to the right at the foot of the hill, through Voisins, would take them to Quincy. They thanked me, wheeled their horses across the road and stood there. I waited to see what was going to happen – small events are interesting here. After a bit one of them said that perhaps I would be wise to step out of the road, which was narrow, as the regiment was coming.

I asked, of course, 'What regiment?' and 'What are they coming for?' and he answered 'The 118th,' and that it was simply 'taking a walk.'

So I sauntered back to my garden, and down to the corner by the hedge, where I was high above the road, and could see in both directions. I had hardly got there when the head of the line came round the corner. In columns of four, knapsacks on their backs, guns on their shoulders, swinging at an easy gait, all looking so brown, so hardy, so clear-eyed, the men from Verdun marched by.

I had thought it cold in spite of the sun, and was well wrapped up, with my hands thrust into my big muff, but these men had beads of perspiration standing on their bronzed faces under their steel helmets.

Before the head of the line reached the turn into Voisins, a long shrill whistle sounded. The line stopped. Someone said: 'At last! My, but this has been a hot march,' and in a second every man had slipped off his knapsack and had a cigarette in his mouth.

Almost all of them dropped to the ground, or lay down against the bank. A few enterprising ones climbed the bank, to the field in front of my lawn, to get a glimpse of the view, and they all said what everyone says: 'I say, this is the best point to see it.'

I wondered what they would say to it if they could see it in summer and autumn if they found it fine with its winter haze.

But that is not what gave me my thrill.

The rest was a short one. Two sharp whistles sounded down the hill. Instantly everyone slipped on his sac, shouldered his gun, and at that minute, down at the corner, the military band struck up 'Chant du Départ'. Every hair on my head stood up. It is the first time I have heard a band since the war broke out, and as the regiment swung down the hill to the blare of brass – well, funnily enough, it seemed less like war than ever. Habit is a deadly thing. I have heard that band – a wonderful one, as such a regiment deserves – many times since, but it never makes my heart thump as it did when, so unexpectedly, it cut the air that sunny afternoon.

I had so often seen those long lines marching in silence, as the English and the French did to the Battle of the Marne, as all our previous regiments have come and gone on the hill-side, and never seen a band or heard military music that I had ceased to associate music with the soldiers, although I knew the bands played in the battles and the bugle calls were a part of it.

We have had all sorts of military shows, which change the atmosphere in which the quiet about us had been for months and months only stirred by the far-off artillery.

One day, we had a review on the broad plain which lies along the watershed between the Marne and the Grande Morin, overlooking the heights on the far side of both valleys, with the Grande Route on one side, and the walls to the wooded park of the handsome Château de Quincy on the other. It was an imposing sight, with thousands of steel-helmeted figures *sac au dos et bayonnette au canon*, marching and counter-marching in the cold sunshine, looking in the distance more like troops of Louis XIII than an evolution from the French conscript of the ante-bellum days of the *pantalon rouge*.

Two days later we had the most magnificent *prise d'armes* on the same plain that I have ever seen, much more stir-ring – though less tear-moving – than the same ceremony in the courtyard of the Invalides at Paris, where most foreign-ers see it. At the Invalides one sees the *mutilés* and the ill. Here one only saw the glory. In Paris, the galleries about the court, inside the walls of the Soldiers' Home, are packed with spectators. Here there were almost none. But here the heroes received their decorations in the presence of the comrades among whom they had been won, in the terrible battles of Verdun. It was a long line of officers, and men from the ranks, who stood so steadily before the commander and his staff, inside the hollow square, about the regimental colors, to have their medals and crosses fastened on their faded coats, receive their accolade, and the bravos of their companions as their citations were read. There were seven who received the Légion d'Honneur.

It was a brave-looking ceremony, and it was a lovely day – even the sun shone on them.

There was one amusing episode. These celebrations are always a surprise to the greater part of the community, and, in a little place like this, it is only by accident that anyone sees the ceremony. The children are always at school, and the rest of the world is at work, so, unless the music attracts someone, there are few spectators. On the day of the *prise d'armes* three old peasants happened to be in a field on the other side of the *route nationale*, which skirts the big plain on the plateau. They heard the music, dropped their work and ran across the road to gape. They were all men on towards eighty – too old to have ever done their military service. Evidently no one had ever told them that all Frenchmen were expected to uncover when the flag went by. Poor things, they should have known! But they didn't, and you should have seen a colonel ride down on them. I thought he was going to cut the woollen caps off their heads with his sabre, at the risk of decapitating them. But I loved what he said to them.

'Don't you know enough to uncover before the flag for which your fellow citizens are dying every day?'

Isn't that nice? I loved the democratic 'fellow citizens' – so pat and oratorically French.

I flung the Stars and Stripes to the French breezes on the 7th in honor of the rupture. It was the first time the flag has been unfurled since Captain Simpson ordered the corporal to take it down two years ago the third of last September. I had a queer sensation as I saw it flying over the gate again, and thought of all that had happened since the little corporal of the King's Own Yorks took it down – and the Germans still only forty-two miles away.

XXXV

What do you suppose I have done since I last wrote to you?

I have actually been to the theater for the first time in four years. Would you ever have believed that I could keep out of the theater such a long time as that? Still, I suppose going to the theater – to a sort of variety show – seems to you, who probably continue to go once or twice a week, a tame experience. Well, you can go to the opera, which I can't do if I like, but you can't see the heroes of Verdun not only applauding a show, but giving it, and that is what I have been doing not only once but twice since I wrote you.

I am sure that I have told you that our ambulance is in the *salle de récréation* of the *commune*, which is a small rectangular room with a stage across one end. It is the only thing approaching a theater which the *commune* boasts. It is well lighted, with big windows in the sides, and a top-light over the stage. It is almost new, and the walls and pointed ceiling are veneered with some Canadian wood, which looks like bird's-eye maple, but isn't.

It is in that hall that the *matinées*, which are given every other Sunday afternoon, take place. They are directed by a lieutenant-colonel, who goes into it with great enthusiasm, and really gets up a first-class programme.

The boys do all the hard work, and the personnel of the ambulance aids and abets with great good humor, though it is very upsetting. But then it is for the army – and what the army wants these days, it must have.

Luckily the men in our ambulance just now are either convalescent, or, at any rate, able to sit up in bed and bear excitement. So the beds of the few who cannot be dressed are pushed close to the stage, and around their cots are the chairs and benches of their convalescent comrades. The rest of the beds are taken out. The big military band is packed into one corner of the room. Chairs are put in for the officers of the staff and their few invited guests – there are rarely more than half a dozen civilians. Behind the reserved seats are a few benches for the captains and lieutenants and the rest of the space is given up to the *poilus*, who are allowed to rush when the doors are opened.

Of course the room is much too small, but it is the best we have. The wide doors are left open. So are the wide windows, and the boys are even allowed to perch on the wall opposite the entrance, from which place they can see the stage.

The entire programme is given by the *poilus*; only one performer had a stripe on his sleeve, though many of them wore a decoration. What seems to me the prettiest of all is that all the officers go, and applaud like mad, even the white-haired generals, who are not a bit backward in crying '*Bis, bis*!' like the rest.

The officers are kind enough to invite me and the card on my chair is marked 'Mistress Aldrich'. Isn't that Shakespearian? I sit among the officers, usually with a commandant on one side and a colonel on the other, with a General de Division, and a Général de Brigade in front of me, and all sorts of gilt stripes about me, which I count with curiosity, now that I have learned what they mean, as I surreptitiously try to discover the marks that war has made on their faces – and don't find them.

The truth is, the *salle* is fully as interesting to me as the performance, good as that is – with a handsome, delicate-looking young professor of music playing the violin, an actor from the Palais Royale showing a diction altogether remarkable, two well-known gymnasts doing wonderful stunts on horizontal bars, a prize pupil from the Conservatory at Nantes acting, as

302

only the French can, in a well-known little comedy, two clever, comic monologists of the La Scala sort, and as good as I ever heard even there, and a regimental band which plays good music remarkably. There is even a Prix de Rome in the regiment, but he is *en congé*, so I've not heard him yet. I wonder if you take it in? Do you realize that these are the soldiers in the ranks of the French defence? Consider what the life in the trenches means to them!

They even have artists among the *poilus* to paint backdrops and make properties. So you see it is one thing to go to the theater and quite another to see the soldiers from Verdun giving a performance before such a public – the men from the trenches going to the play in the highest of spirits and the greatest good humor.

At the first experience of this sort I did long to have you there. It was such a scene as I could not have believed possible in these days and under these conditions if I had not actually taken part in it.

As soon as the officers had filed in and taken their seats the doors and windows were thrown open to admit 'la vague', and we all stood up and faced about to see them come. It was a great sight.

In the aisle down the center of the hall – there is only one – between the back row of reserved seats, stood Mlle. Henriette, in her white uniform, white gloved, with the red cross holding her long white veil to the nurse's *coiffe* which covered her pretty brown hair. Her slight, tall, white figure was the only barrier to prevent "la vague" from sweeping right over the hall to the stage. As they came through the door it did not seem possible that anything could stop them – or even that they could stop themselves – and I expected to see her crushed. Yet two feet from her, the mass stopped – the front line became rigid as steel and held back the rest, and, in a second, the wave had broken into two parts and flowed into the benches at left and right, and, in less time than it takes you to read this, they were packed on the benches, packed in the windows, and hung up on the walls. A queer murmur, half laugh and half applause, ran over the reserved seats, and the tall, thin commandant beside me said softly, 'That is the way they came out of the trenches at Verdun.' As I turned to sit down I had impressed on my memory forever that sea of smiling, clean-shaven, keen-eyed, wave on wave of French faces, all so young and so gay – yet whose eyes had looked on things which will make a new France.

I am sending you the programme of the second *matinée* – I lost that of the first.

I do wish, for many reasons, that you could have heard the recitation by Brochard of Jean Bastia's 'L'Autre Cortège', in which the poet foresees the day 'When Joffre shall return down the Champs Elysées' to the frenzied cries of the populace saluting its victorious army, and greeting with wild applause 'Pétain, who kept Verdun inviolated', 'De Castelnau, who three times in the fray saw a son fall at his side', 'Gouraud, the Fearless', 'Marchand, who rushed on the Boches brandishing his cane', 'Mangin, who retook Douaumont', and 'All those brave young officers, modest even in glory, whose deeds the world knows without knowing their names' and the soldier heroes who held the frontier 'like a wall of steel from Flanders to Alsace', – the heroes of Souchez, of Dixmude, of the Maison du Passeur, of Souain, of Notre Dame de Lorette, and of the great retreat. It made a long list and I could feel the thrill running all over the room full of soldiers who, if they live, will be a part of that triumphal procession, of which no one talks yet except a poet.

But when he had pictured that scene the tempo of the verse changed: the music began softly to play a Schumann

Reverie to the lines beginning: 'But this triumphal cortège is not enough. The return of the army demands another cortège,' – the triumph of the *Mutilés* – the martyrs of the war who have given more than life to the defence of France – the most glorious heroes of the war.

The picture the poet made of this 'other *cortège*' moved the soldiers strangely. The music, which blended wonderfully with Brochard's beautiful voice, was hardly more than a breath, just audible, but always there, and added greatly to the effect of the recitation. There was a sigh in the silence which followed the last line – and an almost whispered 'bravo', before the long shouts of applause broke out.

It is the only number on any programme that has ever touched, even remotely, on war. It came as a surprise – it had not been announced. But the intense, rather painful, feeling which had swept over the audience was instantly removed by a comic monologue, and I need not tell you that these monologues – intended to amuse the men from the trenches and give them a hearty laugh – are usually *very* La Scala – that is to say – *rosse*. But I do love to hear the boys shout with glee over them.

The scene in the narrow streets of Quincy after the show is very picturesque. The road mounts a little to Moulignon, and to see the blue-grey backs of the boys, quite filling the street between the grey walls of the houses, as they go slowly back to their *cantonnements*, makes a very pretty picture.

It does seem a far cry from this to war, doesn't it? Yet isn't it lucky to know and to see that these boys can come out of such a battle as Verdun in this condition? This spirit, you see, is the hope of the future. You know, when you train any kind of a dog to fight, you put him through all the hard paces and force him to them, without breaking his spirit. It seems to me that is just what is being done to the men at the front.

XXXVI

March 1, 1917

Well, I have been very busy for some time now receiving the regiment, and all on account of the flag. It had been going up in the 'dawn's early light', and coming down 'with the twilight's last gleaming' for some weeks when the regiment marched past the gate again. I must tell you the truth – the first man who attempted to cry '*Vivent les Etats-Unis*' was hushed by a cry of '*Attendez-patience – pas encore*,' and the line swung by. That was all right. I could afford to smile – and, at this stage of the game, to wait. You are always telling me what a 'patient man' Wilson is. I don't deny it. Still, there are others.

The first caller that the flag brought me was on the morning after the regiment marched by it. I was upstairs. Amélie called up that there was '*un petit soldat*' at the door. They are all '*les petits soldats*' to her, even when they are six feet tall. She loves to see them coming into the garden. I heard her say to one of them the other day, when he 'did not wish to disturb *madame*, if she is busy,' '*Mais, entrez donc. Les soldats ne gênent jamais ma maîtresse.*'

I went downstairs and found a mere youngster, with a sergeant's stripe on his sleeve, blushing so hard that I wondered how he had got up the courage to come inside the gate. He stammered a moment. Then he pointed to the flag, and, clearing his throat, said:

'You aire an *Américaine*?'

I owned it.

'I haf seen the flag – I haf been so surprised – I haf had to come in.'

I opened the door wide, and said: 'Do', and he did, and almost with tears in his eyes – he was very young, and blonde – he explained that he was a Canadian.

'But,' I said, 'you are a French Canadian?'

'Breton,' he replied, 'but I haf live in Canada since sixteen.' Then he told me that his sister had gone to New Brunswick to teach French seven years ago, and that he had followed, that, when he was old enough, he had taken out his naturalization papers, and become a British subject in order to take up government land; that he had a wheat farm in Northern Canada – 160 acres, all under cultivation; that he was twenty when the war broke out, and that he had enlisted at once; that he had been wounded on the Somme, and came out of the hospital just in season to go through the hard days at Verdun.

As we talked, part of his accent wore away. Before the interview was over he was speaking English really fluently. You see he had been tongue-tied at his own temerity at first. When he was at ease – though he was very modest and scrupulously well-mannered – he talked well.

The incident was interesting to me because I had heard that the French Canadians had not been quick to volunteer, and I could not resist asking him how it happened that he, a British subject, was in the French army.

He reddened, stammered a bit, and finally said: 'After all I am French at heart. Had England fought any other nation but France in a war in which France was not concerned it would have been different, but since England and France are fighting together what difference can it make if my heart turned to the land where I was born?'

Isn't the naturalization question delicate?

I could not help asking myself how England looked at the matter. I don't know. She has winked at a lot of things, and a great many more have happened of late about which no one has ever thought. There are any number of officers in the English army today, enrolled as Englishmen, who are American citizens, and who either had no idea of abandoning their country, or were in too much of a hurry to wait for formalities. I am afraid all this matter will take on another color after 'this cruel war is over'.

This boy looked prosperous, and in no need of anything but kind words in English. He did not even need cigarettes. But I saw him turn his eyes frequently towards the library, and it occurred to me that he might want something to read. I asked him if he did, and you should have seen his eyes shine – and he wanted English at that, and beamed all over his face at a heap of illustrated magazines. So I was able to send him away happy.

The result was, early the next morning two more of them arrived – a tall six-footer, and a smaller chap. It was Sunday morning, and they had real, smiling Sunday faces on. The smaller one addressed me in very good English, and told me that the sergeant had said that there was an American lady who was willing to lend the soldiers books. So I let them loose in the library, and they bubbled, one in English, and the other in French, while they revelled in the books.

Of course I am always curious about the civil lives of these lads, and it is the privilege of my age to put such questions to them. The one who spoke English told me that his home was in London, that he was the head clerk in the correspondence department of an importing house. I asked him how old he was, and he told me twenty-two; that he was in France doing his military service when the war broke out; that he had been very successful in England, and that his employer had opposed his returning to France, and begged him to take out naturalization papers. He said he could not make up his mind to jump his military service, and had promised his employer to return when his time was up – then the war came.

I asked him if he was going back when it was over.

He looked at me a moment, shook his head and said, 'I don't think so. I had never thought of such a thing as a war.

No, I am too French. After this war, if I can get a little capital, I am going into business here. I am only one, but I am afraid France needs us all.'

You see there again is that naturalization question. This war has set the world thinking, and it was high time.

One funny thing about this conversation was that every few minutes he turned to his tall companion and explained to him in French what we were talking about, and I thought it so sweet.

Finally I asked the tall boy – he was a corporal and had been watching his English-speaking chum with such admiration – what he did in civil life.

He turned his big brown eyes, on me, and replied: 'I, *madame*? I never had any civil life.'

I looked puzzled, and he added: 'I come of a military family. I am an orphan, and I am an *enfant de troupe*.'

Now did you know that there were such things today as 'Children of the Regiment'? I own I did not. Yet there he stood before me, a smiling twenty-year old corporal, who had been brought up by the regiment, been a soldier boy from his babyhood.

In the meantime they had decided what they wanted for books. The English-speaking French lad wanted either Shakespeare or Milton, and as I laid the books on the table for him, he told his comrade who the two authors were, and promised to explain it all to him, and there wasn't a sign of show-off in it either. As for the Child of the Regiment, he wanted a Balzac, and when I showed him where they were, he picked out *Eugénie Grandet*, and they both went away happy.

I don't need to tell you that when the news spread that there were books in the house on the hilltop that could be borrowed for the asking, I had a stream of visitors, and one of these visits was a very different matter.

One afternoon I was sitting before the fire. It was getting towards dusk. There was a knock at the door. I opened it. There stood a handsome soldier, with a corporal's stripes on his sleeve. He saluted me with a smile, as he told me that his comrades had told him that there was an American lady here who did not seem to be bored if the soldiers called on her.

'*Alors*,' he added, 'I have come to make you a visit.'

I asked him in.

He accepted the invitation. He thrust his fatigue cap into his pocket, took off his topcoat, threw it on the back of a chair, which he drew up to the fire, beside mine, and at a gesture from me he sat down.

'Hmmm,' I thought. 'This is a new proposition.'

The other soldiers never sit down even when invited. They prefer to keep on their feet.

Ever since I began to see so much of the army, I have asked myself more than once, 'Where are the *fils de famille*?' They can't all be officers, or all in the heavy artillery, or all in the cavalry. But I had never seen one, to know him, in the infantry. This man was in every way a new experience, even among the non-commissioned officers I had seen. He was more at his ease. He stayed nearly two hours. We talked politics, art, literature, even religion – he was a good Catholic – just as one talks at a tea-party when one finds a man who is cultivated, and can talk, and he was evidently cultivated, and he talked awfully well.

He examined the library, borrowed a volume of Flaubert, and finally, after he had asked me all sorts of questions – where I came from; how I happened to be here; and even to 'explain Mr Wilson', I responded by asking him what he did in civil life.

He was leaning against the high mantel, saying a wood fire was delicious. He smiled down on me and replied: 'Nothing.'

'Enfin!' I said to myself. 'Here he is – the "fils de famille" for whom I have been looking.' So I smiled back and asked him, in that case, if it were not too indiscreet – what he did to kill time?

'Well,' he said, 'I have a very pretty, altogether charming wife, and I have three little children. I live part of the time in Paris, and part of the time at Cannes, and I manage to keep busy.'

It seemed becoming for me to say 'Beg pardon and thank you', and he bowed and smiled an '*il n'y a pas de quoi*', thanked me for a pleasant afternoon – an 'unusual kind of pleasure', he added, 'for a soldier in these times', and went away.

It was only when I saw him going that it occurred to me that I ought to have offered him tea – but you know the worth of '*esprit d'escalier*'.

Naturally I was curious about him, so the next time I saw the Canadian I asked him who he was. 'Oh,' he replied, 'he is a nice chap; he is a noble, a vicomte – a millionaire.'

So you see I have found the type – not quite in the infantry ranks, but almost, and if I found one there must be plenty more. It consoled me in these days when one hears so often cries against '*les embusqués*'.

I began to think there was every type in the world in this famous 118th, and I was not far from wrong.

The very next day I got the most delicious type of all – the French-American – very French to look at, but with New York stamped all over him – especially his speech. Of all these boys, this is the one I wish you could see.

Like all the rest of the English-speaking Frenchmen – the Canadian excepted – he brought a comrade to hear him talk to the lady in English. I really must try to give you a graphic idea of that conversation.

When I opened the door for him, he stared at me, and then he threw up both hands and simply shouted, 'My God, it is true! My God, it is an American!!'

Then he thrust out his hand and gave me a hearty shake, simply yelling, 'My God, lady, I'm glad to see you. My God, lady, the sight is good for sore eyes.'

Then he turned to his comrade and explained, '*J'ai dit à la dame*, "*Mon Dieu, Madame*,"' etc., and in the same breath he turned back to me and continued:

'My God, lady, when I saw them Stars and Stripes floating out there, I said to my comrade, "If there is an American man or an American lady here, my God, I am going to look at them," and my God, lady, I'm glad I did. Well, how do you do, anyway?'

I told him that I was very well, and asked him if he wouldn't like to come in.

'My God, lady, you bet your life I do,' and he shook my hand again, and came in, remarking, 'I'm an American myself – from New York – great city, New York – can't be beat. I wish all my comrades could see Broadway – that would amaze them,' and then he turned to his companion to explain, '*J'ai dit à Madame que je voudrais bien que tous les copains pouvaient voir Broadway – c'est la plus belle rue de New York – ils seront épatés – tous*,' and he turned to me to ask '*N'est-ce pas, Madame*?'

I laughed. I had to. I had a vivid picture of his comrades seeing New York for the first time – you know it takes time to get used to the Great White Way, and I remembered the last distinguished Frenchman whom the propaganda took on to the great thoroughfare, and who, at the first sight and sound and feel of it, wanted to lay his head up against Times Square and sob like a baby with fright and amazement. This was one of those flash thoughts. My caller did not give me time for more than that, for he began to cross-examine me – he wanted to know where I lived in America.

It did not seem worthwhile to tell him I did not live there, so I said 'Boston,' and he declared it a 'nice, pretty slow town', he knew it, and, of course, he added, 'But my God, lady, give me New York every time. I've lived there sixteen years – got a nice little wife there – here's her picture – and see here, this is my name,' and he laid an envelope before me with a New York postmark.

'Well,' I said, 'if you are an American citizen, what are you doing here, in a French uniform? The States are not in the war.'

His eyes simply snapped.

'My God, lady, I'm a Frenchman just the same. My God, lady, you don't think I'd see France attacked by Germany and not take a hand in the fight, do you? Not on your life!'

Here is your naturalization business again.

I could not help laughing, but I ventured to ask: 'Well, my lad, what would you have done if it had been France and the States?' He curled his lip, and brushed the question aside with:

'My God, lady! Don't be stupid. That could never be, never, on your life.'

I asked him, when I got a chance to put in a word, what he did in New York, and he told me he was a chauffeur, and that he had a sister who lived 'on Riverside Drive, up by 76th Street', but I did not ask him in what capacity, for before I could, he launched into an enthusiastic description of Riverside Drive, and immediately put it all into French for the benefit of his *copain*, who stood by with his mouth open in amazement at the spirited English of his friend.

When he went away, he shook me again violently by the hand, exclaiming: 'Well, lady, of course you'll soon be going back to the States. So shall I. I can't live away from New

York. No one ever could who had lived there. Great country the States. I'm a voter – I'm a Democrat – always vote the Democratic ticket – voted for Wilson. Well, goodbye, lady.'

As he shook me by the hand again, it seemed suddenly to occur to him that he had forgotten something. He struck a blow on his forehead with his fist, and cried: 'My God, lady, did I understand that you have been here ever since the war began? Then you were here during the battle out there? My God, lady, I'm an American, too, and my God, lady, I'm proud of you! I am indeed.' And he went off down the road, and I heard him explaining to his companion '*J'ai dit à madame*,' etc.

I don't think any comment is necessary on what Broadway does to the French lad of the people.

Last night I saw one of the most beautiful sights that I have ever seen. For several evenings I have been hearing artillery practice of some sort, but I paid no attention to it. We have no difficulty in distinguishing the far-off guns at Soissons and Rheims, which announce an attack, from the more audible, but quite different, sound of the *tir d'exercice*. But last night they sounded so very near – almost as if in the garden – that, at about nine, when I was closing up the house, I stepped out on to the terrace to listen. It was a very dark night, quite black. At first I thought they were in the direction of Quincy, and then I discovered, once I was listening carefully, that they were in the direction of the river. I went round to the north side of the house, and I saw the most wonderful display – more beautiful than any fireworks I had ever seen. The artillery was experimenting with signal lights, and firing colored *fusées volantes*. I had read about them, but never seen one. As near as I could make out, the artillery was on top of the hill of Monthyon – where we saw the battle of the Marne begin – and the line they were observing was the Isles-lès-Villenoy, in the river right at the west of us. When I first saw the exercises, there were half a dozen lovely red and green lights hanging motionless in the sky. I could hear the heavy detonation of the cannon or gun, or whatever they use to throw them, and then see the long arc of light like a chain of gold, which marked the course of the *fusée*, until it burst into color at the end. I wrapped myself up, took my field-glasses, and stayed out an hour watching the scene, and trying to imagine what exactly the same thing, so far as mere beauty went, meant to the men at the front.

In the morning I found that everyone else had heard the guns, but no one had seen anything, because, as it happens, it was from my lawn only that both Monthyon and the Isles-lès-Villenoy could be seen.

XXXVII

March 19, 1917

Such a week of excitement as we have had. But it has been uplifting excitement. I feel as if I had never had an ache or a pain, and Time and Age were not. What with the English advance, the Russian Revolution, and Zeppelins tumbling out of the heavens, every day has been just a little more thrilling than the day before.

I wonder now how 'Willie' – as we used to call him in the days when he was considered a joke – feels over his latest great success – the democratic conversion, or I suppose I should, to be correct, say the conversion to democracy, of all Russia? It must be a queer sensation to set out to accomplish one thing, and to achieve its exact reverse.

Yesterday – it was Sunday – just capped the week of excitement. It was the third beautiful day in the week – full of sunshine, air clear, sky blue.

In the morning, the soldiers began to drop in, to bring back books and get more, to talk a little politics, for even the destruction of the Zeppelin at Compiègne, and the news that the English were at Bapaume, was a bit damped by the untimely fall of Briand.

The boys all looked in prime condition, and they all had new uniforms, even new caps and boots. The Canadian, who usually comes alone, had personally conducted three of his comrades, whom he formally introduced, and, as I led the way into the library, I remarked, '*Mais, comme nous sommes chic aujourd'hui*,' and they all laughed, and explained that it was Sunday and they were dressed for a formal call. If any of them guessed that the new equipment meant anything they made no sign. I imagine they did not suspect any more than

I did, for they all went down the hill to lunch, each with a book under his arm. Yet four hours later they were preparing to advance.

It was exactly four in the afternoon that news came that the French had pierced the line at Soissons – just in front of us – and that Noyon had been retaken – that the cavalry were *à cheval* (that means that the 23d Dragoons have advanced in pursuit) – and, only a quarter of an hour after we got the news, the *assemblage général* was sounded, and the 118th ordered *sac au dos* at half past six.

For half an hour there was a rush up the hill – boys bringing me back my books, coming to shake hands and present me with little souvenirs, and bring the news that the *camions* were coming – which meant that the 118th were going right into action again. When a regiment starts in such a hurry that it must take a direct line, and cannot bother with railroads, the boys know what that means.

I know you'll ask me how they took the order, so I tell you without waiting. I saw a few pale faces – but it was only for a moment. A group of them stood in front of me in the library. I had just received from the front, by post, the silk parachute of a *fusée volante*, on which was written: '*A Miss Mildred Aldrich Ramassé sur le champ de bataille à 20 metres des lignes Boches. Souvenir de la patrouille de Février 22, 1917*,' and the signature of the Aspirant, and that was the only way I knew he had probably been on a dangerous mission.

It was the first time that I had ever seen one any nearer than in the air, during the exercises by night of which I wrote you, and one of the boys was explaining it, and its action, and use, and everyone but me was laughing at the graphic demonstration. I don't know why I didn't laugh. Usually I laugh more than anyone else.

Sometimes I think that I have laughed more in the last two years than in all the rest of my life. The demonstrator looked at me, and asked why I was so grave. I replied that I did not know – perhaps in surprise that they were so gay.

He understood at once. Quite simply he said: 'Well, my dear *madame*, we must be gay. What would we do otherwise? If we thought too often of the comrades who are gone, if we remembered too often that we risked our skins every day, the army would be demoralized. I rarely think of these things except just after an attack. Then I draw a deep breath, look up at the sky, and I laugh, as I say to my soul, "Well, it was not to be this time, perhaps it never will be." Life is dear to each of us, in his own way, and for his own reasons. Luckily it is not so dear to any of us as France or honor.'

I turned away and looked out of the window a moment – I could not trust myself – and the next minute they were all shaking hands, and were off down the road to get ready.

The loaded *camions* began to move just after dark. No one knows the destination, but judging by the direction, they were heading for Soissons. They were moving all night, and the first thing I heard this morning was the bugle in the direction of Quincy, and the news came at breakfast time that the 65th Regiment – the last of the big fighting regiments to go into action at Verdun, and the last to leave, was marching in. The girl from the butcher's brought the news, and 'Oh, *madame*,' she added, 'the Americans are with them.'

'The what?' I exclaimed.

'A big American ambulance corps – any number of ambulance automobiles, and they have put their tents up on the common at Quincy.'

You can imagine how excited I was. I sent someone over to Quincy at once to see if it was true, and word came back that Captain Norton's American *Corps Sanitaire* – forty men who have been with this same division, the 31st Corps – for many months – had arrived from Verdun with the 65th Regiment, and was to follow it into action when it advanced again.

This time the *cantonnement* does not come up to Huiry – only to the foot of the hill at Voisins.

Of course I have not seen our boys yet, but I probably shall in a few days.

XXXVIII

March 28, 1917

Well, all quiet on the hilltop again – all the soldiers gone – no sign of more coming for the present. We are all nervously watching the advance, but controlling our nerves. The German retreat and the organized destruction which accompanies it just strikes one dumb. Of course we all know it is a move meant to break the back of the great offensive, and though we knew, too, that the Allied commanders were prepared for it, it does make you shiver to get a letter from the front telling you that a certain regiment advanced at a certain point thirty kilometres, without seeing a Boche.

As soon as I began to read the account of the destruction, I had a sudden illuminating realization of the meaning of something I saw from the car window the last time I came out from Paris. Perhaps I did not tell you that I was up there for a few days the first of the month?

Of course you don't need to be told that there has been a tremendous amount of work done on the eastern road all through the war. Extra tracks have been laid all the way between Paris and Chelles, the outer line of defenses of the city – and at the stations between Gagny and Chelles the sidings extend so far on the western side of the tracks as to almost reach out of sight. For a long time the work was done by soldiers, but when I went up to Paris, four weeks ago, the work was being done by Annamites in their saffron-colored clothes and queer turbans, and I found the same little people cleaning the streets in Paris. But the surprising thing was the work that was accomplished in the few days that I was in Paris. I came back on March 13, and I was amazed to see all those miles and miles of sidings filled with trucks piled with wood, with great posts, with planks, with steel rails, and what looked the material to build a big city or two. I did not wonder when I saw them that we could not get coal, or other necessities of life, but it was not until I read of the very German-like idea of defending one's self on the property of other people that I realized what all that material meant, and that the Allies were prepared for even this tragic and Boche-like move. I began to get little cards and letters back from the 118th on the twenty-third. The first said simply:

Dear Madame,

Here we are – arrived last night just behind the line – with our eyes strained towards the front, ready to bound forward and join in the pursuit.

Of course I have seen the Americans – a doctor from Schenectady and forty men, almost all youngsters in their early twenties. In fact twenty-two seems to be the popular age. There are boys from Harvard, boys from Yale, New England boys, Virginia boys, boys from Tennessee, from Kentucky, from Louisiana, and American boys from Oxford. It is a first-line ambulance corps – the boys who drive their little Ford ambulances right down to the battlefields and receive the wounded from the *brancardiers*, and who have seen the worst of Verdun, and endured the privations and the cold with the army.

When a Virginia man told me that he had not taken cold this winter, and showed me his little tent on the common, where, from choice, he is still sleeping under canvas, because he 'likes it', I could easily believe him. Do you know – it is absurd – I have not had a cold this winter, either? I, who used to have one tonsilitis per winter, two bronchitis, half a dozen colds in my head, and occasionally a mild specimen of *grip*. This is some record when you consider that since my coal gave out in February we have had some pretty cold weather, and that I have only had imitation fires, which cheer the imagination by way of the eyes without warming the atmosphere. I could fill a book with stories of 'how I made fires in war time', but I spare you because I have more interesting things to tell you.

On the 26th we were informed that we were to have the 65th Regiment cantoned on the hill for a day and a night. They were to move along a bit to make room for the 35th for a few days. It was going to be pretty close quarters for one night, and the adjutant who arranged the *cantonnement* was rather put to it to house his men. The Captain was to be in my house, and I was asked, if, for two days – perhaps less – I could have an officers' kitchen in the house and let them have a place to eat. Well – there the house was – they were welcome to it. So that was arranged, and I put a mattress on the floor in the atelier for the Captain's cook.

We had hardly got that over when the adjutant came back to look over the ground again, and see if it were not possible to canton a *demi-section* in the granges. I went out with him to show him what there was – a grange on the south side, with a loft, which has already had to be braced up with posts, and which I believe to be dangerous. He examined it, and agreed: a grange on the north side, used for coal, wood, and garden stuff, with a loft above in fair condition, but only accessible by ladder from the outside. He put up the ladder, climbed it, unlocked the door, examined it, and decided that it would do, unless they could find something better.

So soldiers came in the afternoon and swept it out, and brought the straw in which they were to sleep, and that was arranged.

It was about seven the next morning when they began to arrive. I heard the tramp of their feet in the road, as they marched, in sections, to their various *cantonnements*. I put a clean cap over my tousled hair, slipped into a wadded gown and was ready just as I heard the '*Halte*', which said that my section had arrived. I heard two growly sounds which I took to be '*A droite, marche!*' – and by the time I got the window open to welcome my section I looked down into an Indian file of smiling bronzed faces, as they marched along the terrace, knapsacks and guns on their backs, and began mounting the ladder.

Soon after, the Captain's cook arrived with his market baskets and took possession of the kitchen, and he was followed by orderlies and the kits, and by the officer who was to be the Captain's table companion.

As Amélie had half a section cantoned in her courtyard she was busy there, and I simply showed the cook where things were, gave him tablecloths and napkins, and left him to follow his own sweet will, free to help himself to anything he needed. If you remember what I told you about my house when I took it, you can guess how small I had to make myself.

I can tell you one thing – on the testimony of Amélie – the officers eat well. But they pay for it themselves, so that is all right. The cook was never idle a minute while he was in the house. I heard him going up to bed, in his felt shoes, at ten o'clock – Amélie said he left the kitchen scrupulously clean – and I heard the kitchen alarm clock, which he carried with him, going off at half past five in the morning.

I had asked the Captain when the regiment was to advance, and he said probably the next morning, but that the order had not come. Twice while I was at dinner in the breakfast room, I heard an orderly come in with despatches, but it was not until nine o'clock that the order *sac au dos* at half past ten the next morning – that was yesterday – was official, and it was not until nine in the morning that they knew that they were leaving in *camions* – which meant that they were really starting in the pursuit, and the American division was to follow them.

The officers had a great breakfast just after nine – half a dozen courses. As they did not know when, if ever, they would sit down to a real meal at a table again they made their possibly last one a feast. As they began just after nine and had to be on the road at half past ten I don't need to tell you that the cook had no time to clear up after himself. He had just time – with his mouth full of food – to throw his apron on the floor, snatch up his gun and his knapsack and buckle himself into shape as he sprinted up the hill to overtake his company.

As for me – I threw on a cape and went across the road to the field, where I could see the Grande Route, and the *chemin Madame* leading to it. All along the *route nationale*, as far as I could see with my field-glass, stood the grey *camions*. On the *chemin Madame* the regiment was waiting. They had stacked their guns and, in groups, with cigarettes between their lips, they chatted quietly, as they waited. Here and there a bicyclist was sprinting with orders.

Suddenly a whistle sounded. There was a rattle of arms as the men unstacked their guns and fell into line, then hundreds of hobnailed boots marked time on the hard road, and the 65th swung along to the waiting *camions*, over the same route I had seen Captain Simpson and the Yorkshire boys take, just before sundown, on that hot September day in 1914.

As I stood watching them all the stupendousness of the times rushed over me that you and I, who have rubbed our noses on historical monuments so often, have chased after emotions on the scenes of past heroism, and applauded mock heroics across the footlights, should be living in days like these, days in which heroism is the common act of every hour. I cannot help wondering what the future generations are going to say of it all; how far-off times are going to judge us; what is going to stand out in the strong limelight of history? I know what I think, but that does not help yet.

Do you know that I had a letter from Paris this week which said: 'I was looking over your letters written while we were tied up in London, in August, 1914, and was amused to find that in one of them you had written "the annoying thing is, that, after this is over, Germany will console herself with the reflection that it took the world to beat her".' It is coming truer than I believed in those days – and then I went back to dishwashing.

You never saw such a looking kitchen as I found. Léon, the officers' cook – a pastry cook before he was a soldier – was a nice, kindly, hard-working chap, but he lacked the quality dear to all good housekeepers – he had never learned to clean up after himself as he went along. He had used every cooking utensil in the house, and such a pile of plates and glasses! It took Amélie and me until two o'clock to clean up after him, and when it was done I felt that I never wanted to see food again as long as I lived. Of course we did not mind, but Amélie had to say, every now and then, '*Vive l'armée!*' just to keep her spirits up. Anyway it was consoling to know that they have more to eat than we do.

The American corps had to leave one of their boys behind in our ambulance, very ill with neuritis – that is to say, painfully ill. As the boys of the American corps are ranked by the French army as officers this case is doubly interesting to the *personnel* of our modest hospital. First he is an American – a tall young Southerner from Tennessee. They never knew an American before. Second, he is not only an honorary officer serving France, he is really a lieutenant in the officers' reserve corps of his own State, and our little ambulance has never sheltered an officer before.

The nurses and the sisters are falling over one another to take care of him – at least, as I always find one or two of them sitting by his bed whenever I go to see him, I imagine they are.

The amusing thing is that he says he can't understand or speak French, and swears that the only words he knows are:

Oui, oui, oui,
Non, non, non,
Si, si, si,
Et voilà,
Merci!

which he sings, in his musical southern voice, to the delight of his admiring nurses. All the same, whenever it is necessary for an interpreter to explain something important to him, I find that he has usually got the hang of it already, so I've my doubts if he has as little French as he pretends. One thing is sure his discharge will leave a big void in the daily life of the ambulance.

This is growing into a long letter – in the quiet that has settled on us I seem to have plenty of time – and the mood – so, before I close, I must say something in reply to your sad sentence in your last letter – the reply to mine of December regarding our first big *cantonnement*. You say 'Oh! the pity of this terrible sacrifice of the youth of the world!! Why aren't the middle-aged sent first – the men who have partly lived their lives, who leave children to continue the race?' Ah, dear old girl – you are indeed too far off to understand such a war as this. Few men of even forty can stand the life. Only the young can bear the strain. They not only bear it, they thrive on it, and, such of them as survive the actual battles, will come out of it in wonderful physical trim. Of course there are a thousand sides to the question. There are hospitals full of the tuberculous and others with like maladies, but those things existed before the war, only less attention was paid to them. It is also a serious question – getting more serious the longer the war goes on – as to how all these men will settle into civil life again – how many will stand sedentary pursuits after years in the open, and how they will settle back into the injustices of class distinctions after years of the equality of the same duty – fighting for their country. Still if the victory is decisive, and the army is satisfied with the peace conditions, I imagine all those things will settle themselves.

Well, Congress meets on Monday. There is no doubt in anyone's mind of the final decision. I only hope it won't drag too long. I have taken my flags down just to have the pleasure of putting them up again.

I had this letter closed when I got my first direct news from the front since the advance.

Do you remember how amused I was when I saw the Aspirant equipped for his march in January? I was told afterward that my idea of a light equipment for the cavalry in battle was 'theoretically beautiful', but in such a war as this absolutely impracticable. Well I hear today that when the cavalry advanced it advanced in a 'theoretically beautiful' manner. It seems that the order was unexpected. It caught the cavalry in the saddle during a manoeuvre, and, just as they were, they wheeled into line and flew off in pursuit of the Boches. They had nothing but what was on their backs – and ammunition, of course. The result was that they had forty-eight hours of real suffering. It was harder on the officers than on the men, and hardest of all on the horses. All the soldiers always have a *bidon* with something in it to drink, and almost invariably they have a bite or so in their sacks. No officer ever has anything on him, and none of them carries a *bidon* except on a march. For forty-eight hours in the chase they suffered from hunger, and, what was worse still, from thirst. As the weather was nasty and they were without shelters of any kind – not even tents – they tasted all the hardships of war. This must comfort the foot soldiers, who are eternally grumbling at the cavalry. However, the officer who brought back the news says the men bore it with philosophical gaiety, even those who on the last day had nothing as well as those who in forty-eight hours had a quarter of a biscuit. The horses were not so philosophical – some of them just lay down and died, poor beasts. I assure you I shall never laugh again at a cavalryman's 'battle array'.

XXXIX

The sun shines, and my heart is high. This is a great day. The Stars and Stripes are flying at my gate, and they are flying over all France. What is more they will soon be flying – if they are not already – over Westminster, for the first time in history. The mighty, unruly child, who never could quite forgive the parent it defied, and never has been wholly pardoned, is to come back to the family table, if only long enough to settle the future manners of the nations about the board, put in, I suppose, a few 'don'ts', like 'don't grab'; 'don't take a bigger mouthful than you can becomingly chew'; 'don't jab your knife into your neighbor – it is not for that purpose'; 'don't eat out of your neighbor's plate – you have one of your own' – in fact 'Thou shalt not – even though thou art a Kaiser – take the name of the Lord thy God in vain'; 'thou shalt not steal'; 'thou shalt not kill'; 'thou shalt not covet' and so on. Trite, I know, but in thousands of years we have not improved on it.

So the Stars and Stripes are flying over France to greet the long delayed and ardently awaited, long ago inevitable declaration which puts the States shoulder to shoulder with the other great nations in the Defence of the Rights of Man, the Sacredness of Property, the Honor of Humanity, and the news has been received with such enthusiasm as has not been seen in France since war broke over it. Judging by the cables the same enthusiasm which has set the air throbbing here is mounting to the skies on your side of the ocean. We are a strangely lucky nation – we are the first to go into the great fight to the shouts of the populace; to be received like a star performer, with 'thunders of applause'.

Well – God's in his heaven, All's right with the world' – and – *we are no longer in the war zone.* As soon as a few formalities are filled, and I can get a *carte d'identité*, I shall be once more free to circulate. After sixteen months of a situation but one step removed from being interned, it will be good to be able to move about – even if I don't want to.

To give you some idea how the men at the front welcome the news, here is a letter which has just come – written before Congress had voted, but when everyone was sure of the final decision.

At the Front, April 4, 1917

Dear Madame,

It has been a long time since I sent you my news. The neglect has not been my fault, but due to the exceptional circumstances of the war.

At last we have advanced, and this time as real cavalry. We have had the satisfaction of pursuing the Boches – keeping on their flying heels until we drove them into Saint-Quentin. From the 18th to the 28th of March the war became once more a battle in the open, which was a great relief to the soldiers and permitted them to once more demonstrate their real military qualities. I lived through a dozen days filled to overflowing with emotions – sorrow, joy, enthusiasm. At last I have really known what war is – with all its misery and all its beauty. What joy it was for us of the cavalry to pass over the trenches and fly across the plains in the pursuit of the Germans! The first few days everything went off wonderfully. The Boches fled before us, not daring to turn and face us. But our advance was so rapid, our impetuosity such, that, long before they expected us, we overtook the main body of the enemy. They were visibly amazed at being caught before they could cross the canal at Saint-Quentin, as was their plan, and they were obliged to turn and attempt to check our advance, in order to gain sufficient time to permit their artillery to cross the canal and escape complete disaster.

It was there that we fought, forcing them across the canal to entrench themselves hastily in unprepared positions, from which, at the hour I write, our wonderful infantry and our heavy artillery, in collaboration with the British, are dislodging them.

Alas! The battles were costly, and many of our comrades paid with their lives for our audacious advance. Be sure that we avenged them, and cruel as are our losses they were not in vain. They are more than compensated by the results of the sacrifice – the strip of our native soil snatched from the enemy. They died like heroes, and for a noble cause.

Since then we have been resting, but waiting impatiently to advance and pursue them again, until we can finally push them over their own frontier.

Today's paper brings us great and comforting news. At last, dear madame! At last your marvelous country is going to march beside us in this terrible war. With a full heart I present to you my heartiest congratulations. At last Wilson understands, and the American people – so noble, and always so generous – will no longer hesitate to support us with all their resources. How wonderfully this is going to *aid us to obtain the decisive victory we must have, and perhaps to shorten the war.*

Here, in the army, the joy is tremendous at the idea that we have behind us the support of a nation so great, and all our admiration, all our gratitude goes out to your compatriots, to the citizens of the great Republic, which is going to enter voluntarily into this Holy War, and so bravely expose itself to its known horrors.

Bravo! et vivent les Etats-Unis!

My greetings to Amélie and Papa: a caress for Khaki and Didine, and a pat for Dick.

Receive, madame, *the assurance of my most respectful homage.*

I am feeling today as if it were no matter that the winter had been so hard; that we have no fuel but twigs; that the winter wheat was frozen; that we have eaten part of our seed potatoes and that another part of them was frostbitten; that butter is a dollar a pound (and none to be had, even at that price, for days at a time); that wood alcohol is sixty-five cents a litre, and so on and so forth. I even feel that it is not important that this war came, since it could not be escaped, and that what alone is important is – that the major part of the peoples of the world are standing upright on their feet, lifting their arms with a great shout for Liberty, Justice, and Honor; that a war of brute force for conquest has defeated itself, and set free those who were to have been its victims. It is not, I know, today or tomorrow that it will all end; it is not next year, or in many years, that poor Poland's three mutilated parts can be joined and healed into harmony; and oh! how long it is going to be before all the sorrow and hatred that Germany has brought on the world can be either comforted or forgotten! But at least we are sure now of the course the treatment is going to take – so the sun shines and my heart is high, and I do believe that though joy may lead nowhere, sorrow is never in vain.

Biographical Note

Mildred Aldrich was born in Providence, Rhode Island, in 1853. Having grown up in Boston, she went on to become a teacher and then a journalist. Writing for various Boston papers she eventually began working for the *Boston Herald*.

In 1898, she moved to France, where she took up roles as a foreign correspondent and translator. She was to move to Huiry, near Paris, in 1914 into a house on a hillside that gave her a bird's eye view of the Marne valley. The letters she wrote to her friends detailed her experiences of the war – and were published in several volumes from 1915 to 1919. Aldrich would also write a couple of novels and an autobiography, *Confessions of a Breadwinner*.

Aldrich suffered a heart attack in February 1928 and died a few days later in Neuilly.

HESPERUS PRESS

Under our three imprints, Hesperus Press publishes over 300 books by many of the greatest figures in worldwide literary history, as well as contemporary and debut authors well worth discovering.

Hesperus Classics handpicks the best of worldwide and translated literature, introducing forgotten and neglected books to new generations.

Hesperus Nova showcases quality contemporary fiction and non-fiction designed to entertain and inspire.

Hesperus Minor rediscovers well-loved children's books from the past – these are books which will bring back fond memories for adults, which they will want to share with their children and loved ones.

To find out more visit **www.hesperuspress.com**

@HesperusPress